W9-DBV-087

WOMEN
AND
WORK

John Deutsch Institute
for the Study of Economic Policy
Queen's University

Published for the School of Policy Studies, Queen's University
by McGill-Queen's University Press
Montreal & Kingston • London • Ithaca

This project was financially assisted
by the Labour-Management Partnerships Program

Le Programme de partenariat syndical-patronal a
contribué financièrement à la réalisation de ce projet

 Government Gouvernement
of Canada du Canada

 Gouvernement Government
du Canada of Canada

The views expressed in this document
do not necessarily reflect those of the Government of Canada

Les opinions exprimées dans ce document ne reflètent
pas nécessairement celles du gouvernement du Canada

ISBN: 0-88911-806-X (bound)   ISBN: 0-88911-808-6 (pbk.)
© 1999   John Deutsch Institute for the Study of Economic Policy
Queen's University, Kingston, Ontario K7L 3N6
Telephone: (613) 533-2294   FAX: (613) 533-6025
Printed and bound in Canada
Cover design: Mark Howes
Cover photo: Richard P. Chaykowski
Cover Art: "Heads" by Luke Anowtalik

Canadian Cataloguing in Publication Data

Main entry under title:

Women and work

Proceedings of a conference held at Queen's University, April 5-7, 1998.
Includes bibliographical references.
ISBN   0-88911-806-X (bound)   ISBN   0-88911-808-6 (pbk.)

1. Women - Employment - Canada - Congresses. I. Chaykowski,
Richard P. (Richard Paul), 1958-   . II. Powell, Lisa M. (Lisa Marie),
1966-   . III. John Deutsch Institute for the Study of Economic Policy.

HD6099.W625 1999   331.4'0971   C99-931274-X

Acknowledgement

The John Deutsch Institute is pleased to be able to publish *Women and Work*. Central to the JDI's mandate is its role as a publishing venue for policy issues of national interest. The essays that follow clearly meet this standard both individually and as a collection. In terms of the latter, the range of areas covered (technological change, income distribution, school-to-work transitions, equality legislation, among several others) serves to provide a valuable integrative approach to policy issues relating to women and the labour market.

On behalf of the JDI, I would like to express our thanks and appreciation to the editors, Richard Chaykowski and Lisa Powell, for preparing the general manuscript for publication. I also acknowledge the financial support from the Canadian Workplace Research Network and the Labour-Management Partnerships Program of Human Resources Development Canada.

On our side, it is a pleasure to recognize again the efforts of Sharon Sullivan in her roles as manuscript coordinator and publication overseer. Marilyn Banting provided the style editing and the School of Policy Studies publication unit helped out with various tasks including cover design.

We trust that *Women and Work* will be well received and make an important and timely contribution to Canadian policy. With areas such as productivity, union distribution and technology high in terms of our national policy priorities, the manner in which these relate to women and work must assume pride of place in this agenda.

Thomas J. Courchene
Director
John Deutsch Institute

Preface

While the remarkable trends occurring over the latter half of the twentieth century with respect to the changing roles of women in the labour market are quite well-documented, many of the implications of these developments are somewhat less well understood. In addition, with the extent and depth of economic restructuring that has occurred in Canada over the last decades of this century, there are a range of new challenges confronting women in the labour market. With these developments in mind, we thought that the time was propitious to embark upon a project centred around the theme of "Women and Work" in the Canadian labour market.

In late 1997, we agreed that a useful approach would be to host a conference on this theme, followed by the publication of the research. A conference on "Women and Work" was organized by the John Deutsch Institute of Queen's University, in 1998, and co-sponsored by the Canadian Workplace Research Network and the John Deutsch Institute. We gratefully acknowledge the financial support of the Canadian Workplace Research Network and the Labour-Management Partnerships Program of Human Resources Development Canada, and the John Deutsch Institute of Queen's University, for both the conference and the publication of this volume. These sponsors have enthusiastically and substantively supported this project from the outset.

The papers included in this research volume cover a range of important themes relating to women and the labour market, including: technological change, skills and the workplace; income security programs and the work decisions of lone parents; evidence on female labour supply and school-to-work transitions; remuneration, benefits and workplace conditions; and labour policy relating to women. In many cases, the papers were intended to be more extensive, in-depth treatments of subject matter than is typically available in most journals. In addition, the approaches used to consider the different issues vary across the papers; while some papers are empirical analyses, others provide an institutional examination of the issue at hand. Taken together, they offer fresh empirical evidence and new insights into many of the major trends and issues affecting women and the labour market. The papers in this volume have benefited from reviews provided by discussants at the "Women and Work" conference. We gratefully acknowledge the benefit of very constructive and useful comments provided by Anil Verma (University of Toronto), Douglas Hyatt (University of Toronto), Nicole Fortin (Université de Montréal), Frances Woolley (Carleton University), Michael Abbott (Queen's University), Audrey Kobayashi (Queen's University) and Brenda Lautsch (Simon Fraser University). In addition, beneficial input was provided at the conference by Akivah Starkman (Human Resources Development Canada), Allen Zeesman (Human Resources Development Canada), Charles Beach (Queen's University), Roberta Robb (Brock University) and Garnett Picot (Statistics Canada).

Throughout the course of the project we, as editors, have benefited from the assistance and input of many individuals. We are particularly indebted to Sharon Sullivan of the John Deutsch Institute for her most able assistance in organizing and managing the conference. We are also indebted to Sharon for her exceptional editorial and development work in producing the volume, and to the team of Mark Howes of the Queen's School of Policy Studies and Marilyn Banting for their creative and editorial contributions. We are also very grateful to Tom Courchene of the John Deutsch Institute for his strong interest in this project — and for lending his support to it — from the very beginning. Finally, at the Canadian Workplace Research Network, we are very appreciative of the support provided by Akivah Starkman and Linda L'Heureux.

Richard Chaykowski
and
Lisa Powell

Contents

Contributors

The Gender Earnings Gap Amongst Canadian Bachelor's Level University Graduates: A Cross-Cohort, Longitudinal Analysis

Ross Finnie and Ted Wannell

Introduction

There now exists a substantial body of research on the gender earnings gap in Canada. Some of this work looks at broad groups of workers using general databases such as the Census, the Survey of Consumer Finances and the Labour Market Activity Survey, while other studies focus on narrower groups of workers using more specialized databases. Altogether, we now

This research was made possible by financial support received from the Human Capital and Education Studies Division in the Applied Research Branch of Human Resources Development Canada. A Social Sciences and Humanities Research Council grant awarded to Finnie provided assistance for an earlier phase of the work. Helpful comments were received from Doug Giddings, Philip Jennings, and the editors of this volume. Excellent research assistance was provided by Marc Frenette.

1

have quite a good understanding of the extent and structure of male-female differences in earnings and how these patterns have evolved over time.[1]

There remain, however, various specific aspects of the gender earnings gap worth exploring, while given the continually changing nature of the situation it is almost always worth updating the record with new data. In this context, this paper presents the findings of an empirical analysis of the gender earnings gap and other job outcomes amongst recent Bachelor's level university graduates based on three waves of the National Graduates Survey (NGS) databases.

The NGS databases used here comprise large, representative databases of individuals who have successfully completed their programs at Canadian colleges and universities in 1982, 1986 and 1990, with information gathered during interviews conducted two and five years after graduation for each group of graduates (1984-87, 1988-92, 1990-95). These data thus allow for the longitudinal analysis of outcomes for each class of graduates, as well as comparisons of these earnings dynamics from one cohort to another. Further-more, the databases contain a range of variables of both a conventional type (employment status, earnings, etc.) and others which are especially pertinent to recent university graduates, such as the job-education skill match, the comparison of the individual's schooling to the qualifications required for the job, and so on, which allow for a relatively detailed and somewhat novel analysis of the factors underlying the gender differences in earnings. In short, the size and representative structure of the NGS databases, their panel nature, the existence of three cohorts of data, and the interesting variables available on the files provide the opportunity to conduct a relatively extensive dynamic analysis of the gender earnings gap for this particular group of Canadian workers from the early 1980s into the mid-1990s.

Furthermore, the focus of the NGS databases on recent graduates as they enter the labour market with relatively little previous experience and freshly minted human capital permits us to isolate the emerging trends which are being driven at the entry-point margins of the market more than do more general databases which include workers of all ages, thus portending the sorts of changes which are likely to occur on a more general scale over time.

---

[1]Gunderson (1985, 1989) and Gunderson and Riddell (1991) provide good overviews of the gender earnings gap in terms of the relevant estimation issues, the empirical evidence, and the related policy issues, while more recent work includes Christofides and Swidinsky (1994); Doiron and Riddell (1994); Kidd and Shannon (1994, 1996); and Miller (1987).

Ross Finnie and Ted Wannell

In our case, probably the most important findings are that there have been significant increases in the starting earnings levels of female graduates, but declines for men, thus causing a significant narrowing of the gender earnings gap over a period of just eight years (from 1984 through 1988 to 1992), but that there have not been commensurate changes in the patterns of earnings growth from two to five years following graduation, suggesting that women's catching up might not happen as quickly or in as sustained a fashion as the immediate post-graduation earnings levels might suggest.[2]

There are two main sections to the empirical analysis. The first consists of a comparison of a variety of indicators of employment status and job characteristics of male and female graduates as of the two points in time corresponding to the interview dates for each of the three cohorts of graduates. These include traditional measures, such as unemployment rates and employment status (part-time/full-time, temporary/permanent, self-employed/paid worker) as well as some of the less conventional types mentioned above (the job-education skill match, over- and under-qualification, job satisfaction).

Earnings patterns are also analyzed in this first section, leading into the second part of the analysis, which consists of an econometric analysis of the gender earnings gap for each of the six periods of time covered by the data. Using standard regression models and decomposition methods, the overall difference in mean earnings is divided into the part due to differences in the mean values of the explanatory variables and the part due to the differences in the associated coefficient estimates. In this way, we are able to describe the structure of the earnings gap at each point in time, its evolution from two

---

[2]This paper is part of a series on the school-to-work transition and early years in the labour market of postsecondary graduates. Finnie (1999a) documents the employment and earnings patterns of graduates at all levels (College, Bachelor's, Master's, PhD); Finnie (1999b) analyzes the changes in the structure of graduates' earnings using standard decomposition techniques based on regression models; Finnie (1999c) focuses on the dynamic aspects of graduates' school-to-work transition; and Finnie (1999d, e) explore outcomes by field of study amongst Bachelor's graduates in a descriptive manner and then more econometrically. Other joint work includes Betts, Ferrall and Finnie (1998, 1999), the first using a hazard model framework to look at the time to the first job, and the second studying the effects of school quality on graduates' earnings. Lavoie and Finnie (1999) focus on the performance of science and technology graduates in particular. Other work is currently in progress.

to five years following graduation, and the shifts in this structure across cohorts.

The analysis thus exploits a unique and under-used set of databases to provide a somewhat novel perspective of the gender earnings gap amongst a particularly interesting group of workers — recent Bachelor's level university graduates. The next section introduces the NGS databases and outlines the selection of the samples used in the analysis. The third section presents the descriptive statistics, while the fourth covers the decomposition analysis. The final section includes a summary of the major results, some broad implications of these findings, and some direction for further research.

The NGS Data and the Construction of the Working Samples

The National Graduates Surveys

The National Graduates Surveys (and Follow-Up) databases, developed by Statistics Canada in conjunction with Human Resources Development Canada, are well suited to this analysis for a number of reasons. First, the NGS files are representative of the underlying national population of trade, college, and university graduates in the given years and include large numbers of observations — more than 30,000 individuals in each survey in total, and close to 10,000 at the Bachelor's level alone, thus providing abundant samples for the analysis of post-graduation labour market outcomes.[3]

Second, the NGS databases have a longitudinal element, being derived from the two interviews carried out for each cohort, two and five years after graduation. This allows for a dynamic analysis of the school-to-work transition covering the seminal years of graduates' working careers. This dynamic aspect is especially interesting in the present context, as it allows us to observe the evolution of outcomes by gender in the early post-schooling

---

[3]The NGS databases are based on a stratified sampling scheme, with stratifications by degree level, discipline and province. The sample framework is established through the use of institutions' administrative files on graduates, with those records also providing some of the basic educational information on the NGS files, such as program and discipline of study.

Ross Finnie and Ted Wannell

years and to analyze the factors which underlie the substantial growth in the gender earnings gap which is observed over this interval.

Third, the availability of data for three separate cohorts of graduates — representing those who successfully completed their university programs in 1982, 1986 and 1990 — permits the comparison of outcomes over a period typically thought to have been characterized by important changes in the labour market experiences of younger workers, as well as a time during which women generally continued to catch up to men in terms of earnings, while also bringing the record up to the fairly recent past.[4]

Finally, the NGS databases possess interesting arrays of variables covering the educational experiences, employment profiles, job characteristics, and basic demographic information and other attributes of graduates. These include not only more conventional measures, such as field of study, employment status, and earnings levels, but also others which are more specifically related to the particular experiences of recent postsecondary graduates and the school-to-work transition, such as the educational prerequisites of the job as compared to the level of schooling attained, the extent to which the skills learned at school were being used in the job, and evaluations of the current job with respect to earnings levels and on a more overall basis. The variables used in the analysis are described in the Appendix.

In summary, the three NGS databases provide for a detailed, dynamic analysis of early labour market outcomes generally, and the gender earnings gap in particular, amongst Canadian university graduates in the critical years just following graduation from the early 1980s into the mid-1990s. The NGS data are, furthermore, interesting and unique not only in a Canadian context, but to the best of these authors' understanding they are unequalled in the world in terms of offering large representative surveys of postsecondary graduates covering various elements of the school-to-work transition over the last decade and a half.

---

[4]The first survey of 1995 graduates has been carried out, but those data were not ready for analysis at the time of writing and the second interview data will not be available until they are collected in the year 2000.

Selection of the Working Samples

First, the entire analysis excludes graduates who had previously accumulated five or more years of full-time work experience by the time of graduation from the program in question or who were 35 years of age or older upon completing their studies, thus focusing the analysis on "fresh" graduates who have followed more or less conventional career profiles with respect to school and work. These deletions exclude, in particular, women returning to school after having spent time raising children, as well as both men and women who have made mid-career switches involving major re-tooling in terms of education. While such individuals certainly comprise interesting groups of graduates, their study is best left to a separate project.

Second, graduates who obtained an additional degree by one of the two interview dates were deleted from the analysis at that point.[5] This was done, first of all, because many such graduates no longer belonged to the original education group (e.g., a Bachelor's graduate might have become a Master's graduate and perhaps changed disciplines) and had in any event been mixing school and work in a way likely to affect the labour market outcomes upon

---

[5]That is, graduates who had obtained a new degree/certificate/diploma by the first interview were deleted from both periods' analysis, while those who obtained a new diploma only by the second interview were included in the first period calculations (as long as they met the other selection criteria) but not the second. This selection procedure results in samples which are as inclusive as possible for each survey year, which is especially important in a context where going on to further schooling could be related to early labour market outcomes, a hypothesis which finds support in the case of engineering graduates in Finnie and Lavoie (1997).

Essentially all formal postsecondary degree/certificate/diploma programs were considered in this selection. Exceptions include the following: "interest"/recreation-type courses, which typically do not represent any sort of formal human capital investment and which should not generally have a direct effect on early labour market outcomes; banking and insurance certificates, which are normally gained largely as a matter of a course by those on certain career paths; non-professional health certificates which, by their very designation, are not generally career related; high school diplomas, which are deemed to largely represent an accreditation formality without direct effects on labour market outcomes for those already possessing postsecondary diplomas; and registered apprenticeships, which are again seen to be part of a normal career path rather than additional formal schooling per se.

Ross Finnie and Ted Wannell

which this analysis is focused. A second, related reason for this selection rule is that including "additional degree graduates" would have thrown off the precise post-graduation time frame corresponding to the two interview dates (i.e., two and five years after graduation) which holds for the non-continuing group. Finally, it is impossible to identify the specific field of study in which any new degree was obtained as of the 1984 survey for the 1982 graduates.

Third, part-time workers who cited school as the reason for their partial involvement in the labour market were excluded from the analysis of all the employment-related outcomes on the grounds that such individuals were — by definition — still principally students and had therefore not yet entered the school-to-work transition phase of their careers in earnest.[6] Other part-time workers were, on the other hand, generally included in the analysis, thus lending it a broad sample base.

Fourth, the small number (less than one-half of 1% in each year) of "other" workers (i.e., not paid, not self-employed) were also eliminated from the entire analysis of job outcomes, since employment status, earnings levels, and other job outcomes of such family workers, volunteers and other non-standard workers would be expected to depart from those of others (as verified empirically). A similarly small number of workers deemed to have unreasonably low earnings were also deleted.[7]

Finally, observations were dropped if the required information was missing for any of the variables used in the analysis, resulting in a further very small number of deletions. The results of the major sample selection criteria as applied to male and female graduates of the three cohorts are shown in Table 1.

---

[6]An analysis of the 1982 cohort, for which enrolment status as of the interview dates is given in the NGS files (which was not the case for the later cohorts), revealed that most individuals eliminated by this restriction (part-time — student) were in fact full-time students and, conversely, that most full-time students were eliminated by this condition, precisely as wished.

[7]Full-time workers with less than $5,000 in annual earnings (the equivalent of a wage of about $3.20 per hour for 30 hours of work per week over 52 weeks) were deleted. This affected no more than approximately one-half of 1% of the sample in each year, with a relatively high proportion of the first interview cases (where there were generally more such low earners) being individuals who then obtained a new diploma by the subsequent interview (who were otherwise eliminated from most of the analysis, see above), suggesting the relevant jobs were research assistantships or other such atypical jobs.

Table 1: Sample Sizes[1]

| | 1982 Cohort | | | | 1986 Cohort | | | | 1990 Cohort | | | |
| | 1984 | | 1987 | | 1988 | | 1991 | | 1992 | | 1995 | |
	% Deleted	# Left	% Deleted	# Left	% Deleted	# Left	% Deleted	# Left	% Deleted	# Left	% Deleted	# Left
Unweighted												
Males												
Original sample		4,202		3,645		4,695		4,053		4,236		3,498
New diploma	16	3,542	34	2,395	12	4,112	19	3,279	15	3,593	35	2,260
Student-PT	2	3,468	1	2,341	2	4,002	2	3,206	2	3,525	1	2,231
Females												
Original sample		3,949		3,450		4,782		4,145		4,643		3,983
New diploma	17	3,283	32	2,337	14	4,095	21	3,257	16	3,882	36	2,560
Student-PT	2	3,214	2	2,275	2	3,985	2	3,177	2	3,783	2	2,499
Weighted												
Males												
Original sample		35,212		34,169		39,477		38,837		39,764		37,602
New diploma	17	29,100	36	21,863	13	34,193	20	30,892	16	33,452	35	24,324
Student-PT	2	28,441	1	21,380	2	33,296	2	30,148	2	32,814	1	24,016
Females												
Original sample		35,136		34,226		43,000		42,105		46,244		45,443
New diploma	21	27,875	35	22,134	17	35,797	24	32,011	17	38,544	36	29,087
Student-PT	2	27,253	2	21,481	3	34,526	2	31,300	2	37,388	2	28,362

Note: [1] A very small number of non-wage, non-self-employed workers (i.e., family, volunteer workers) were also deleted in each year.

Ross Finnie and Ted Wannell

Employment Status and Job Outcomes

The Distribution of Graduates by Field of Study and Sex

We begin with the distribution of male and female graduates by field of study (Table 2a) and the share of female graduates within each field (Table 2b). The distributions by field were relatively stable across cohorts, with the only significant shifts being a moderate decline in the percentage of engineering graduates amongst men, and declines in elementary and secondary teaching and fine arts and humanities graduates and an increase in the percentage of commerce graduates amongst women.

The figures thus show some enduring differences in the distribution of graduates by sex. Female graduates have been significantly overrepresented in teaching/education, fine arts/humanities, the general social sciences and other health disciplines (i.e., apart from doctors, dentists, pharmacists, optometrists, and the like — dominated by nursing graduates). Women have, on the other hand, been underrepresented in economics, engineering, computer science, and mathematics and the physical sciences. The other fields have had more or less similar numbers of male and female graduates (agricultural and biological sciences, veterinary sciences, medical professions), or have seen women catch up to men over time (commerce, law). Not surprisingly, these male-female differences in the distribution of graduates by field are of central importance to the overall differences in outcomes by gender seen below.

Unemployment Rates and Employment Status

Unemployment Rates. We now turn to indicators of labour force status and job outcomes shown in Table 3. Unemployment rates were generally quite low, ranging from 4 to 11% across the various interview periods, with the rates generally dropping quite significantly from two to five years following graduation, from the 10 to 11% range down to 4 or 5%. The rates show no clear trend across cohorts, with the unemployment levels of the first group of graduates virtually identical to those of the last set, interviewed at

Table 2a: The Distribution of Graduates by Field of Study[1]

	1982 Cohort	1986 Cohort	1990 Cohort
	%	%	%
Males			
No specialization	2	4	3
Elem./secon. teaching	4	5	5
Other education	5	4	5
Fine Arts & Humanities	10	11	12
Commerce	15	15	15
Economics	6	5	6
Law	5	3	4
Other social sciences	13	11	14
Agricultural & bio. sc.	6	6	6
Veterinary	1	1	1
Engineering	19	17	15
Medical professions	5	4	4
Other health	-	-	1
Computer sciences	3	5	4
Math. & other phys. sc.	6	7	6
	100	**100**	**100**
Females			
No specialization	2	3	3
Elem./secon. teaching	16	12	12
Other education	9	6	7
Fine Arts & Humanities	17	18	17
Commerce	9	11	12
Economics	2	2	2
Law	4	3	3
Other social sciences	18	21	22
Agricultural & bio. sc.	6	6	7
Veterinary	1	1	1
Engineering	2	2	2
Medical professions	4	3	3
Other health	6	6	6
Computer sciences	1	2	1
Math. & other phys. sc.	2	3	3
	100	**100**	**100**

Note: [1] In this and all following tables, a dash indicates too few observations to report (see text for an explanation of the reporting rules).

Ross Finnie and Ted Wannell

Table 2b: The Percentage of Female Graduates by Field of Study

	1982 Cohort	1986 Cohort	1990 Cohort
	%	%	%
No specialization	49	51	50
Elem./secon. teaching	79	73	72
Other education	66	64	65
Fine Arts & Humanities	63	63	61
Commerce	38	44	47
Economics	21	33	28
Law	43	46	52
Other social sciences	57	67	64
Agricultural & bio. sc.	51	52	58
Veterinary	47	42	56
Engineering	11	13	15
Medical professions	44	46	49
Other health	97	94	89
Computer sciences	24	31	20
Math. & other phys. sc.	30	30	36

roughly comparable points in the business cycle.[8] Of particular pertinence to this paper, unemployment rates were more or less equal for male and female graduates.

---

[8]The first interview of the class of 1982 (in 1984) took place during a very deep, but relatively brief recession, so that by the time of the second interview in 1987, the economy was in the midst of a strong upswing. The class of 1986 matriculated on the cusp of this upswing, but was then experiencing the protracted downturn of the early 1990s when interviewed a second time in 1991. The class of 1990 first faced the 1990s recession (1992 interview), and then a soft stage of the fitful recovery from this downturn for the second interview in 1995. We thus generalize that the first and last cohorts graduated at approximately similar points in the business cycle, although the general climate improved more quickly for the first cohort than the later one.

A number of other broad changes also occurred over this period. In the course of the 1980s recession, relative youth earnings generally declined and then remained low (in an historical context) thereafter. Perhaps at least partly as a result, age-specific participation rates in postsecondary education climbed over the first part of this period, slowing only after the turn of the decade — a time when provincial governments were cutting back on funding. Employment and pay equity legislation was introduced (and in one case, later rescinded) in a number of jurisdictions. A North American free trade zone was created. A national value-added tax was introduced, and so on.

The Gender Earnings Gap Amongst Recent Bachelor's Graduates   *11*

Table 3: Employment Status, Job Characteristics, and Overall Evaluation of the Educational Program[1]

	1982 Cohort		1986 Cohort		1990 Cohort	
	1984	1987	1988	1991	1992	1995
Males						
Employment Status						
Unemp. rate (%)	10	4	11	8	10	5
% PT	6	4	4	2	6	3
% PT involuntarily (PT workers)	86	-	71	67	80	74
% Temporary	23	7	19	9	22	9
% Self-employed	8	12	7	11	7	13
Job Outcomes						
% Over-qualified	31	28	31	26	28	26
% Under-qualified	2	4	3	6	3	4
Job satisfaction (overall) index	78	80	78	81	80	80
Job satisfaction (earnings) index	66	67	64	66	67	66
Program Evaluation Index	-	74	79	77	76	73
Females						
Employment Status						
Unemp. rate (%)	10	5	10	8	10	5
% PT	12	14	11	12	11	11
% PT involuntarily (PT workers)	78	43	64	34	78	50
% Temporary	29	11	24	15	26	14
% Self-employed	4	7	3	7	4	7
Job Outcomes						
% Over-qualified	34	28	37	29	30	26
% Under-qualified	1	4	3	5	3	3
Job satisfaction (overall) index	76	78	76	80	79	79
Job satisfaction (earnings) index	65	65	61	66	66	66
Program Evaluation Index		72	78	75	72	69

Note   [1] In this and all following tables, the samples exclude those who obtained a new diploma by the relevant interview, those who were part-time workers due to school, and "other" workers.

Part-Time Employment.[9] Rates of part-time employment (Figure 1) have, not surprisingly, been much higher for female graduates than males, varying between 12 and 14% for the former, versus 2 to 6% for the latter. Furthermore, these gender differences grew in the years following graduation, with

---

[9] Recall that individuals working part-time precisely because they were in school are excluded from the analysis.

Ross Finnie and Ted Wannell

Figure 1: Part-Time Employment

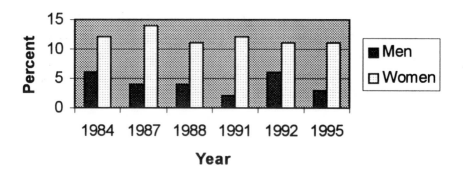

the proportion of female graduates in part-time jobs remaining stable or edging upward slightly from the first interview to the second in each case, while the males' rates declined two or three points from their already lower levels.

The men's rates — their general levels and their declines over time — primarily reflect the employment opportunities they faced and the improvements in these conditions in the years following graduation (the figures indicate that most male part-time workers held that job status involuntarily). The female rates, on the other hand, also reflect labour supply decisions related to having and raising children and other factors related to a looser labour force attachment in general, as reflected in the lower rates of involuntary part-time work, especially as of the second interview. The gender differences in preferences are not, however, sufficient to explain fully the associated differences in the rates of part-time work, meaning that a significant "gender part-time employment status gap" has indeed existed amongst graduates no matter how the status is viewed.[10]

---

[10]Multiplying the part-time rates by the involuntary part-time percentages generates involuntary part-time rates of 5.2/2.6%, 2.8/1.3% and 4.8/2.2% for the three cohorts of male graduates as each of the interview dates, versus rates of 9.4/6.0%, 7.0/4.1% and 8.6/5.5% for the female graduates. See the Appendix for certain reservations regarding the comparability of the rates of involuntary part-time work between the first two and third cohorts.

As with the unemployment rates, there was no clear trend in the rates of part-time work across cohorts, with comparisons of the first and last cohorts indicating either stable or slightly lower rates for the later graduates (males, females as of two and five years following graduation).[11] At a time when it is often taken for granted that there have been increases in "non-standard work" in general, and especially amongst the young, these data provide no empirical evidence of this phenomenon in the form of part-time work amongst Bachelor's level university graduates.

Temporary Employment. There were uniformly large declines in the rates of temporary employment (Figure 2) from two to five years following graduation, with the men's rates falling from the 19 to 23% range to 7 to 9%, while for women the rates fell from the 24 to 29% range to 11 to 15%, presumably again reflecting the improvements in job opportunities over this interval. The data might, however, hint at a moderate shift in these dynamics across cohorts, with the percentage of graduates with temporary jobs as of the second interview, in particular, remaining slightly higher for the third cohort of graduates relative to the earliest group.

Figure 2: Temporary Employment

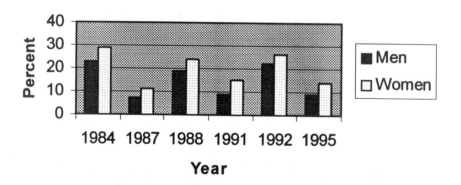

---

[11]The involuntary part-time rates (see above) are uniformly lower for the third cohort.

Ross Finnie and Ted Wannell

Women were more commonly in temporary jobs than men. And while it might be tempting to ascribe these differences to supply-side factors, any such explanation comes up against the fact that for the one year such data are available, the proportions of men and women in temporary jobs voluntarily were at similar levels (see Finnie, 1999c). In short, the gender differences in rates of temporary employment would appear to be generally due to a relative penury of permanent job opportunities for women rather than a matter of choice — another element of the gender gap.

Self-Employment. Being self-employed — as opposed to being a wage or salary worker — could stem from a variety of reasons, and it is beyond the scope of this paper to attempt a full accounting of why some graduates enter self-employment. It is, however, another outcome which differs substantially for men and women (Figure 3).

In every period, the percentage of individuals who were self-employed was roughly twice as great for men (8 to 13%) as women (3 to 7%). Since the rates generally increased from two years to five years following graduation, and when we consider that labour market opportunities frequently tended to improve over this interval (as discussed above), these results might suggest that self-employment has more often stemmed from the advantages of the self-employment option rather than the lack of suitable opportunities with respect to wage and salary positions (at least at the margin), and that male graduates have had advantages over female graduates in this regard.

Figure 3: Self Employment

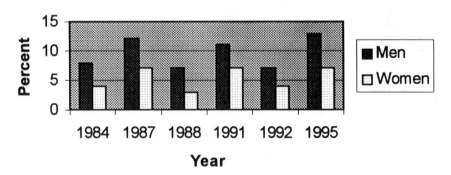

No cross-cohort trends are evident — again indicating that there has been no general increase in non-standard work amongst Bachelor's graduates over time.

Usual Hours of Work (1986 and 1990 Cohorts)

In addition to the information on full- and part-time employment status, the 1986 and 1990 graduates were asked about the usual hours of work in their current jobs and it turns out that differences in hours play an important role in the overall gender earnings gap and its growth from two years to following graduation beyond what is captured by the simpler part-time versus full-time differentiation. In this section we concentrate on gender differences in usual hours amongst full-time workers.

At all time points, full-time men (overall) averaged at least two hours more work per week than female graduates, with the gap growing over time within each cohort (Table 4a and Figure 4). Amongst 1986 graduates, average hours for men increased from 44.3 in 1988 to 45.1 in 1991, while female hours increased from 41.8 to 42.4, with the hours gap thus widening from 2.5 to 2.7. For the 1990 graduates, average male hours went from 44.7 in 1992 to 45.3 in 1995, the average female workweek remained steady at 41.8 hours in both years, and the hours gap grew commensurately from 2.9 to 3.5. The differences in hours worked were, therefore, greater and increased more over time for the later cohort — thus running counter to the convergence seen in some of the other employment-related outcomes (including earnings) across subsequent cohorts of graduates.

The major reason for the hours gap — in the accounting sense — is that many more male than female graduates worked very long hours (i.e., more than 50 hours per week), with more than one-quarter of full-time employed men working greater than 50 hours per week in each cohort, as compared to just 17.1% of the female graduates in 1988 and 19.3% in 1992 (Table 4b). Furthermore, the gap grew in the subsequent three years amongst both sets of graduates: for men, the incidence of long hours increased to over 30% in both cohorts, while for women the rate grew from 17 to 20% for the earlier class and inched up just half a point for the later group. Thus, within five years of graduation, half again as many men were working very long hours as women.

It may seem reasonable to ascribe the different work hours of male and female graduates to a greater burden of familial responsibilities being placed on women — the care of children in particular. But although the hours gap

Ross Finnie and Ted Wannell

Table 4a: Average Weekly Hours by Life Cycle Status (Full-Time Only)

		Two Years After		Five Years After	
		1988	1992	1991	1995
Men	Single no children	43.9	44.4	44.9	45.0
	Married no children	44.9	45.6	44.9	45.2
	Married with children	46.3	45.5	45.7	45.9
	All men	44.3	44.7	45.1	45.3
Women	Single no children	42.1	41.6	43.1	42.6
	Married no children	41.3	42.3	42.4	42.4
	Married with children	41.8	41.5	40.6	39.5
	All women	41.8	41.8	42.4	41.8
Difference	Single no children	1.8	2.8	1.8	2.4
	Married no children	3.6	3.3	2.5	2.8
	Married with children	4.5	4.0	5.1	6.4
	All	2.5	2.9	2.7	3.5

Figure 4: Average Weekly Hours
Full-time Workers

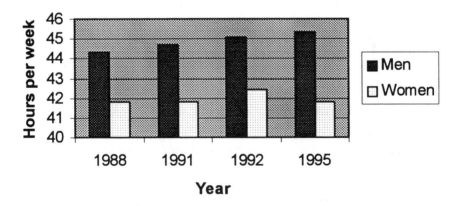

Table 4b: Working Long Hours
% of Full-Time Working More than 50 Hours per Week

	Two Years After		Five Years After	
	1988	*1992*	*1991*	*1995*
	%	%	%	%
Men	26	31	28	33
Women	17	20	19	20

is greatest amongst married graduates with children, there is also a sizable gap amongst single, childless graduates. For the class of 1986, unattached males averaged 1.8 hours per week more than their female counterparts in both 1988 and 1991, and the gap was even higher in the class of 1990: 2.8 hours per week in 1992 and 2.4 hours per week in 1995.

The gender gap was greater, but the cross-cohort patterns of full-time hours were steadier amongst married graduates with no children. In both cohorts, women worked approximately three-and-a-half fewer hours per week than their male counterparts as of two years following graduation and about two-and-a-half hours less at the five-year mark, with this reduction perhaps reflecting a self-selection process whereby more career-minded women remained in the married-no-children group and others chose the "mommy-track".

Finally, the data clearly indicate that female graduates bear a greater responsibility when children are present, with the hours gap being the greatest amongst married graduates with children. Married women with children in full-time work averaged at least four hours less work per week than their male counterparts as of two years following graduation, with the difference increasing to 5.1 hours by the second interview for the 1986 cohort and to 6.4 hours for the 1990 group.

Alternative Measures of Job Quality: Skill Matches and Job Satisfaction

Educational Prerequisites and Graduates' Qualifications. The first measure of the job-education skill match available on the NGS is the relationship between the educational prerequisites of the job and the individual's level of attainment. Overall, a substantial number of graduates appear to have been overqualified for their positions, with these rates varying from 26 to 37% across the various periods for male and female graduates (Table 3). These results could, however, reflect a certain ambiguity regarding the formal prerequisites versus the true requirements of many jobs. It might, for example, often be the case that a Bachelor's degree is not formally required, but is needed to compete successfully for a position, thus resulting in an artificially high rate of "overqualification". In short, although the questions posed and the related construction should generate a fairly "objective" comparison of the educational prerequisites of the job and the individual's qualifications, there is some room for the individual's perception to play a role in the resulting measures.

However, the rates generally declined a little from the first interview to the second — consistent with a situation where graduates were moving into positions for which they were more aptly qualified, gaining promotions, and generally moving forward in their careers. Along the other time dimension, rates of overqualification were slightly lower for the latest cohort relative to earlier ones and, while it is again difficult to know exactly how to interpret these findings, we can at least say that they do not support the notion that the quality of jobs being found by graduates has been deteriorating.[12]

Finally, even if we cannot be too sure of the ultimate meaning of this measure, the gender comparisons should reflect the kinds of jobs that male and female graduates have been obtaining. The rates of being overqualified (underemployed?) range from being equal (1987 and 1995) to being slightly to moderately higher for women (the other years), with the differences being greater for the middle cohort than the other groups of graduates.

The Job-Education Skill Use Index. The other skill use measure reported here is the job-education skill match index which has been created from the information available in the NGS databases, with higher values indicating greater use of the skills acquired during the education program in the current job (see the Appendix). The results should be directly comparable across interview years for a given cohort and between the first two cohorts, but not between the first two and last groups of graduates due to a somewhat changed set of response options given in the NGS questionnaires.

---

[12]On the other hand, the apparently increasing educational levels required in the jobs that graduates have been finding could also represent "qualification creep" — in a weak labour market, requirements may have been arbitrarily raised for some positions.

The reported scores suggest that the great majority of graduates were using skills they had learned at school in their current jobs. The mean scores in the 82- to 88-point range for the earlier cohorts (1984-87, 1988-91) represent corresponding percentages of graduates who responded in the affirmative to the simple "yes"/"no" question regarding their use of the skills learned at school in the current job asked in those years, while the 68- to 71-point range for the 1990 cohort (1992-95) represents an average response of slightly more than "to some extent" where the other options were "not at all" "very little" and "to a great extent" (see the Appendix).

Perhaps surprisingly, there were no dramatic changes in the index scores from two to five years following graduation — but this could reflect the ambiguities related to the underlying question and the construction and interpretation of the resulting measure more than the actual underlying job-education skill match relationship per se.[13]

Thus, we again have a measure whose absolute interpretation is somewhat problematic, but for which the relevant gender comparisons mean at least something. This time, the gender differences are even smaller (never more than two points) with no clear male-female pattern across the various survey years.[14]

---

[13]Indeed, even the underlying concept is problematic — what is a "skill"? One might also wonder how well graduates can identify what was learned at school, what is used in the job, and the relationship between the two? Thus, while the questions that were posed are reasonable, the results need to be interpreted with care. For example, and with regard to the dynamic element in particular, it is possible that by five years after finishing their programs, graduates are less able to identify what they learned in school and have difficulty in differentiating their current skill sets in terms of what was developed during their formal schooling, what was gained on the job, and what was a combination of the two. It is also possible that some graduates were using different skills than those that were gained at school, but ones which could never have been developed except by building upon that more fundamental base; how would such graduates respond? In short, there is information in these results — after all, the responses are hardly random, and the results generally make sense — but the findings need to be interpreted with great care.

[14]Standard deviations of the means have been calculated and are very small, typically under one point, but the indicated differences are so small as to be uninteresting, even if they might be statistically significant.

Overall Job Satisfaction. Similar to the skill-match measure, the job satisfaction index scores reported in the tables are constructed such that higher scores indicate greater satisfaction (see the Appendix). Overall, graduates appear to have been what we might describe as "quite" satisfied with their jobs, with the range of mean scores around the 80-point mark indicating that given the response options of "very satisfied", "satisfied", "dissatisfied" (or "not satisfied" in certain years), "very dissatisfied" (or "not at all satisfied"), the average responses were generally just under half-way between the two most favourable evaluations.[15]

Despite the extent to which job characteristics and outcomes generally evolve in a favourable fashion from two to five years following graduation (as seen above and as will be seen further regarding earnings below), the associated levels of job satisfaction remained almost perfectly stable over this interval. This presumably reflects the relative/subjective nature of individuals' responses to the satisfaction question: they would presumably *expect* to have better jobs over time, and thus express no greater satisfaction when those expectations are realized.

The job satisfaction scores generally remained stable or rose slightly from the first cohort to the third, thus lending further evidence to the idea that there has not been any significant decline in the quality of jobs that graduates have been finding over this period — although it is again difficult to know what role expectations are playing in these patterns.

Finally, despite the gender differences in job characteristics seen above and the differences in earnings shown below, overall job satisfaction levels were very similar for male and female graduates. Taken at face value, these results would presumably suggest that female graduates were happy with the job opportunities (and outcomes) they faced and that gender differences in earnings (and other outcomes) have been stemming from supply side influences — that is, that the earnings differences are the result of different choices being made by men and women in terms of employment status and the specific jobs they take, rather than being due to discrimination per se. On the other hand, if respondents' frames of reference differ by gender, this interpretation is no longer possible: that is, women might face reduced opportunities and then express their satisfaction in terms relative to those

---

[15]The four categories have index scores of 0, 33.3, 66.7, and 100 respectively (see the Appendix), meaning that the score half-way between the two most favourable responses would be 83.4, which compares to the mean scores of 76 to 81 reported in the table.

lower expectations, thus being equally "satisfied" with objectively less attractive jobs. Attempting to resolve these competing hypotheses would be a very interesting exercise, but one that lies beyond the scope of this paper and perhaps the limits of the NGS data themselves.

Earnings Satisfaction. The earnings satisfaction scores are generally lower than those for the more global measure just seen, thus suggesting that the scores mean *something*, but otherwise show the same patterns as before. Men and women express similar levels of satisfaction, despite their different earnings levels; earnings satisfaction changed only slightly from the first to second interview, despite the significant increases in earnings and other job characteristics which generally occurred over this interval; and there is no clear trend across cohorts, even in the presence of some significant shifts in real earnings levels (downward for men, upward for women), suggesting that graduates were expressing their satisfaction relative to the conditions faced by their own particular cohort rather than earlier graduates or some more timeless and perhaps more objective scale.

Earnings Patterns by Sex

Mean Earnings of Men and Women. Table 5 reports the earnings levels of graduates in 1995 constant dollars. These are presented in a number of ways: the mean earnings of all graduates who were working (and otherwise met the relevant sample inclusion criteria) as of each of the interview dates; the mean earnings of just those who were working full-time; median earnings for the same groups (all workers, full-time only); and mean earnings by quintile for the two sets of workers.

We focus, however, on the first set of figures — the mean earnings of all workers taken together (also shown in Figure 5) — due to their broader representativeness and because they provide the best context for the decomposition analysis presented below, which is based on similarly broad samples. Furthermore, the key elements of the patterns discussed here are generally similar to what is found in the medians and more detailed break-downs and the full-time groups.

The mean earnings of male graduates ranged from $32,800 to $35,200 as of the first interview to $45,800 to $42,100 as of the second, while female graduates' earnings varied between $28,600 and $30,500 as of the first point and $34,600 and $35,500 as of the second. The NGS data thus allow us to

Table 5: Earnings (1995 Constant Dollars)[1]

	1982 Cohort			1986 Cohort			1990 Cohort		
	1984	1987	Change	1988	1991	Change	1992	1995	1995
	$	$	%	$	$	%	$	$	%
Males									
Mean earnings									
All workers	35,000	45,800	31	35,200	43,100	22	32,800	42,100	28
Full-time workers	35,800	47,100	32	35,700	44,800	25	33,700	43,500	29
Median earnings									
All workers	33,200	40,900	23	32,000	39,100	22	31,300	39,000	25
Full-time workers	33,200	40,900	23	32,000	40,200	26	31,300	40,000	28
Mean earnings by quintile									
All workers									
Top	55,400[a]	76,600[a]	38	55,400[a]	67,700[a]	22	50,100[a]	66,800[b]	33
4th	39,200	48,100	23	37,200	45,000	21	36,500	46,000	26
3rd	32,600	40,500	24	31,700	39,000	23	30,800	38,500	25
2nd	25,400	33,600	32	25,800	32,200	25	22,300	30,900	39
Bottom	15,600	21,300	37	15,800	20,400	29	10,200	18,200	78
Full-time workers									
Top	55,800[a]	78,500[b]	41	55,600[a]	69,300[a]	25	50,700[a]	67,800[b]	34
4th	39,500	49,100	24	37,600	45,800	22	37,000	46,600	26
3rd	33,300	41,500	25	32,200	39,900	24	31,400	39,700	26
2nd	26,400	35,000	33	26,700	33,700	26	24,100	32,500	35
Bottom	17,700	24,000	36	17,400	23,000	32	12,900	20,100	56
Females									
Mean earnings									
All workers	28,600	34,600	21	29,700	35,100	18	30,500	35,500	16
Full-time workers	30,000	36,500	22	30,700	36,900	20	31,600	36,900	17
Median earnings									
All workers	28,900	32,000	11	29,500	33,800	15	28,100	33,500	19
Full-time workers	28,900	34,500	19	29,500	34,900	18	29,200	35,000	20
Mean earnings by quintile									
All workers									
Top	43,200	53,000[a]	23	46,200[a]	54,500[a]	18	47,200[a]	53,800[a]	14
4th	34,100	38,400	13	33,100	38,900	18	33,700	39,400	17
3rd	28,400	33,000	16	28,700	33,400	16	28,400	33,500	18
2nd	21,100	26,100	24	22,200	25,800	16	19,100	26,000	36
Bottom	12,100	14,500	20	12,800	11,800	-8	7,600	13,800	82
Full-time workers									
Top	43,600	55,100[a]	26	46,300[a]	58,000[a]	25	47,500[a]	55,300[a]	16
4th	34,800	40,000	15	33,900	40,200	19	34,100	40,400	18
3rd	29,600	34,400	16	29,600	34,400	16	29,300	35,100	20
2nd	23,200	28,700	24	23,900	28,000	17	22,000	28,300	29
Bottom	15,400	18,000	17	15,700	15,100	-4	11,600	16,600	43

Note: [1] In this and all following tables, the means with no letter superscript have standard
errors below 1, those with an *a* have standard errors between 1 and 2 and those
with a *b* have standard errors between 2 and 3.

The Gender Earnings Gap Amongst Recent Bachelor's Graduates   23

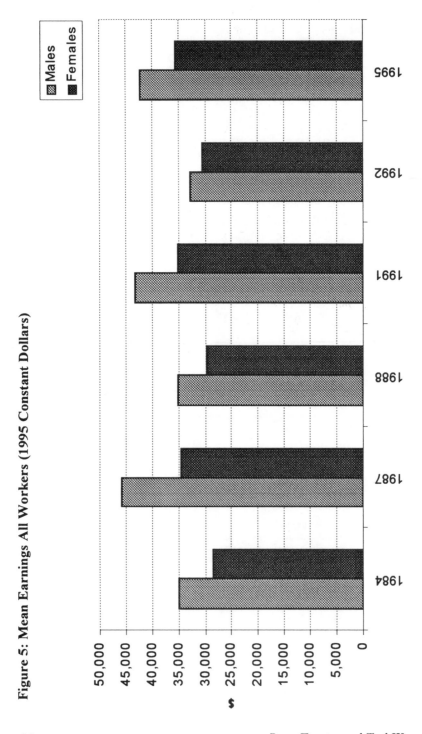

Figure 5: Mean Earnings All Workers (1995 Constant Dollars)

Ross Finnie and Ted Wannell

see rather precisely how graduates' earnings rose over the early years in the labour market and — of particular relevance to this paper — how male graduates' growth rates outstripped those of females in every case: 31 versus 21% for the first cohort, 22 as against 18% in the second, and 28 as opposed to 16% for the final group of graduates (see the relevant columns in Table 5).

The cross-cohort trends, on the other hand, clearly favoured female graduates. Male graduates' earnings generally declined over time, with the mean earnings of the third group of graduates laying 6.3% below those of the first cohort as of the first interview, and 8.1% lower as of the second interview (at roughly comparable points in the economic cycle). The mean earnings of the female graduates of the third cohort were, in contrast, 6.7 and 2.6% above those of the first cohort as of the first and second interviews respectively.

The Gender Earnings Gap. Male graduates' mean earnings were, not surprisingly, higher than female graduates' in every survey year. More interesting, however, are the magnitudes of those gaps and their movements over time. Given the time trends in earnings seen above, it is hardly surprising to see that the gender gap generally widened from the first interview to the second for each set of graduates, but was narrower for each subsequent cohort relative to the preceding one as of each of the interview dates.

More precisely, female mean earnings were 82 and 76% as high as male's earnings as of the first and second interviews, respectively, for the first cohort; they were 84 and 81% as high as at the same points following graduation amongst the graduates of the second cohort; and they were 93 and 84% as high at the two dates for the final set of graduates: that is, progressions of 82, 84 and 93 (first interview), and of 76, 81 and 84 (second interview). The gender earnings gap as of two years following graduation was, therefore, reduced by 61% over the relevant eight-year period, and by a still significant, but considerably smaller, 33%, as of five years following graduation.[16]

---

[16]These gaps compare to relative earnings levels ranging from 0.10 to 0.40 found for other groups of workers, with the gap generally being greater for broader groups of workers, smaller for more specific groups, and narrowing over time (Gunderson, 1985).

The gender earnings gap amongst Bachelor's graduates thus narrowed steadily across cohorts, but the *growth* in the gap from two to five years following graduation was actually greatest of all for the most recent group of graduates. In other words, although the gender earnings gap started off smaller for each more recent cohort, it continued to widen in the post-graduation years much as it had in the past — or even more so. These findings have potentially significant implications for the longer-term earnings profiles of graduates, as they suggest that longer-run ("permanent") reductions in the earnings gap amongst recent cohorts of graduates might not be nearly as great as the immediate post-graduation record suggests.

In this analysis, we are placing considerable emphasis on comparisons of the first and last groups of graduates due to their entering the market at roughly comparable points in the business cycle. Conversely, we are surmising that the somewhat different dynamics observed for the middle group — especially the much smaller widening of the gender earnings gap from two to five years following graduation — is probably related to the business cycle. We emphasize, however, that these results represent the record for just three graduating classes and a single business cycle, and acknowledge that our discussions of longer-run tendencies must be significantly tempered by the obvious fact that more years of data will need to be analyzed before firmer statements can be made about secular trends, business cycle effects, and other patterns over time.

Nevertheless, the data provide at least some evidence that while female graduates' earnings profiles appear to have been shifting up towards males' with each succeeding cohort in terms of starting *levels*, the relative *slopes* of those profiles might not have changed commensurately. In the decomposition analysis which follows, we will explore the factors underlying these trends.

The Gender Earnings Gap by Field of Study. Male and female mean earnings patterns by field of study are shown in Table 6. The cross field patterns per se are analyzed in detail in Finnie (1999c), and here we only look at the differences in the gender earnings gap by field and the related trends over time, seen most clearly in Figures 6a and 6b. The most interesting finding is that although the gender gap has varied across fields, with these patterns often shifting to a fairly significant degree from one cohort (and even interview) to the next, the overall trend was clearly towards more equal earnings within almost every discipline over time (i.e., in the later cohorts). The only cases where this was not true is other education and commerce as of the five-year interviews and computer science and mathematics

Table 6: Mean Earnings by Field (1995 Constant Dollars)

	1982 Cohort			1986 Cohort			1990 Cohort		
	1984	1987	Change	1988	1991	Change	1992	1995	1995
	$	$	%	$	$	%	$	$	%
Males									
No specialization	24,900[a]	35,600[a]	43	34,200[a]	43,000[a]	26	28,700[a]	36,800[a]	28
Elem./secon. teaching	32,800	38,300	17	34,500	37,200	8	33,900	37,700	11
Other education	29,700	34,300	15	31,600	37,900	20	28,700	35,600	24
Fine Arts &Humanities	25,500	35,500[a]	39	28,300	33,100	17	23,400	31,400	34
Commerce	34,200	44,200	29	34,900	43,600	25	32,700	42,300	29
Economics	32,100	45,000[a]	40	32,800[a]	39,100	19	32,900	43,300[a]	32
Law	38,100[a]	54,600[a]	43	36,600	58,800[a]	61	37,800	51,300[a]	36
Other social sciences	30,200	41,000	36	29,800	35,900	20	28,100	36,200	29
Agricultural & bio. sc.	29,700	41,700[a]	40	27,500	39,300	43	26,800	34,800[a]	30
Veterinary	33,700[b]	-	-	39,000[b]	-	-	-	-	-
Engineering	38,800	45,900	18	36,900	44,400	20	37,400	45,500	22
Medical professions	62,100[b]	86,800[b]	40	66,500[b]	76,900[b]	16	50,800[a]	76,600[b]	51
Other health	-	-	-	-	-	-	-	-	-
Computer sciences	39,000	47,400	22	34,300	43,500	27	37,900	46,400	22
Math. & other phys. sc.	35,800	45,600	27	33,900	42,500	25	33,200	42,100[a]	27
Females									
No specialization	24,300[a]	-	-	28,200	32,200	14	22,800	33,700[a]	48
Elem./secon. teaching	27,900	31,000	11	29,700	32,300	9	32,600	35,300	8
Other education	26,600	30,700	15	26,700	31,400	18	27,500	30,000	9
Fine Arts &Humanities	23,900	29,400	23	24,200	28,800	19	26,400	31,100	18
Commerce	29,700	37,700	27	30,600	38,500	26	31,300	36,200	16
Economics	31,700[a]	-	-	32,800[a]	33,100	1	-	-	-
Law	31,900	45,400[a]	42	35,900	48,500[a]	35	36,600[a]	54,000[b]	48
Other social sciences	25,000	31,100	24	26,300	32,500	24	26,600	31,400	18
Agricultural & bio. sc.	27,000	32,400	20	25,000	31,500[a]	26	26,300	32,400	23
Veterinary	-	-	-	-	-	-	-	-	-
Engineering	35,200	41,300[a]	17	35,200	41,200	17	37,300[a]	42,000	13
Medical professions	42,900	56,300[a]	31	49,300[a]	62,900[b]	28	50,400[a]	59,300[a]	18
Other health	34,800	35,600	2	34,200	35,900	5	35,000	37,500	7
Computer sciences	38,500[a]	45,100[a]	17	32,100	40,600	26	36,000[a]	41,700[a]	16
Math. & other phys. sc.	33,200	41,000[a]	23	32,000	37,900[a]	18	30,100	38,000[a]	26

Note: [1] In this and all following tables, a dash indicates too few observations to report (see text for an explanation of the reporting rules). The means with no letter superscript have standard errors below 1, those with an *a* have standard errors between 1 and 2 and those with a *b* have standard errors between 2 and 3.

Figure 6a: Mean Earnings Ratios by Field
1st Interviews

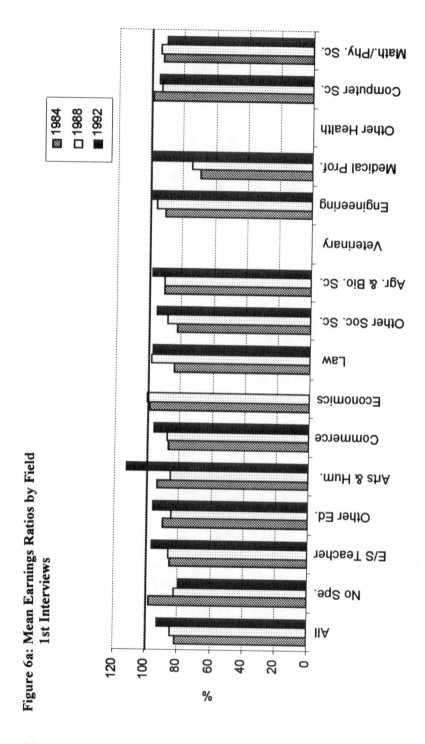

Ross Finnie and Ted Wannell

Figure 6b: Mean Earnings Ratios by Field
2nd Interviews

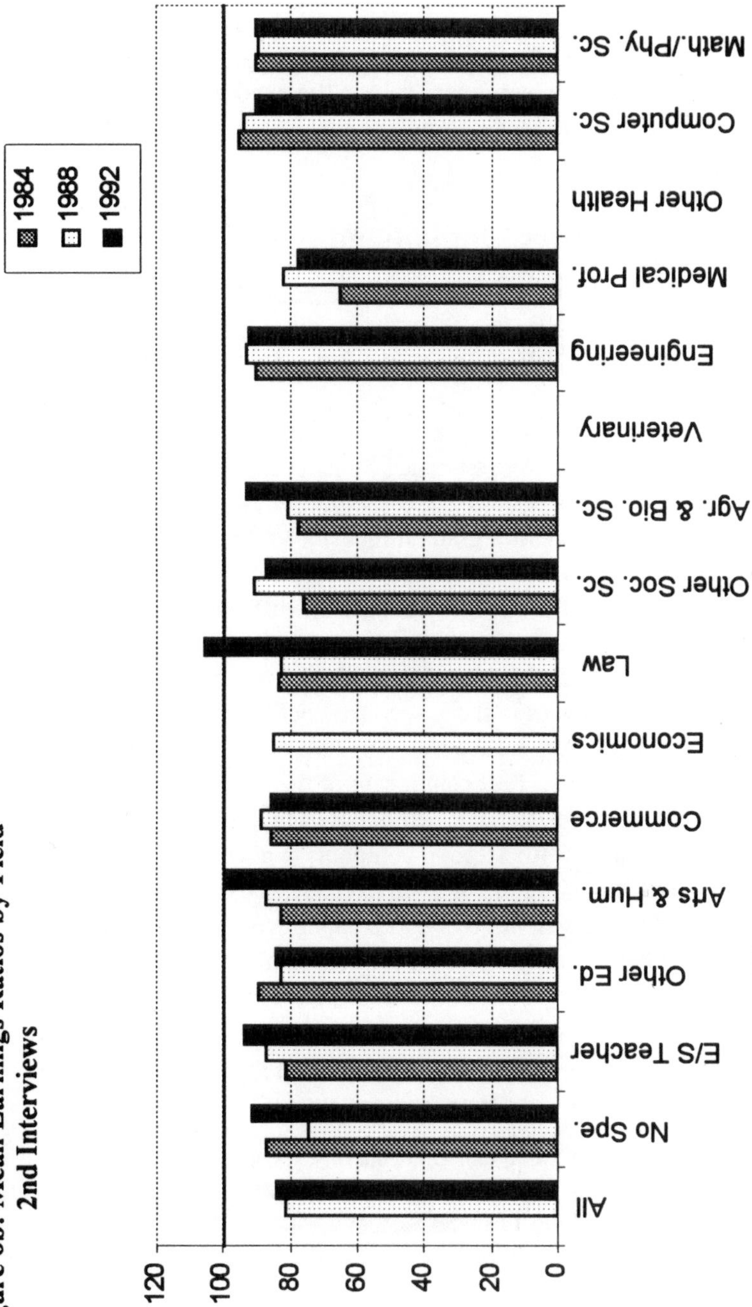
1984
1988
1992
%
120
100
80
60
40
20
0
All
No Spe.
E/S Teacher
Other Ed.
Arts & Hum.
Commerce
Economics
Law
Other Soc. Sc.
Agr. & Bio. Sc.
Veterinary
Engineering
Medical Prof.
Other Health
Computer Sc.
Math./Phy. Sc.

and physics as of both interview dates. We shall see below in the decomposition analysis that differences in the distribution of male and female graduates by field of study play a significant role in the gender earnings gap and its widening in the years following graduation.

The Decomposition Method and the Econometric Models

The Decomposition Analysis

The decomposition analysis essentially follows standard conventions.[17] First, separate earnings models were estimated for male and female graduates using the information gathered during the two interviews carried out for each cohort two and five years after graduation (1984-87 for the 1982 graduates, 1986-91 for the 1986 graduates and 1992-95 for the 1990 graduates). These results were then used to decompose the gender differences into the part due to differences in the mean values of the explanatory variables (field of study, job experience, province of residence, individual characteristics, etc.) and the part due to the differences in the associated coefficient estimates.[18]

Following the usual procedures, the effects of the differences in the explanatory variables (the first component of the decomposition) have been evaluated using the male coefficient estimates, while the effects of the different coefficient estimates (the second component) have been evaluated using the female mean levels. As in any such exercise, the decomposition algebra could have been reversed, but this approach allows us to view the earnings gap in terms of how much less women earn due to the "discriminatory" rates of return applied to their given sets of characteristics and how much less they

---

[17]See Cain (1986) for a thorough general exposition of the decomposition method employed here, Gunderson (1989) for another general review in the context of the gender earnings gap per se, and Gunderson (1985) and Gunderson and Riddell (1991) for a focus on Canadian studies of the gender earnings gap.

[18]The models are estimated in the spirit of a rigorous descriptive exercise rather than as part of any attempt to capture the more complex set of structural relationships underlying the earnings generation processes.

Ross Finnie and Ted Wannell

earn due to their different characteristics evaluated at "fair" market rates of return.

The Form of the Earnings Models

The regression models used in the analysis conform to standard conventions adapted to the post-graduation period captured by the NGS data, with earnings taken to be a function of a series of variables representing the individual's human capital and other factors that affect earnings.

It is important to note that the earnings variable available on the NGS databases represents what the person would earn on an annual basis were the job held at the time of the interview to last the full year, regardless of the actual job status. In adjusting for irregular work patterns in this manner, the measure represents the individual's rate of pay as measured on an annual basis, rather than the amount necessarily earned. It is a somewhat unconventional measure, but well-defined, analytically interesting, and presumably well reported (being a figure individuals should either know or be able to calculate rather easily). All earnings values are expressed in constant 1995 dollars, rounded to the nearest thousand, and capped at the $99,000 upper limit which characterizes the 1984 data (the lowest bound in the six databases), or $143,035 in constant 1995 dollars.[19]

---

[19]Failing to apply a common cap would distort comparisons of earnings levels across survey years because the years with the higher caps (generally the later ones — although there was some inflation-based erosion of the cap value in the most recent periods) tend to have higher earnings values simply due to the capping effects per se (as verified empirically). Applying a common cap thus provides a consistent measure of earnings across years — at least for earnings values below the cap. Following up on this latter point, however, this consistency comes at the cost of a general downward bias in measured mean earnings levels; furthermore, with the cap applied, any male-female differences at the highest earnings levels (i.e., beyond the cap) are not observed and are, therefore, effectively set to zero, which could affect the gender comparisons of average earnings levels and/or the decomposition exercise. Any attempt to eliminate this problem by deleting all relevant observations would introduce a competing set of biases. Faced with these trade-offs and the associated choices of (i) simply using the variable caps which were applied to each year of data, (ii) deleting the problem observations (i.e., those beyond the caps), and (iii) applying a common cap to all years of data, the latter approach was adopted here. In practice, very few graduates

Again following standard practice, the models were specified in log-linear form, meaning that the coefficient estimates can be interpreted as the proportional effect on earnings of a one unit change in the given independent variable (for small changes), with the decompositions framed in a similar context. Furthermore, with earnings levels generally fairly similar across cohorts, any changes in the estimated percentage effects from one group of graduates to another will reflect changes in the absolute (real) dollar effects of approximately similar magnitudes (e.g., an effect of x percent will be worth approximately the same dollar amount). Such a straightforward relationship between percentage and dollar effects will not, however, hold so closely from the results for the first and second interviews, since mean earnings rise substantially over this interval (see below).

The Variables Included in the Models

The earnings models include variables meant to capture (i) the amount — and type — of education-related human capital, such as field of study and already holding a more advanced degree; (ii) on-the-job acquisitions of human capital and other earnings influences (e.g., the outcomes of search/matching processes) related to early work experience; (iii) working part-time (perhaps an especially important variable when looking at annual earnings rather than hourly wage rates); (iv) the effects of being in a temporary job or self-employed; (v) marital status and the presence of children, which might further reflect human capital influences (e.g., the intensity of the investment component of past labour market experience) and/or supply-side choices (e.g., the precise number of hours worked beyond the broad full/part-time cut-off and other aspects of labour supply and work "effort"); and (vi) province/region of employment and language first spoken at home.

It was deemed desirable to restrict the models to variables that could more easily be presumed to be exogenous so as to obviate the need to deal with issues relating to the potential endogeneity of the regressors and to allow the coefficients to be interpreted in terms of the effects of the explanatory

---

had earnings beyond the cap: never more than one-half of 1% of the sample in any given year; on the other hand, tests show that this is a sufficient number of observations to significantly affect certain calculations/comparisons — thus verifying the importance of the capping exercise.

Ross Finnie and Ted Wannell

variables on earnings rather than as "associated outcomes". In particular, industry and occupation were omitted from the models (although models with industry and occupation included have been estimated and are available from the authors upon request).

Hours of work dummies are, on the other hand, included in one set of regressions. While there may be some issue of the endogeneity of hours worked, this should be much less of a concern in a context where the dependent variable is annual earnings rather than the hourly wage.[20] Furthermore, hours have an important direct influence on annual earnings and — it turns out — an important role in the gender earnings gap, meaning that it is important to include hours in the models. Finally, tests indicated that hours were in fact not endogenous and could thus be included in a straightforward manner in the models.[21]

Based on these basic principles, the regression models contain the following variables, all of which are defined in a consistent fashion across all three cohorts. The Appendix includes more detailed documentation of the variables where appropriate.

Educational Characteristics

- *Field of study:* 15 discipline groups, reflecting fields of roughly similar natures with respect to subject material, approach, etc., and comparable mean earnings patterns as determined through a preliminary analysis focused on this issue. (*"Other" (general) social sciences* is the omitted group in the regressions.)

---

[20]That is, while the number of hours usually worked in a week are generally likely to be a function of the hourly wage (standard labour supply theory), it is much less obvious as to why hours worked would be a function of annual earnings.

[21]An empirical examination of alternative regression models using a specification link test (Stata Corporation, 1997) showed optimal results for the model presented (log of annual earnings as the dependent variable, hours dummies on the right-hand side) compared to several alternative specifications. The alternatives included models with the log of estimated hourly wage as the dependent variable; reported annual earnings as the dependent variable with hour dummies on the right-hand side; the log of annual earnings as the dependent variable and reported hours as an independent variable; and the log of annual earnings or the dependent variable with no hours variable on the right-hand side.

- *A previously obtained higher degree:* a dummy variable indicating that the individual held a higher degree (Master's or PhD) before completing the Bachelor's degree which represents the basis for the individual's inclusion in the NGS survey (i.e., in 1982, 1986 or 1990).

Post-Graduation Work Experience
- Proxied with the part-time and full-time employment status at various points in time since graduation — two dates between graduation and the first interview in the case of the first interview regressions (October in the year following graduation (1983/87/91) and June of the year after that (1984/88/92)) and the addition of the first interview employment status to the second interview regressions. (*Working full-time* is the omitted category in each case.)

Part-Time Employment Status and Hours of Work
- A dummy variable indicating that the individual normally worked less than 30 hours per week (the standard definition).
- For 1986 and 1990 graduates, a separate set of models includes a series of dummy variables representing the usual hours of work. (This information was not collected for the 1982 graduates.) Hours dummies rather than the number of hours are used for two reasons: such a specification allows for non-linear and/or threshold effects, while the inclusion of a linear hours variable tends to introduce different scaling effects (essentially shifting the intercept) which makes comparisons across years somewhat less straightforward. The hours dummies used are: < 20 hours, 20-29 hours, 30-34 hours, 35-39 hours, 40 hours (the omitted group), 41-44 hours, 45-49 hours, and 50 or greater hours.

Job Characteristics
- *Temporary job status:* a dummy variable indicating that the individual held a temporary (as opposed to permanent) job.
- *Self-employed:* a dummy variable indicating the individual was self-employed (as opposed to being a paid worker).

Marital Status/Number of Children
The specific variables included allow for the effects of children to vary by marital status:
- *Single (never married), with/without children.*
- *Married, with/without children.*

Ross Finnie and Ted Wannell

- *Widowed/Separated/Divorced, with/without children.*

(*Single, no children* is the omitted category in the regressions.)

Province/Language

The choice of variables allows for "majority" and "minority" language effects along with provincial/regional differences, with the language variable representing the one first spoken by the individual.[22]

- *Atlantic Canada, Quebec, Ontario, Manitoba/Saskatchewan, Alberta, British Columbia and the Territories*: a series of indicator variables reflecting the graduate's current province of residence (*Ontario* is the omitted category.)
- *Quebec-English*: captures the effect of being an anglophone in Quebec, leaving the Quebec variable alone (above) to represent (primarily) francophone Québecois.
- *Minority French*: captures the effect of being a francophone outside Quebec, leaving the provincial/regional indicators noted above to represent anglophones in those areas (assuming a common effect across provinces).
- *Other language*: captures non-French/English speakers (again assuming a common effect across provinces — including Quebec).

The Decomposition Results

Models Including the Part-Time Dummy Variable (All Cohorts). Table 7a reports the first set of decomposition results, with the effects associated with each of the variables included in the regressions grouped into the following categories: the intercept; educational characteristics (predominantly field of study, but also including whether the person already held a degree beyond the Bachelor's); work experience since graduation (dummy variables to capture the differences in earnings between those who were in full-time work versus those in part-time work or not in the labour force as of selected dates following graduation); part-time employment status in the current job; other current job characteristics (self-employed, temporary position); marital status and the presence of children; province and language. Following

---

[22]There are other language indicators available on the NGS databases, but this is the most clearly defined and consistent measure across the various surveys.

Table 7a: Decomposition Results

	1st Interview			2nd Interview		
	Beta	X	Total	Beta	X	Total
	%	%	%	%	%	%
1982 Cohort						
Intercept	18.7	0.0	18.7	22.8	0.0	22.8
Educational characteristics	-6.3	3.8	-2.5	-8.0	6.0	-2.0
Work experience	0.1	-0.2	-0.1	-5.7	2.0	-3.7
Part-time work	0.5	2.8	3.4	1.7	3.6	5.3
Job characteristics	-2.3	1.3	-1.0	0.5	2.0	2.5
Marital/children	1.9	0.3	2.2	1.9	0.7	2.6
Province/language	-0.8	0.3	-0.5	-0.1	-0.1	-0.2
Total	11.7	8.3	20.1	13.1	14.2	27.3
1986 Cohort						
Intercept	12.9	0.0	12.9	11.0	0.0	11.0
Educational characteristics	-3.3	2.4	-0.9	-0.3	3.2	2.9
Work experience	1.3	0.2	1.5	-4.0	1.8	-2.2
Part-time work	-2.0	4.2	2.2	1.1	7.0	8.1
Job characteristics	-1.4	1.5	0.1	1.0	1.3	2.3
Marital/children	0.7	-0.2	0.5	4.3	-0.5	3.8
Province/language	1.2	0.1	1.3	-2.9	-0.3	-3.2
Total	8.1	8.0	16.1	10.1	12.5	22.6
1990 Cohort						
Intercept	0.3	0.0	0.3	4.0	0.0	4.0
Educational characteristics	2.6	3.3	5.9	2.7	3.7	6.5
Work experience	1.0	-0.4	0.7	-0.7	0.9	0.2
Part-time workers	-1.0	3.7	2.7	-1.9	6.7	4.8
Job characteristics	-1.9	1.3	-0.6	0.4	1.6	2.0
Marital/children	-0.5	-0.3	-0.8	0.0	-0.5	-0.5
Province/language	1.2	0.1	1.4	-0.1	0.6	0.5
Total	0.6	7.6	8.2	4.5	12.5	17.0

convention, results are presented in terms of the effects of the differences in the coefficients ("Beta"), the effects of the explanatory variables ("X"), and the total effect associated with each group of variables. These sum to the overall gender earnings gaps, expressed in the percentage terms which conform to the log earnings model specification used in the regressions.[23]

The Beta effects associated with the intercept terms indicate the existence of large general differences in the earnings of men and women unrelated to any of the explanatory variables included in the models.[24] These general effects were largest for the first cohort and then declined over time, being associated with gender earnings differences of 18.7 and 22.8% as of two and five years following graduation for the 1982 cohort; differences of 12.9 and 11% as of the same points in time percent for the class of 1986; but much lower differences of just 0.3 and 4.0% for the last set of graduates. Thus, as a large proportion of the relatively large gender earnings gap which existed for the earlier groups of graduates appears to have been quite generalized, so was much of the catching up to male graduates which female graduates accomplished across cohorts.[25]

---

[23]The overall gaps are not exactly the same as those implied by the mean earnings tabulations shown above due to the slightly different samples used in the regressions (observations with missing values of the explanatory variables were deleted) and due to the approximation which is implicit in the log-linear regression specification (the indicated "percentage effects" hold precisely only for small changes in the independent variables in the neighbourhood of the sample means).

[24]Strictly speaking, the decomposition intercept effects represent the contribution to the overall gender earnings gap of the differences in earnings amongst males and females with all the explanatory (dummy) variables set to zero.

[25]It should also be recognized that as in any such exercise, the intercept term will absorb various general male-female effects not otherwise captured by the variables included in the models. In particular, to the degree the regressors do not perfectly represent individuals' investments in human capital at the detailed level (such as the specific field of study within the discipline groups used or any other characteristics of the educational program, the individual's post-graduation work experience profile, and so on), the overall intercept will tend to absorb these influences to the degree they affect male-female earnings patterns at a general level, with some of these effects likely spilling over to the discipline effects (which together encompass all graduates) as well. That said, the models should capture

The set of educational characteristic variables (predominantly the field of study indicators) had mixed effects on the overall earnings gap. The negative Beta effects for the first two cohorts — representing influences which tended to diminish the earnings gap — indicate that the earnings patterns between the baseline social science group and graduates in other disciplines generally favoured women; that is, earnings were, on average, relatively higher for women in the other disciplines than was the case for men. This was, however, no longer the case for the 1990 cohort, where the educational Beta effects are positive. On the other hand, the associated X effects indicate that women have tended to be overrepresented in disciplines which have generally low earnings, with the impact of these differences growing from two to five years following graduation, especially for the earlier cohorts.

Taking the intercept and field effects together, in every period at least one-half of the gender earnings gap is related to the intercept term and the field of study effects. In other words, a large portion of the gender earnings gap amongst recent graduates has been associated with a general tendency for female graduates to have lower earnings than males within a given field (the Beta effects on the intercept and for the educational characteristics category of variables) regardless of the specific nature of their current job characteristics, post-graduation work experience, or personal attributes, as well as due to women tending to be more concentrated in the lower paying disciplines (the associated X effects).

Furthermore, this non-specific component grew significantly from two to five years following graduation, meaning that much of the increase in the overall gender earnings gap over this interval has been widespread, independent of specific post-graduation career profiles or personal characteristics. On the other hand, the narrowing of the gender earnings gap across cohorts was equally widespread — seen in the declines of the intercept and educational characteristic effects from the earlier to later groups of graduates.

One consistently important specific factor, however, has been part-time work, with women's typically shorter workweek hours driving their overall earnings levels from 2.8 to 7.0% lower (depending on the particular period) than those of men. Furthermore, the part-time effects are uniformly larger for the second interview decompositions than the earlier ones, meaning that

---

at least the largest such effects, such as those related to post-graduation labour market experience, working part-time or being in a temporary job, being married or having children, and so on.

Ross Finnie and Ted Wannell

gender divergences in part-time work patterns have been a significant factor in the widening of the gender earnings gap from two to five years following graduation. The part-time Beta effects are, on the other hand, more mixed and generally smaller (and sometimes negative), meaning that the penalties for working part-time in terms of reduced annual earnings have sometimes been greater for men but, in other cases, greater for women.

The effects of the other variables included in the models have been generally smaller and less consistent across the different periods. The job characteristic effects are, for example, quite mixed as of the first interview, but then become somewhat more consistent — although still fairly small — contributors to the gender earnings gap by the later period in each case, reflecting both a greater incidence of holding permanent jobs and being self-employed amongst men, and due to the returns to self-employment (in particular) being greater for males than females (generating the small, but positive Beta effects for the job characteristic variables in the second interview decompositions).

The influences of marital status and the presence of children — after controlling for past work experience, current part-time work status, and the other influences captured by the variables included in the models — account for moderate portions of the earnings gap for the first cohort (both points in time), and for the later year for the second cohort, but have substantially no (direct) effect for the third cohort. The work experience variables — which capture the effects of having had periods of working only part-time work or of being completely out of the labour force between graduation and the current interview — also show varying effects across periods, with the negative Beta effects in 1987 and 1991 suggesting that female graduates' earnings have not suffered as much as men's from past breaks from full-time work.[26] The province and language effects are mostly quite small, indicating that the distribution of graduates across the provinces and the related earnings effects have been quite similar for male and female graduates.

Finally, we note that the total of the Beta effects was effectively zero for the 1990 graduates as of the first interview, suggesting a fully "non-discriminatory" earnings-generation process, with the male-female earnings gap completely "explained" by differences in field of study, the rate of part-

---

[26]The relatively small effects of the experience variables may be at least partly due to the proxy aspect of the measures employed, necessitated by the fact that the NGS databases lack direct measures of work experience following graduation.

time work, and job characteristics. This was, however, no longer true by the second interview, although even here almost the entire total Beta effect was associated with the intercept, as opposed to specific labour force outcomes or personal characteristics.

Models Including Usual Hours Worked (1986 and 1990 Cohorts Only). We now turn to the models that replace the single part- versus full-time indicator used above with a series of dummy variables representing hours of work (Table 7b). Note first that the overall earnings gap changes at each

Table 7b: Decomposition Results

	1st Interview			2nd Interview		
	Beta	X	Total	Beta	X	Total
	%	%	%	%	%	%
1986 Cohort						
Intercept	10.9	0.0	10.9	11.0	0.0	11.0
Educational characteristics	-2.8	2.3	-0.5	-0.2	2.8	2.6
Work experience	1.5	0.2	1.6	-3.4	1.5	-1.9
Hours of work	-1.1	5.3	4.2	1.0	8.6	9.6
Job characteristics	-1.2	1.4	0.2	0.9	1.1	2.0
Marital/children	0.3	-0.2	0.1	3.1	-0.5	2.6
Province/language	0.7	0.1	0.9	-2.8	-0.3	-3.1
Total	8.3	9.1	17.4	9.6	13.3	22.9
1990 Cohort						
Intercept	-3.9	0.0	-3.9	5.0	0.0	5.0
Educational characteristics	3.0	3.1	6.1	1.6	4.0	5.6
Work experience	0.7	-0.4	0.3	-0.9	0.7	-0.2
Hours of work	0.9	5.9	6.8	-1.9	9.3	7.4
Job characteristics	-1.7	1.3	-0.5	-0.4	1.4	1.0
Marital/children	-0.5	-0.3	-0.8	-1.0	-0.4	-1.4
Province/language	1.7	0.1	1.8	-0.2	0.5	0.3
Total	0.0	9.7	9.7	2.3	15.4	17.7

Ross Finnie and Ted Wannell

time point with the addition of the hours dummies. This is the result of dropping observations where the usual hours of work information was missing. The differences are, however, not great.

Given the differences in usual hours worked of men and women noted earlier and the presumed importance of such differences on earnings, it should come as no surprise that the proportion of the total gender earnings gap accounted for by the X effects is now greater than was the case where only the simple part- versus full-time differentiation was permitted, with in every case these effects growing from the first interview to the second, as average hours by gender diverged significantly over the early years in the labour market.

The 5.3% effect of the male-female difference in hours worked "explains" 31% of the total gender earnings gap amongst 1986 graduates two years after graduation, while the 8.6% effect accounts for 38% of the considerably larger gap which held five years after graduation. These effects were even greater for the class of 1990: the two-year effect of 5.9% represents 61% of the total earnings gap in 1992, and the five-year effect of 9.3% represents 53% of the 1995 gap. Male-female differences in hours were, therefore, central factors in accounting for the overall gender earnings gap and its increase over the early years in the labour market, for the 1986 and 1990 graduates for which this information is available — an important finding.

Adding the hours dummies also affects the estimated effects of some of the other variables, but the differences are generally not very large and the earlier discussions still hold. This in itself is interesting; one might have thought, for example, that the family status variables in particular would have changed significantly as the better measures of hours were included in the models (on the assumption that the hours effects were at least partially captured by those variables in the absence of the more precise measure), but the differences are not very great. In fact, this might have been anticipated in light of the earlier finding that hours of work already diverged quite significantly for unattached men and women, as well as the more expected results of there being substantial differences amongst those who were married or had children.

Conclusion

In this paper we set out to compare the employment outcomes of three recent cohorts (1982, 1986 and 1990) of male and female Bachelor's level university graduates using the National Graduates Surveys. These data are well suited to studying the evolution of outcomes over the early years in the labour market for each class and for making comparisons from one cohort to another, while controlling for important individual characteristics.

The major findings may be summarized as follows:

- The distributions of graduates by field of study were relatively stable over the eight years spanned by the three cohorts of graduates, but the share of female graduates did increase significantly in commerce, law, and veterinary science from 1982 to 1990. On the other hand, women continued to be poorly represented in engineering, computer sciences, mathematics and the physical sciences and economics. Since graduates of at least several of these fields are considered to be in short supply, attracting women into these areas would presumably help to ease a perceived labour market problem as well as perhaps help to address an equity concern.
- Male and female graduates differed little in terms of unemployment rates, the job-education skill, the relationship between the schooling prerequisites of the job and the level held, and job satisfaction. Men tended to be overrepresented among the self-employed, while women were more likely to hold temporary jobs. The general levels of these variables and their gender patterns remained relatively constant across cohorts.
- There were, however, more important male-female differences in the number of hours worked, both initially, and then even more substantially as of five years following graduation, with these divergences having actually been the greatest for the most recent cohort.
- In contrast, there was a substantial narrowing of the overall gender earnings gap across cohorts — the result of increases in female graduates' earnings and decreases in male/graduates' earnings. The narrowing of the gap was, however, much greater as of the initial interviews, and men's earnings grew considerably more strongly than women's out to the five-year mark, even for the later groups of graduates — indeed, the earnings gap increased by as much from two to five years following graduation for the 1990 cohort as it did for the 1982 cohort. Thus, while

Ross Finnie and Ted Wannell

female graduates started out on a much more equal footing in the 1990s, their earnings quickly began to trail behind those of their male classmates.

- Based on the decomposition analysis, a large part of the gender earnings gap at each interview date, and much of the increase in the overall earnings gap from two to five years following graduation, appears to have been of a generalized nature, unrelated to specific job characteristics, experience profiles, or individual attributes. At the same time, much of the narrowing of the gap across cohorts has been of a similarly general nature.

- As for more specific influences, hours of work has clearly been an important determinant of the earnings gap at each point in time, as well as of its increase in the years following graduation.

- Other factors, such as past work experience, specific job characteristics, family status, and province of residence and language spoken, have played only smaller and generally more mixed roles in the gender gap amongst these Bachelor's graduates.

Probably the most interesting and important result is the extent to which the gender earnings gap has increased so significantly from two to five years following graduation for each set of graduates, with this dynamic continuing even as the initial post-graduation gap has narrowed significantly from one cohort to the next. The obvious question is "why?" In particular, if certain forces — be they on the demand side or the supply side — have been causing such a significant shift in starting earnings levels, why have these same forces not affected the male-female patterns of earnings growth as well?

One clue to these dynamics is perhaps found in the relatively important role that hours of work appear to have played in the initial earnings gap and its widening in the subsequent post-graduation years. One straightforward interpretation of these results would be that men and women have been making — and, it would appear, continue to make — different labour supply decisions which have had important direct effects on their earnings levels. Put most simply, women have been working fewer hours than men and have been receiving commensurately lower earnings levels — with, in particular, the widening of the hours gap from two to five years following graduation driving a substantial portion of the increased earnings gap over this period.

At the same time, the hours effects explain only a portion of the observed earnings patterns, and thus we need to search further for the other underlying causes of these dynamics. Furthermore, the hours patterns, as well as any other "explanatory" factors, might themselves be at least partly determined by a larger set of processes which might include various types of discrimination — directly in the labour market itself, in other institutions (including schools and universities), or on a broader social level. Addressing such issues is, of course, one of the great challenges in modern social science research, and represents a task which obviously lays beyond the scope of this paper.

The narrower issues of probing further the structure of the gender earnings gap at a given point in time and pursuing more deeply what underlies the significant widening of the gap between two and five years following graduation are, however, topics which could indeed be investigated further using the NGS data employed here — thus pointing us in the direction of future research projects.

Appendix
Variables Used in the Analysis

1. Variables Used in the Regression Analysis

Some of the variables used in the regression analysis are fully explained in the text. Those which merit further documentation include the following.

Earnings
Based on the question: "Working your usual number of hours, approximately what would be your annual earnings before taxes and deductions at that job?" The variable thus represents what the person would earn on an annual basis were the job to last the full year, regardless of the actual job status. Earnings values are expressed in constant 1995 dollars, rounded to the nearest thousand, and capped at the $99,000 upper limit which characterizes the 1984 data (the lowest bound in the six databases), or $143,035 in constant 1995 dollars.

Field of Study
The field of study variables are as follows:
> No Specialization
> Elementary/Secondary Teaching
> Other Education
> Fine Arts and Humanities
> Commerce
> Economics
> Law (including Jurisprudence)
> Social Sciences (excluding economics)
> Agricultural and Biological Sciences
> Veterinary Sciences
> Engineering
> Medical Professions (Doctors, Dentists, Pharmacists, *etc.*)
> Other Health (nurses and other health professionals)
> Computer Sciences
> Mathematics and Physical Sciences

This classification scheme is the result of an attempt to keep the specification parsimonious while capturing important cross-field differences in earnings levels. The decision process began by using the standard USIS field groupings employed in the NGS data as a starting point, but then conducting a preliminary analysis of cross-field earnings patterns (a key outcome) at a more detailed level across the different survey years (by sex).

Part-Time Employment Status

Based on a direct question to this effect, with the 30 hour cut-off being conventional.

Temporary Job

Based on a direct question to this effect: "Is this [the current (main) job] a temporary or permanent position?" (In 1984, the question was slightly different: "Did you have a permanent position?", but the results should be directly comparable.) A slight problem with this variable in the 1987 data means that the number of temporary jobs is under-estimated (see Finnie, 1999c), but the error is small enough that this should not affect the regression results or associated decompositions to any substantial degree.

Self-Employment

Based on a direct question regarding the class of worker, with the response options being paid worker, self-employed, and "other" (including family workers, volunteer work, etc.), with workers of the latter type deleted from the analysis.

2. Other Outcome Variables

Labour Forces Status: Unemployment

The labour force status variables in the NGS databases generally follow standard Statistics Canada conventions. The one exception is with respect to ongoing students: full-time students looking for work are included with the other unemployed, which is not usually the case, since enrolment status as of the interview dates is, surprisingly, missing from most years of the NGS data, thus precluding the usual adjustment. The resulting unemployment rates are, therefore, slightly biased upwards relative to what would be obtained with the more conventional definition.

Employed Part-Time Involuntarily

The categorization of individuals into voluntary versus involuntary part-time workers is based on a specific question to this effect, with the responses classified by the author as follows: *voluntary*: personal/family reasons, school, didn't want a full-time job; *involuntary*: could only find a part-time job, business conditions, contract work, shortage of work. Individuals who responded "illness/disability", "full-time job less than 30 hours", "other reason", or "multiple jobs" were excluded from the calculations on the grounds that such responses could not be safely considered as either voluntary or involuntary.

The response options were, however, not perfectly consistent across all surveys. In 1984, 1987, 1988 and 1991, they were identical, consisting of the three voluntary categories listed above, a single "could only find a part-time job" involuntary category, and the first three of the non-classified responses. In 1992, however, the "illness/disability" and "full-time job less than 30 hours" non-classified categories were not included. In 1995, the seven original response categories were again included, but the final three involuntary options listed above ("business conditions", "contract work", "shortage of work") were also available, as was the final non-classified category ("multiple jobs").

Thus, the results should be directly comparable for the first four survey years (1984-87, 1988-91). The 1992 results are, however, only directly comparable to these others to the degree individuals who would have chosen one of the missing categories in that year ("illness/disability" and "full-time job less than 30 hours") chose "other" instead, as this would make the aggregate of the "voluntary" responses comparable to those in the earlier periods. The 1995 results are comparable to the earlier periods to the degree that individuals who chose one of the additional "involuntary" responses ("business conditions", "contract work", "shortage of work") would have responded "could only find a part-time job" in the earlier years, and if individuals who chose the "missing jobs" response would have given one of the non-classifiable reasons in an earlier survey (presumably the "other" category).

In summary, the results are directly comparable for the first four surveys, and it would seem reasonable on logical grounds to assume that the results for the later two periods are also quite comparable to those of the earlier periods (and each other), but this cannot be verified empirically, leaving a margin of doubt in this regard.

Educational Prerequisites of the Current Job
Based on the question: "When you were hired ... what were the minimum educational qualifications required?" The over/under/even-qualified measures were then created by comparing the response with the level of the program completed in the graduation year with the more detailed categories available post-1984 reduced to the broader "College", "Bachelor's", Master's", and PhD" categories available in that earlier year in order to focus on more significant differences and to have a consistent measure across all surveys.

The Job-Education Skill Match Index
Based on the question: "Do you use any of the skills acquired through the education program ... in your job?" For the 1982 and 1986 cohorts, the response options were "yes" and "no"; for the 1990 cohort, the response options were "to a great extent", "to some extent", "very little", "not at all". The responses were assigned scores between 0 and 100: the 1982 and 1986 cohort scores were assigned either 0 ("no") or 100 ("yes"), while the 1990 scores range from 0 ("not at all"), to 33 1/3 ("very little"), through 66 2/3 ("to some extent"), to 100 ("to a great extent"). The tables report the mean values of these scores, with higher scores representing closer job-education skill matches. See the last part of this Appendix for further discussion of the various index variables of this type used in the analysis. Given the underlying response options, the scores should be generally comparable across interview years (two and five years after graduation) for a given cohort, and also comparable between the 1982 and 1986 cohorts, but not directly comparable across the first two cohorts and the last cohort.

Job Satisfaction Index (Earnings, Overall)
Based on the questions: "Considering the duties and responsibilities of your job, how satisfied are you with the money you make?", and "Considering all aspects of your job,

how satisfied are you with it?". The response options were similar in all years: "very satisfied", "satisfied", "dissatisfied", "very dissatisfied" in the 1986 and 1990 survey years (1988-91 and 1992-95); and the last two options differing very slightly for the first cohort: "not satisfied", "not at all satisfied". The responses were assigned values from 0 to 100 in the same manner as the job-education skill match variable, and the tables report the mean values of these scores, with higher values indicating greater job satisfaction. See the last part of this Appendix for further discussion of the various index variables of this type used in the analysis.

3. Other Education Variable Used in the Selection Criteria

New Diplomas
Essentially all formal postsecondary degree/certificate/diploma programs were considered in this selection. Exceptions include the following: "interest"/recreation-type courses, which typically do not represent any sort of formal human capital investment and which should not generally have a direct effect on early labour market outcomes: banking and insurance certificates, which are normally gained largely as a matter of a course by those on certain career paths; non-professional health certificates which, by their very designation, are not generally career related; high school diplomas, which were deemed to largely represent an accreditation formality without direct effects on employment opportunities for those already possessing postsecondary diplomas; and registered apprenticeships, which were again seen to be part of a normal career path rather than additional formal schooling per se.

4. Further Notes on the Index Variables

Each of the index variables mentioned (the job-education skill match and the job satisfaction measures) above may be thought of as based upon more fundamental sets of evaluations regarding the overall evaluation of the educational program, the job-education skill match, or the level of job satisfaction. The data collection process and the construction of the indexes described above may thus be thought of as first reducing those more underlying evaluations to a series of discrete choices (the original response options contained in the NGS databases) and then transforming these categorical responses into the indexes whose mean scores are reported in the tables. Higher values thus indicate greater levels of satisfaction with the choice of field of study, closer job-education skill matches, or greater job satisfaction.

In short, the original responses given in the NGS data are transformed into a scalar measure which can be thought of as an index of the "average" level of the underlying evaluations. The constructed indexes have the distinct advantage of significantly reducing the dimensionality of the underlying evaluations and thereby facilitating much easier and more direct comparisons across groups and over time relative to what would be required working with the full set of categorical responses.

References

Betts, J., C. Ferrall and R. Finnie (1998), "Time to First Job — A Hazard Model Approach Using the National Graduates Survey" (working title), Working Paper (Ottawa: Analytical Studies Branch, Statistics Canada), forthcoming.

_____ (1999), "The Effect of University Quality on Graduates' Earnings in Canada" (working title), Working Paper (Ottawa: Analytical Studies Branch, Statistics Canada), forthcoming.

Cain, G. (1986), "The Economic Analysis of Labor Market Discrimination: A Survey", in O. Ashenfelter and R. Layard (eds.), *Handbook of Labor Economics*, Vol. 1 (Oxford: North-Holland), 693-785.

Christofides, L.N. and R. Swidinsky (1994), "Wage Determination by Gender and Minority Status: Evidence from the LMAS", *Canadian Public Policy/Analyse de Politiques* 20, 34-51.

Doiron, D. and C. Riddell (1994), "The Impact of Unionization on Male-Female Earnings Differences in Canada", *Journal of Human Resources* 29(2), 504-535.

Finnie, R. (1999a), "Holding Their Own: The Employment Patterns and Earnings of Canadian Post-Secondary Graduates in the 1980s and 1990s", *Canadian Business Economics*, forthcoming.

_____ (1999b), "Changes in the Structure of Post-Secondary Graduates' Earnings in the 1980s and 1990s" (working title), Working Paper (Ottawa: Applied Research Branch, Human Resources Development Canada), forthcoming.

_____ (1999c), "A Dynamic Analysis of the School-to-Work Transition of Post-Secondary Graduates in Canada in the 1980s and 1990s" (working title), Working Paper (Ottawa: Applied Research Branch, Human Resources Development Canada), forthcoming.

_____ (1999d), "Fields of Plenty, Fields of Lean: A Cross-Cohort, Longitudinal Analysis of Early Labour Market Outcomes of Canadian University Graduates by Discipline" (working title), Working Paper (Ottawa: Applied Research Branch, Human Resources Development Canada), forthcoming.

_____ (1999e), "Earnings Differences by Field of Study Amongst Recent Canadian University Graduates" (working title), Working Paper (Ottawa: Applied Research Branch, Human Resources Development Canada), forthcoming.

Finnie, R. and M. Lavoie (1997), "The School-to-Work Transition of Engineering Graduates: A Cross-Cohort, Longitudinal Analysis of Four Major Decisions in the Engineering Career", Research Paper R-97-4E (Ottawa: Applied Research Branch, Human Resources Development Canada).

Gunderson, M. (1985), "Discrimination, Equal Pay, and Equal Opportunities in the Labour Market", in C. Riddell (ed.), *Work and Pay: The Canadian Labour Market* (Toronto: University of Toronto Press), 219-265.

_____ (1989), "Male-Female Wage Differentials and Policy Responses", *Journal of Economic Literature* 27(1), 46-72.

Gunderson, M. and C. Riddell (1991), "Economics of Women's Wages in Canada", in S.L. Willborn (ed.), *International Review of Comparative Public Policy*, Vol. 3: *Women's Wages - Stability and Change in Six Industrialized Countries* (Greenwich, CT: JAI Press), 151-176.

Kidd, M.P. and M. Shannon (1994), "An Update and Extension of the Canadian Evidence on Gender Wage Differentials", *Canadian Journal of Economics* 27(4), 918-938.

_____ (1996), "The Gender Wage Gap: A Comparison of Australia and Canada", *Industrial and Labour Relations Review* 49(4), 729-745.

Krahn, H. (1996), "School-Work Transitions: Changing Patterns and Research Needs", discussion paper prepared for the Applied Research Branch of Human Resources Development Canada.

Lavoie, M. and R. Finnie (1999), "Is it Worth Doing a Science or Technology Degree in Canada? Empirical Evidence and Policy Implications", *Canadian Public Policy/Analyse de Politiques* 25(1), 101-121.

Miller, P. (1987), "Gender Differences in Observed and Offered Wages in Canada, 1980", *Canadian Journal of Economics* 20, 225-244.

Stata Corporation (1997), *Stata Reference Manual*, Release 5, Vol. 2, 329-334.

Women and Men's Entitlement to Workplace Benefits: The Influence of Work Arrangements

Brenda Lipsett and Mark Reesor

Introduction

Supplemental health and dental plans and employer-sponsored pension plans (ESPP) are non-wage benefits that many consider to be a basic element in employee compensation and worker and family security. These plans contribute to workers' current and future well being by supplementing the basic coverage provided through federal and provincial retirement income and medical care programs.[1] For employers, benefit plans are an important

---

[1] Employer-sponsored pension benefits can make the difference between financial precariousness and financial well-being in old age for many Canadians. Government transfers alone are not sufficient to provide Canadians with a prosperous retirement and they were not designed with such a goal in mind. To illustrate, with the maximum Canada Pension Plan (CPP) monthly benefit of $736.81 and a maximum Old Age Security (OAS) benefit of $405.00, the maximum annual income from these sources is $13,701.72. This falls below the 1996 low-income cut-off for a single individual living in a moderate sized urban centre (population 100,000 to 499,999) at $14,591.00. For a husband and wife family in which the husband receives maximum CPP and OAS benefits, and the wife receives maximum OAS benefits, total family income from these sources

incentive device in labour contracts, affecting employee turnover, work effort and the timing of retirement. Employers who acquire a reputation for taking care of their employees' supplemental medical and retirement needs may find it easier to recruit and retain higher quality employees.

The challenge, according to the Labour Secretariat of the Commission for Labour Cooperation, is for North American countries to improve the living standards of workers by encouraging the development of employment benefits that are transferable from one job to another, that can benefit workers in non-standard jobs and that can provide adequate, lifelong benefits in a cost-effective manner. To meet this challenge, there is a need for better information on the types and levels of benefits that workers receive. In addition, with increasing numbers of workers in non-standard work arrangements, it is important to understand the relative levels of security which are associated with different employment forms.[2] Given that women are overrepresented in non-standard work arrangements, the gender dimension merits particular attention.

Previous research on entitlement to workplace benefits (reviewed and extended in Currie and Chaykowski, 1995) has focused on the role of gender concentration in jobs, wages, unions, industry, public versus private sector, marriage and child bearing, male/female occupational segregation and compensation differentials, and observable personal characteristics such as age and education. The purpose of this paper is to provide a comprehensive assessment of the determinants of entitlement to employer-sponsored benefit plans for Canadian men and women employees and to specifically address the information gap on the role of work arrangements in benefits coverage. Using bivariate and multivariate analysis of the 1995 Survey of Work Arrangements (SWA), we examine the personal and job-related characteristics of non-student employees that are associated with three non-wage

---

would total $18,561.72. This is only $200.00 higher than the 1996 low-income cut-off for a two-person family living in a moderate urban centre at $18,367.00. Alternative sources of retirement income — registered pension plans (RPPs), registered retirement savings plans (RRSPs) and other savings — are imperative for a good standard of living in old age. However, only RPPs (and C/QPP) insure against the possibility of living long enough to exhaust savings.

[2]Together part-time, temporary (proxied by short-tenure) and own-account self-employment have gradually risen from 25% of total employment in 1976 to 32% in 1997 according to Labour Force Survey data.

benefits — extended health and dental plans and employer-sponsored pension plans.

The second section of the paper describes the data used in this analysis, gives *a priori* reasoning for examining the effects of certain job and personal characteristics on entitlement to *direct* benefit coverage and provides aggregate bivariate results. Some additional evidence on the potential *indirect* coverage of married workers by spousal benefits, drawing on data from Statistics Canada's SWA family file, is also provided. The third section introduces the logistic regression model, reports the results, and identifies the characteristics of employers, jobs and individuals that influence the chances of being entitled to coverage. The influence of part-time and non-permanent work arrangements on the entitlement to benefits, controlling for other factors such as job tenure, is an important goal of the multivariate analysis. Conclusions follow in the final section.

Who's Entitled: Evidence from the 1995 Survey of Work Arrangements

This section presents a bivariate description of the job and personal characteristics of those entitled to employer-sponsored benefits using data from the nationally representative survey. It builds a series of workplace demand and employee supply factors that can influence who is entitled to non-wage benefits into the empirical model that is tested in the third section. The overall bivariate results reveal that, excluding full-time students, 63% of Canadian employees are entitled to an extended health plan through their employer while 59% of employees are entitled to a dental plan, and 55% to a pension plan or group RRSP (ESPP). Women are less likely than men to be entitled to these benefits. Some non-covered workers have access to these benefits through a family member.

The Data

The analysis is based on the 1995 SWA, an addendum to the November 1995 Labour Force Survey. Full-time students are excluded in order to concentrate on employees with a prime attachment to the labour market, and not to detract from the importance of part-time and temporary work arrangements on entitlement to benefit coverage.[3]

The SWA workplace benefit question explicitly asked: *"Through his/her employer, is ... entitled to a health plan other than provincial medicare?; a dental plan?; a pension plan or group RRSP other than C/QPP?"* Thus, the potential for confusion between provincial medicare, individually purchased insurance and employer-sponsored health plans was controlled for, as was the potential confusion between employer-sponsored pension plans and the Canada/Quebec Pension Plans.

It is important to note that the SWA focuses on entitlement to workplace benefits and not on actual coverage through participation in benefit plans. It does not provide any information on whether employees not entitled to these workplace benefits are self-insuring through other vehicles. There were no further questions addressing the quality of the plans. Certainly, specific details on aspects such as drugs and home care would be of interest to policymakers looking at national approaches to pharmacare and home-care plans. Furthermore, there were no questions regarding specific attributes of the ESPPs, such as portability or the rights of spouses and survivors, the extent of the employer contributions to the plans, or whether employees had access to a union-sponsored pension plan.[4] Additionally, participation in flexible benefit plans would be of interest to human resource managers exploring tools to increase employee productivity.[5] However, these aspects cannot be addressed with the SWA data.

---

[3]In total there were 25,721 respondents to the SWA. Of these, 21,261 were paid workers in their main job and the remaining 4,460 were self-employed. The self-employed are excluded from this analysis since benefit coverage through an employer does not pertain to their situation. Additional screens reduced the sample used in the analysis to 18,540 — 9,498 males and 9,042 females. Any records that had missing values for any of: union status; permanent/non-permanent status; firm size; RPP coverage; health coverage other than provincial medicare; and dental plan coverage were excluded from the analysis. This excluded 1,293 records or about 6.5% of the sample of non-full-time students.

[4]According to Frenken (1996, p. 71), in 1995, 7% of RPPs were union-negotiated, covering 16% of all members.

[5]For a discussion of the growing importance of flexible benefit packages see Johnson (1996).

Empirical Framework and Descriptive Results

Overall, the SWA shows 63% of Canadian non-student employees are entitled to an extended health plan, 59% to a dental plan, and 55% to a pension plan through their employer. Women are less likely than men to be entitled to these benefits with 69%, 59% and 58% of males entitled to an extended health, dental and pension plan, respectively, compared with 58%, 54% and 52%, respectively, of females.[6] The gender differences evident in the overall workplace benefit entitlement rates are reflected in gender differences in industry and occupation concentration, shares of part-time, non-permanent, small firm and unionized workers, and dissimilar wage distributions.

Viewed within a framework of total compensation, a number of demand and supply factors potentially influence who is entitled to workplace benefits. The relationship between wages and benefits, holding total compensation fixed, is negative according to Hedonic wage theory. Direct observation of the trade-off between higher wages and entitlement to benefits is obscured by the observation that firms that pay high wages usually also offer good benefit packages. However, this casual observation does not take into account the influence of other observable and unobservable factors that influence total compensation, such as the demands and risks of the job and the quality of workers involved. With increasing total compensation, employees may prefer to take a larger share of income in the form of workplace benefits, especially if there are tax advantages to doing so, thereby contributing to the observed positive association between wages and benefits. However, from a policy development perspective, it is important to keep the negative relationship in mind — workers pay for their workplace benefits. Policies designed to improve entitlement to employee benefits might well be paid for by workers in the form of lower future wage increases or fewer job opportunities in sectors or work arrangements that previously did not offer benefits.

In an empirical model of entitlement to workplace benefits, theory would suggest that job and personal characteristics and wages would comprise the

---

[6]The Appendix contains detailed tables: A1, the proportion of employees with benefit coverage broken down by the variables used in the multivariate analysis; A2, married workers with possible spousal benefits by worker type; A3, variable names and descriptions used in the regression models; and finally, A4, the parameter estimates of the regression models for the three workplace benefits for each gender.

explanatory factors. Thus, logit regression models examining the effects of certain observable job and personal characteristics on the probability of entitlement to extended health, dental and ESPP coverage are developed for women and men. The expected effects of these characteristics on benefit coverage are detailed below, providing a basis for their inclusion in the models estimated later in the third section. Preliminary checks of these effects are made by referring to the bivariate (not controlling for the effects of other variables) percentages of women and men employees entitled to ESPP, extended health and dental plan coverage classified according to each of the characteristics (see Table 1 in Appendix A.1 for the bivariate results).

Job-Related Characteristics

Part-Time and Non-Permanent Work Arrangements. It has been suggested that non-standard employment is one way for employers to circumvent the increased trend in non-wage labour costs since, historically, non-standard workers have not received most benefits. In a changing workplace environment, where part-time and non-permanent workers provide flexibility to respond to the daily, weekly, annual and cyclical variations in demand (contingent and peripheral employment), where employers wish to reduce labour costs or shift these costs from fixed to variable, and where they may be less concerned about incentives to reduce turnover and increase work effort, we would expect that these part-time and non-permanent workers are less likely to have extended health, dental or pension coverage than permanent full-time workers.

Overall, the bivariate results show that, among full-timers, 69%, 64% and 60% have extended health, dental and ESPP coverage, respectively, compared with just 26%, 23% and 28%, respectively, of part-timers.[7] Furthermore, permanent workers are roughly three times as likely to have extended health, dental or ESPP coverage as non-permanent workers. Both men and women in part-time and non-permanent jobs have low coverage. In fact, part-time female employees are more likely to be covered than male part-timers. The gender dimension of the issue is that more women than men are employed on a part-time or non-permanent basis (19% of women are

---

[7]The General Social Survey (GSS) reveals that, among full-timers, 70% and 59% have extended health and dental coverage, respectively, compared with just 26% and 20%, respectively, for part-timers (Krahn, 1992).

Figure 1: The Shares of Female and Male Employees Entitled to Supplemental Benefit Plans Through their Employer by Work Arrangement

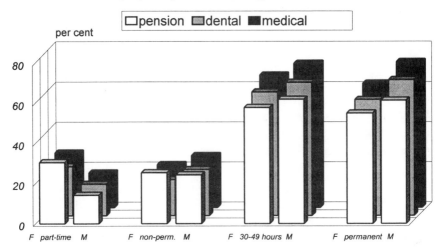

Source: Calculations based on Statistics Canada's 1995 Work Arrangements Survey

employed part-time versus 5% of men and 11% of women are employed in non-permanent jobs versus 8.5% of men).

The coverage of non-standard workers may be changing, with the extension of benefits to part-timers becoming increasingly common. Additionally, the length of many non-permanent jobs suggest an implicit contract arrangement that may involve entitlement to benefits (Polivka, 1996).[8] For example, recent pension reforms by the provincial governments and the Office of the Superintendent of Financial Institutions has improved part-time

---

[8]The question from the SWA regarding job permanency asked "Is ... job permanent, or is there some way that it is not permanent?" This question led to many respondents who classified themselves as non-permanent having job tenures of more than one year (41% of non-permanent workers have a job tenure of more than one year and 16% of non-permanent workers have a tenure of *more than five years*). This challenges the notion that non-permanent jobs are of short duration.

workers' entitlement to registered pension plan coverage.[9] However, many part-time workers likely do not meet the requirements for coverage in many legislative jurisdictions. Although many non-permanent workers have a job tenure of more than one year, the majority of these workers may not meet the continuous service requirement for RPP coverage. To the extent that these part-time and non-permanent jobs represent transitions to full-time permanent jobs, the implications for long-term financial insecurity will be mitigated.

Model Employers of Non-standard Workers. With the growth of non-standard or contingent work forms, it becomes increasingly important to recognize the variation in quality of jobs and outcomes for workers across non-standard employment. This variation is influenced by occupation and skill as well as by the different ways firms design and manage contingent jobs. The SWA can shed some light on who are the model employers providing benefits to their part-time and non-permanent employees.

First, part-time work comprises a variety of arrangements that affect entitlement to benefits. Part-time work can be permanent or temporary or have relatively few or a substantial number of hours per week. The reasons for working in part-time jobs also vary. Focusing on women workers (since some cell sizes for men become too small to report), the closer these part-timers resemble the characteristics of core workers — if they are permanent employees and work between 20 and 30 hours a week — the more likely they are to be entitled to benefits. The distinction between voluntary and involuntary part-time workers does not have an overall effect on benefit coverage. Therefore, there is no evidence suggesting that women work in part-time jobs voluntarily because they have access to benefits. By industry, the model

---

[9]An example of such legislation is the 1993 amendment to the Saskatchewan Pension Benefits Act. This amendment extended employee eligibility for pension coverage to part-time employees with 2 years or 24 months continuous service and who have earned at least 35% of the Year's Maximum Pensionable Earnings (YMPE) or worked 700 hours or more in each of two consecutive calendar years. Prior to this amendment, the Saskatchewan Pension Benefits Act had no legislation requiring that companies offering a pension plan to full-time employees also offer similar coverage to their part-time workers. The other provinces, along with the Office of the Superintendent of Financial Institutions, have passed similar legislation in the 1980s and 1990s (Statistics Canada, 1996a).

Figure 2: Which Part-time Female Employees get Benefits?

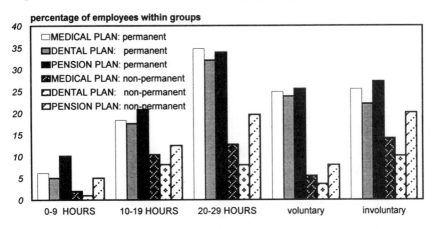

Source: Calculations based on Statistics Canada's 1995 Work Arrangements Survey

employers tend to be in public or publicly regulated sectors (federal and provincial administration, health, education, finance industries, insurance carriers, electrical power, gas and water utilities and communication industries).

Full-time non-permanent work arrangements likewise represent a diverse group. Women in full-time temporary, term or contract jobs are more likely to be entitled to workplace benefits than those working in seasonal or casual jobs or for a temporary-help agency. By industry, the model employers again tend to be in public or publicly regulated sectors (federal and provincial administration, education and related, insurance carriers, electrical power, gas and water utilities and communication industries). By occupation, for both part-time and non-permanent women workers, high-skilled white collar employees are more likely to be entitled to benefit coverage (officials and administrators in government, management and administration related, mathematics, statistics, systems analysts architecture and engineering, elementary, secondary and university teachers, nursing therapy, medicine and health).

Access to Workplace Benefits Through a Family Member. A proviso to the regression analysis that follows in the third section is introduced by the fact that some workers without employer-sponsored benefit plan coverage of their own may be covered by the plans of a working spouse or parent. By

Figure 3: Which Full-time Female Non-permanent Employees Get Benefits?

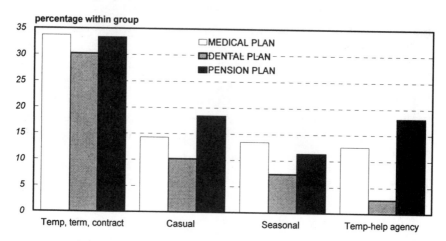

Note: The figure is based on data for full-time, non-permanent employees.
Source: Calculations based on Statistics Canada's 1995 Work Arrangements Survey.

examining extended health and dental plan coverage by family units,[10] we can calculate the extent to which married workers, who are not entitled to workplace benefits at their own place of employment, are potentially covered through spousal insurance. Taking employer-sponsored health plan access as an example, by classifying workers into one of three categories — own coverage (are entitled to their own insurance), possible coverage, (no personal coverage but at least one person in the family unit has coverage), and no coverage (nobody in the family unit has coverage) — an additional 16% of married employees are possibly covered through a spousal employer-

---

[10]A family, as defined by the Labour Force Survey, is any number of people living in the same household who are related either by blood or by marriage. For example, if there are three generations of married couples living in the same household, then these people are considered to be one family (Reesor and Lipsett, 1997). A family for the purpose of benefit coverage would include only husband, wife and children.

Brenda Lipsett and Mark Reesor

sponsored health plan.[11] This raises the percentage of married workers who may have extended health coverage to 82%, up from 66% (see Appendix 2 Tables of Married Workers and Benefit Coverage for full information by gender and workplace benefit according to work arrangement). As indicated in the figures below, employed married men are less likely to access workplace benefits through their spouse than are employed married women. This interdependence between spouses in entitlement to workplace benefits can facilitate non-standard employment arrangements and may play a role in family labour supply decisions. However, it remains clear that part-time and temporary workers are much less likely to have access to workplace benefits than full-time permanent workers.

Union Status, Firm Size and Public/Private Sector Workers. Union status and firm size are expected to influence entitlement to workplace benefit coverage. Unionized workers should be more likely to be entitled to benefits because of the influence of unions in the collective bargaining process (Freeman and Medoff, 1984).[12] Due to economies of scale, large firms should be more able to offer benefits to their employees than smaller firms. Another contributing factor to the lower coverage rates in small firms, given the role of profitability and age of firms in the provision of benefits, is recent policy that has tried to foster employment growth through the development and expansion of small firms. A further point to note is that large firms are more likely to be unionized than small firms, raising the issue of the effect of

---

[11]We say "possible coverage" for the following reason. It is possible for two married couples (all four paid workers) to be in the same family. If only one of these four workers has health coverage, then three of these four would be classified as "possible coverage" (the spouse and the other married couple). In reality only one of them (the spouse) would be covered, while the other couple would have no coverage. Thus, the estimated number of spouses who have health coverage through a spousal plan (i.e., possible coverage) is an overestimate of the actual number (although probably only slightly high). Through similar reasoning, it is easily seen that the number of married workers who are not covered is a slight underestimate.

[12]Unionized workers, for the purpose of this analysis, refer to those who are union members or are covered by a union contract or collective agreement at their place of employment. According to the SWA, 33.4% of employees are union members while an additional 4.4% are covered by a union contract or collective agreement (Lipsett and Reesor, 1997a).

Women and Men's Entitlement to Workplace Benefits

Figure 4: Married Women's Access to Employer-Sponsored Health Plans, by Work Arrangement

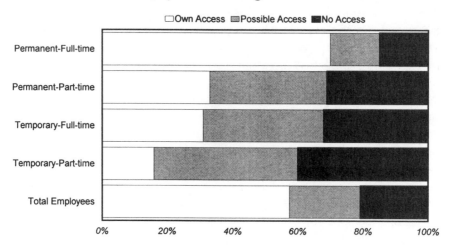

Source: Calculations based on Statistics Canada's 1995 Survey of Work Arrangements, family file.

Figure 5: Married Men's Access to Employer-Sponsored Health Plans, by Work Arrangement

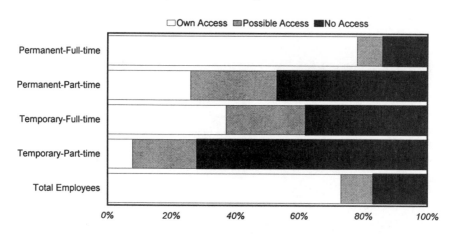

Source: Calculations based on Statistics Canada's 1995 Survey of Work Arrangements, family file.

Brenda Lipsett and Mark Reesor

unionization on benefits at firms of different sizes. Therefore, an interaction term of union status and firm size is included in the regression models.

The bivariate coverage rates from the SWA, Table 1, support these expected effects, in that unionized workers and those in large firms are more likely to have health, dental and ESPP coverage than are non-unionized workers and those employed in small firms. Furthermore, an "equalization" effect of unionization is evident in the entitlement rates (i.e., benefit coverage rates of workers in unionized small firms are closer to the coverage rates of workers in unionized large firms than the corresponding coverage rates of workers in non-unionized firms).[13]

There are strong perceptions about the "generosity" of the highly unionized public sector's non-wage benefits. The data in Table 1 support these perceptions, as public sector employees are more likely to be entitled to extended health, dental and ESPP coverage than private sector employees (81%, 74% and 85%, respectively, of public sector employees versus 59%, 55% and 48%, respectively, of private sector employees). However, the incidence of unionization is much higher in the public sector. Controlling for union status alone, public sector employees remain only somewhat better off in terms of extended health, dental and ESPP coverage than private sector employees. To formally test whether public and private sector unions have differing effects on the probability of health, dental or ESPP coverage, a union status and public/private sector employment interaction term is included in the model.

Job Tenure. Job tenure is a proxy for firm-specific experience (seniority) and may signal the success of an employee-employer match. It may also serve as a proxy for promotion into job categories where benefits are available (especially in non-union settings) and the age and financial viability of private sector firms. Thus, we expect that the longer the job tenure, the higher the probability of entitlement to workplace benefits. Furthermore, in many firms, new employees' access to non-wage benefits are restricted before completion of a probationary period of employment, reinforcing the notion that short-tenured (probationary) workers would be less likely to have

---

[13]Results from the GSS support these findings, as unionized workers are more likely to have health and dental plan coverage than their non-unionized counterparts. Furthermore, the coverage rates of both health and dental plans increase monotonically with firm size (Krahn, 1992).

coverage. The obvious potential correlation between job tenure, permanent/non-permanent status and age will be examined using the regression model.

Entitlement to extended health, dental and ESPP coverage by job tenure, reported in Table 1, indicates a greater likelihood of benefit coverage for longer job tenures, as the coverage rates of all benefits increase monotonically with job tenure.

Industry and Occupation. In addition to the job-related characteristics mentioned thus far, many unaccounted for job characteristics, such as work environment and risk, affect the incentives for employers to offer benefit coverage and vary by industry and occupation. To capture these effects, industry and occupation needs to be controlled for in the regression models.

The industrial sectors with the lowest coverage rates are agriculture, business, personal and miscellaneous services, wholesale and retail trade and construction, while employees in the generally federally regulated industries — utilities, communications and finance and public administration — have the highest coverage rates (see Table 1). The low coverage rates in the private services, trade and construction industries are a concern, as more than one in three workers in Canada are employed in these industries. Furthermore, since service and trade are rapidly growing sectors of the economy, the share of paid workers in these industries, along with the percentage of workers without benefit coverage, is likely to increase.

Entitlement to workplace benefits also varies considerably across occupations. Low coverage occupations include the artistic, primary, sales and service groups. Occupations with high rates of coverage include medicine, natural sciences, social sciences and religion, other crafts and teaching. Furthermore, for *each* occupation, a higher percentage of males than females are entitled to employer-sponsored benefit coverage.

Personal Characteristics

Education. Workplace benefits are often targeted to act as a recruitment incentive for particular types of workers. It is, therefore, expected that personal characteristics, such as education attainment, would be positively associated with the receipt of benefits as firms use compensation packages to attract employees with enhanced skills. Workers commanding high wages, correlated with higher education, are also likely to choose a larger portion of compensation in the form of benefits, especially if those benefits offer tax savings. The data from the SWA (Table 1) support the link between higher

Brenda Lipsett and Mark Reesor

education and better employment conditions, with the proportion of workers entitled to benefits increasing monotonically with education level.

Age, Marital Status and Presence of Dependents. Age, marital status and child-bearing are associated with differences in wages and job tenure but can have independent effects on benefit coverage. Age can be used as a proxy for general labour market experience and, as such, one could expect to be compensated for such experience through higher wages and/or employer-sponsored benefits. As people grow older (marry and have children) financial stability and security become increasingly important, shifting worker preferences towards a job that provides medical insurance and deferred retirement income. Firms interested in acquiring a stable, dependable work-force can offer benefits on a non-discriminatory basis to attract these mature adults. Offering benefits that are of much more value to the group of workers it is trying to attract, such as family coverage in extended health plans, emphasizes the importance of detailed information on the quality of benefit plans, which is not available in the Survey of Work Arrangements.

The data from Table 1 show that younger workers (under age 25 years) are roughly two times less likely than older workers (age 25 years and over) to be entitled to extended health, dental and ESPP coverage. When examining the effect of family status on entitlement to benefits, married workers with children are more likely to have coverage than those without children. For single people, those with children are roughly half as likely as other singles to have health (dental) coverage. The prevalence of part-time work among lone parents partially explains this result.

Province. Regulations regarding workplace benefits falls primarily under provincial jurisdiction. Health care is a responsibility of provincial govern-ments and some aspects of provincial health-care plans vary by province. Therefore, it is reasonable to expect interprovincial variations in private extended medical/dental coverage as substitution takes place between the workplace and public plans. Also, many of the laws regarding pension plans fall under provincial jurisdictions and can cause coverage rates to vary by province.

Data from the SWA exhibit this variation (Table 1) and therefore provincial effects need to be controlled for in the regression models. For example, Ontario has both the highest percentage of workers with extended health coverage at 67% and the highest percentage of workers with dental coverage at 66%. On the other hand, Saskatchewan has the lowest percentage of employees with extended health coverage at 48%, and Quebec has the lowest percentage with dental plan coverage at 45%. Low extended health coverage in Saskatchewan may be due to the extent of coverage of prescription drugs in the public health plan. Low dental coverage in Quebec may be due to a public health plan that covers dental care for children under age 7 and the unique tax treatment of employer contributions to plans as the imputed taxable income of employees for provincial income tax purposes (i.e., no tax advantage associated with taking a portion of total compensation in benefits). Manitoba has the highest percentage of workers with ESPP coverage at 61% and New Brunswick the lowest at 49%. This is due in part to Manitoba's legislated extensions of registered pension plan (RPP) coverage to part-timers in 1984 *and* the inability of workers in Manitoba to opt out of RPP programs, while New Brunswick was one of the final provinces to extend eligibility for RPPs to part-time workers, doing so only in 1991 and leaving the option for coverage to the employee (Statistics Canada, 1996a).

Wages

As discussed above, employee compensation is split between wages and workplace benefits. The relationship between wages and benefits can be viewed in a sequential fashion with the need for wages being satisfied before other elements in the compensation package become important. While this hierarchy primarily reflects the concerns of employees, it can be relevant to the employers' ability to recruit and retain employees. Thus, we would expect entitlement to benefits to increase with wages. The data from Table 1 supports this casual association between wages and the entitlement to benefits.

In the case of workplace pensions, representing deferred income, the association between low wages and lack of entitlement to ESPP may be the result of rational decision making: if receipt of public retirement benefits is means tested then it may not be in a low-wage earner's interest to join a plan. Additionally, J. Pesando (1992) suggests that firms that sponsor pensions are more inclined to pay efficiency wages (above market wages) which could also help explain the long tenure of those covered by workplace pensions.

Multivariate Analysis of the Determinants of Entitlement to Workplace Benefits

This section presents the logistic regression model and the multivariate results. The independent effects of the job and personal characteristics on the likelihood of entitlement to benefits are estimated, controlling for other factors. It reveals that the main determinants of workplace benefit coverage are part/full-time hours, permanent/non-permanent employment status, union status, firm size, job tenure and wages for men and women. The most financially insecure workers today (the non-permanent, part-time, non-unionized, short-tenured, low-wage earners working in small firms) are *much* less likely to have coverage than those who have been working in a permanent, full-time, unionized, high-wage position in a large firm for many years.

The Logistic Regression Model

Based on the empirical framework above, a logistic regression model is estimated by maximum likelihood to determine the relationship between the dependent variable (entitlement to the three workplace benefits) and the independent variables. The independent variables are contained in the vector $x=(JOB, PERS, W)$. *JOB* contains information on work arrangements and other workplace characteristics — weekly hours worked (part-/full-/long-time), permanent/non-permanent status, industry, occupation, union status, seniority (job tenure), class of worker (public/private sector) and firm size; *PERS* contains information on observable personal characteristics — age, education, marital status, presence of dependent children and province of residence; and *W* contains hourly wage groupings.[14]

---

[14]From the discussion in the second section it is clear that wages and benefits are jointly determined components of total compensation. Therefore, at issue is the endogeneity of wages in the model indicating that wage be instrumented. Instruments that have been used include the average annual percentage wage increase, unanticipated inflation and lagged values of the current wage (Currie and Chaykowski, 1995). However, no valid instruments exist in the SWA dataset. Nonetheless, it is important to control for wages when examining entitlement to benefit coverage to reduce the extent of omitted variables bias (Currie and Chaykowski, 1995).

With $\pi(x)$ defined as the probability of entitlement to benefit coverage (conditional on x), then $(1-\pi(x))$ is the probability of no coverage (conditional on x). The *odds* of entitlement to coverage are defined as $\pi(x)/(1-\pi(x))$ — the ratio of the conditional probability of coverage to the conditional probability of no coverage — and the *log-odds* is the natural logarithm of the odds, namely $\ln\{\pi(x)/(1-\pi(x))\}$. The logistic regression model is then:

$$(1) \qquad \ln\left(\frac{\pi(x)}{1-\pi(x)}\right) = \beta_0 + \beta_1 JOB + \beta_2 PERS + \beta_3 W ,$$

where: β_0 is an intercept parameter;

β_1 is a vector of unknown parameters detailing the effect of job-related characteristics on entitlement to workplace benefits;

β_2 is a vector of unknown parameters detailing the effect of personal characteristics on entitlement to workplace benefits; and

β_3 is a vector of unknown parameters detailing the effect of wages on entitlement to workplace benefits.

The results from estimating the logistic model are presented in the form of relative odds, or odds ratios. Odds ratios are defined to be the ratio of the odds of extended health, dental and ESPP coverage, respectively, between two or more groups, namely;

$$(2) \qquad Odds\ Ratio = \frac{\pi_1/(1 - \pi_1)}{\pi_2/(1 - \pi_2)} ,$$

where the subscripts 1 and 2 refer to the two groups being compared.[15]

---

[15]Odds ratios are preferred on statistical grounds to probability ratios (the distributional properties of the estimators are better) and they have the added advantage of not varying with the choice of reference group. However, relative odds exaggerates (or minimizes) the differences between groups and the interpretation is less straightforward.

Brenda Lipsett and Mark Reesor

The Multivariate Results

Generally, the independent effects of work arrangements and other characteristics on the likelihood of entitlement to workplace benefits are confirmed by the results of the regression models. Non-standard work arrangements remain a major determinant of entitlement to workplace benefits even when the effects of other factors, including job tenure, age, education, industry and occupation, are controlled for. Tables of the regression results are included in Appendix 3. Selected results are charted below to illustrate the salient points.

Job-Related Characteristics

Union Status, Firm Size and Public/Private Sector Workers. Union status and firm size are major factors in determining the probability of entitlement to workplace benefit coverage (significant at the 0.001 level). Their effects are as expected, with unionized workers and those working in large firms having better odds of entitlement to coverage than their counterparts. The larger the firm, the greater the likelihood that an employee is entitled to workplace benefits in both unionized and non-unionized settings. In addition, the interaction effect of union status and firm size is significant (0.001 level) for both genders, confirming the "equalization" effect of unionization across firm size on the likelihood of entitlement to workplace benefits. This is illustrated in Figure 6 on the relative odds of ESPP coverage by union status and firm size. The lengths of the bars, which represent the relative odds of ESPP coverage, are relatively more equal across unionized firm sizes than non-unionized firm sizes. For example, female non-unionized employees of large firms (over 500 employees) are 12 times more likely to be entitled to a pension plan than female non-unionized employees of small firms (less than 20 employees). However, unionized women in large firms are only 3.4 times as likely to be entitled to a pension plan than unionized women in small firms. Thus, unionization has an equalization effect on the entitlement to benefits across firm size, removing some of the insecurity of working in a small firm.

The interaction term used to explore the effect of public and private sector unions on entitlement to workplace benefits is insignificant at the 0.1 level for extended health and dental plans and insignificant at the 0.05 level for ESPPs for both genders. This suggests that the ability or preference of

Figure 6: Relative Odds of ESPP Coverage by Union Status and Firm Size

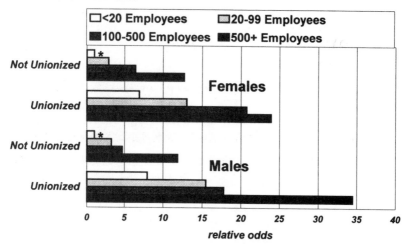

Note: * Denotes the reference group used for the calculation of relative odds.
Source: Survey of Work Arrangements, 1995.

unions to negotiate benefit coverage is no different in the public and private sectors. Thus, the discrepancy in entitlement rates between public and private sector workers is mostly due to the differences in unionization rates, not because the public sector is necessarily a more "generous" employer or has more powerful unions.

Part-Time and Non-Permanent Work Arrangements. Both part-time and non-permanent job status have the expected effect on the probability of entitlement to workplace benefits — part-time and non-permanent workers have lower odds of extended health, dental and ESPP coverage, respectively, than full-time and permanent workers.[16] When personal and job

---

[16]Permanent/non-permanent job status is highly correlated with age and seniority (job tenure) and this variable tends to dampen the effects of the others (and vice-versa). However, since these variables (age, tenure, permanent/non-permanent status) are not perfectly correlated with one another, and because of prior reasoning for inclusion of each of these variables in the models (second section), all three are retained in the models. If one of these variables were removed, we would be losing some information on the determinants of entitlement to workplace benefits, even though the effects of the other two would be more pronounced.

Brenda Lipsett and Mark Reesor

Figure 7: Relative Odds of Employer-Sponsored Benefit Plans, by Part-Time and Full-Time Hours

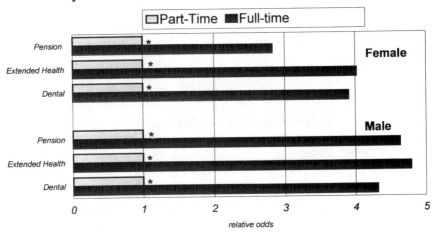

Note: * Denotes the reference group used for the calculation of relative odds.
Source: Survey of Work Arrangements, 1995.

Figure 8: Relative Odds of Employer-Sponsored Benefit Plans, by Permanent and Non-Permanent Job Status

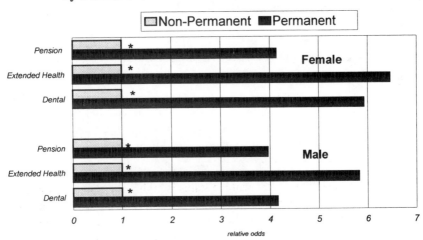

Note: * Denotes the reference group used for the calculation of relative odds.
Source: Survey of Work Arrangements, 1995.

Women and Men's Entitlement to Workplace Benefits   *71*

characteristics are controlled for, these results suggest a clear bias against the provision of benefits to part-time and non-permanent workers. The marked difference between permanent and full-time workers on the one hand, and temporary and part-time workers on the other suggests a general difference in the degree of commitment to core versus peripheral employees. The general availability of well-qualified temporary and part-time workers to whom benefits do not have to be offered may be a function of overall slack in the labour market. (Although many of the people working part-time do so voluntarily, there is a growing number of involuntary part-time workers.) In a tighter labour market, it would be harder to find available temporary and part-time workers, and they may be able to demand workplace benefits.

Job Tenure. Seniority's (job tenure) effect in the multivariate analysis is consistent with its expected effect — the odds of extended health, dental and ESPP coverage, respectively, increases with seniority. The one exception is that the odds of dental plan coverage for workers with 20+ years experience are less than the odds for workers with 11-20 years of seniority. An important implication of job tenure is that it determines the portability of pensions and can affect the mobility of workers. Reduced mobility of workers is only a problem if pensions fail to enhance productivity by reducing hiring and training costs and by enhancing work effort. The fact that job tenure is an important explanatory variable after the first year of employment, which allows for a probation period before entitlement to workplace benefits, suggests that job tenure may be serving as a proxy for other factors. Promotion into job categories where benefits are available, especially in non-union settings, and the age and financial viability of the firm, are two possible explanatory factors.

Occupation and Industry. Occupation and industry are both statistically significant (0.001 level) in the regression models.[17] By occupation, the relative odds of entitlement to extended health and dental coverage are highest for women in machining and managers and administrators and lowest in transportation, construction and processing. For men, occupation makes less of a difference. The highest relative odds of dental coverage is found in

---

[17]The reader is referred to the Appendix tables of regression results for more detailed information about the effect of each industry/occupation on entitlement to extended health, dental and ESPP coverage.

Brenda Lipsett and Mark Reesor

Figure 9: Relative Odds of Women's Workplace Benefit Coverage by Job Tenure

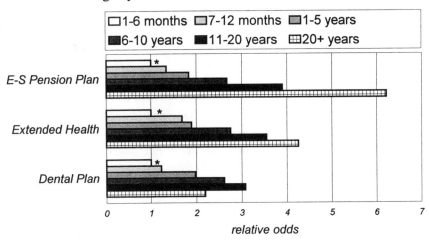

Note: * Denotes the reference group used for the calculation of relative odds.
Source: Survey of Work Arrangements, 1995.

natural and social science occupations and of extended health coverage, among managers and administrators. The relative odds of entitlement to ESPPs are highest for women in teaching, natural and social science, management and administration, other crafts and clerical occupations. For men, material handling replaces other crafts in the top five occupations. The lowest ESPP coverage for women is among those in material handling, transportation, processing, fabricating and machining. For men, the lowest odds of entitlement to ESPP coverage is also found in transportation and fabricating and, unlike women, in medicine, artistic and other crafts occupations.

By industry, holding other factors constant, the highest relative odds of entitlement to extended health and dental plans for women is clearly in utilities, while the lowest is in business and personal services. For men, the highest relative odds of dental coverage is in manufacturing and, for extended health coverage, in primary industries other than agriculture. The lowest relative odds of male dental coverage are in community service while lowest extended health coverage is in the communications industry. Health risks could be one factor playing a role in interindustry differences. The odds of entitlement to an ESPP is lowest in business and personal services, agriculture, miscellaneous services, wholesale and retail trade and construction and highest in public administration, community services and finance, insurance and real estate (FIRE) for both men and women.

Personal Characteristics

Age, Marital Status and Presence of Dependents. Age, marital status and presence of dependents are not major determinants of entitlement to workplace benefits. Much of the proposed effect of age is accounted for by other variables such as tenure, union status and permanent/non-permanent status. Age is insignificant for males at the 0.25 level and, although it is significant for females, the differences in the odds of coverage between age groups is not large. One age effect to note is that older workers (55-69 years) have a significantly lower odds of entitlement to workplace benefits than all younger workers. A possible contributing factor would be the earlier retirement ages of workers with long-term participation in workplace pensions, so that only uncovered older workers tend to be working.

Although marital status and the presence of dependents (and their interactions) are statistically significant, their effect on the relative odds of entitlement to workplace benefit coverage is small. One interesting point is that the coverage rates of single parents is quite comparable to those in other family types when other factors are controlled for, suggesting that their lack of benefits is related to factors such as education and job tenure. Therefore, there is sparse evidence that marriage and children provide strong incentives to "choose" a job that includes workplace benefits, and medical coverage in particular, as part of the overall compensation package. Given that age, marital status and the presence of children have an impact on the use of, and desirability of, extended health and dental benefits, an alternative explanation could be that what is an incentive for the employee (benefits) is a disincentive for the employer (costs).

Education. Education is a statistically significant determinant of entitlement to extended health and dental benefits although the differences between educational attainment groups is not large. Generally, the odds of extended health and dental coverage increase, although not monotonically, with educational attainment. The odds of ESPP coverage increase monotonically with educational attainment for males (0.001 level of significance). However, for females, other variables such as occupation, industry, wages and unionization dampen the effect of education on ESPP coverage, rendering it statistically insignificant (0.25 level) in the regression model.

Province. The variability of coverage rates by province, noted in the second section, is reinforced in the regression analysis with province of residence a significant (0.001 level for both genders) determinant of entitlement to extended health, dental and ESPP coverage. Workers in the province of Saskatchewan have the lowest odds of extended health coverage among all of the provinces. Quebec workers' have the lowest odds of dental plan coverage compared with other Canadians. Workers in the Atlantic province have the highest relative odds of extended health coverage while (female) workers in Saskatchewan have the highest relative odds of entitlement to dental coverage. The highest odds of entitlement to ESPPs is found in the small provinces of Newfoundland, Prince Edward Island, Manitoba and Saskatchewan for women and, additionally, New Brunswick for men. Province specific policies and preferences clearly play an independent role in entitlement to workplace benefits.

Figure 10: Relative Odds of ESPP Coverage by Hourly Wage

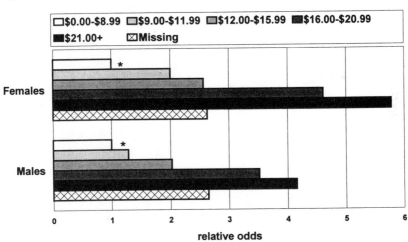

Note: * Denotes the reference group used for the calculation of relative odds.
Source: Survey of Work Arrangements, 1995.

Wages

Wages and benefits go hand in hand — the likelihood of entitlement to workplace benefits increases monotonically with wages. Wages have a significant (0.001 level for both genders) effect on the odds of extended health, dental and ESPP entitlement. These results underline the multiple sources of insecurity for workers in low-wage jobs. Not only do workers earning higher wages have greater financial security today but, given the ESPP entitlement rates among wage groups, this difference will persist into retirement.

Conclusion

Vulnerability and insecurity emerge as principal themes in this analysis of workplace benefits. Workplace benefits critically influence future retirement income, standard of living and security for today's workers. Lack of access to extended health and dental benefits and employer-sponsored pension plans for some groups of workers is the main policy issue. The major determinants of entitlement to extended health, dental and pension plan coverage are permanent/non-permanent job status, part/full-time hours, unionization, firm size, seniority (as proxied by job tenure) and wages. Secondary determinants of coverage include class of worker (public/private sector), industry, occupation, age, education, province of residence, marital status and presence of dependents.

Overall results show that extended health, dental and ESPP coverage applies to 63%, 59% and 55%, respectively, of paid workers. Additionally, some married workers, particularly women, potentially access health and dental plans through spousal plans and may have partial access to spousal ESPPs. The analysis indicates that the low rates of entitlement to workplace benefits are not the result of students in the analysis and secondary wage-earners being covered by a spouse. Moreover, the most financially insecure workers today (the non-permanent, part-time, non-unionized, short-tenured, low-wage earners working in small firms) are the least likely to have access to employer-sponsored benefits. Although improvements have been made in the entitlement to workplace benefits of part-timers, it still lags that of permanent full-time workers.

In looking to the future, the areas where employment has grown significantly in recent years — in small firms and non-standard employment arrangements — are negatively associated with entitlement to workplace benefits. The changes in employment shares away from jobs with high eligibility rates for employer-sponsored benefits (e.g., public sector, large firms) towards those with low eligibility rates (e.g., part-time, temporary, small firms and, in particular, a shift to self-employment) suggest that more workers will lack these benefits in the future. As a result, there will be a greater reliance on public medical and retirement benefit programs and individual resources. As the Canadian labour market continues to evolve, with continued trends to more non-standard employment, the advantages of a strong universal and comprehensive health-care system attached to the individual rather than the job become more apparent. The limited coverage, as well as the limited portability, of ESPPs emphasizes the importance of maintaining a strong, portable public pension system to complement private efforts.

For workers without entitlement to workplace medical coverage or ESPPs, private insurance (or personal savings and RRSPs) is available, but more affordable for those with higher wages. This could result in a greater difference in "actual" private coverage rates between the high and low wage earners. As such, the increased family market income inequality observed over the 1990s likely understates the inequality in living standards — an inequality which will persist into retirement — by excluding entitlement to these employer-sponsored benefits. This inequality further underlines the importance of a strong public health and pension system in promoting security and equity.

This analysis of entitlement to benefit plans through employers reveals a number of questions requiring further research. What is the impact of workplace benefits on a firm's ability to attract and retain quality staff? What is their impact on employee productivity? Is there a gap between actual benefit coverage rates and employee awareness of coverage? What role do workplace benefits have in influencing the rate of social assistance recidivism, especially for lone parents? What is the quality of extended health plan coverage (e.g., comprehensiveness of health services covered, employee contribution in the form of deductables and/or co-payments)? What is the effect on the overall coverage of Canadian workers of the recent decline in employment in sectors with a high probability of entitlement to these benefits (e.g., the shift from public to private sector and from paid to self-employment)? Additionally, further research is required on the dynamics of benefit coverage as workers move between school and work, jobs, and work and retirement, and the extent to which part-time and temporary jobs of lower quality are stepping stones to better jobs. If workers remain in jobs of low quality (low wages and few benefits) for long periods of time, their current and future security will be compromised accordingly.

The revised Labour Force Survey is a key data source for future research because it includes the SWA question on workplace benefits in its November work arrangements module. Additionally, the longitudinal Survey of Labour and Income Dynamics provides useful information on transitions between non-standard and full-time paid employment. However, it provides specific data only on employer-sponsored pension plans. Further data development would be required to determine whether employees not eligible for workplace benefits through their employers were self-insuring through other vehicles, the quality of employee plans, and the extent of participation in flexible benefit plans.

Brenda Lipsett and Mark Reesor

Appendix

A.1 Table 1: Percent of Paid Employees with Entitlement to Employer-sponsored Pension Plan, Extended Health and Dental Plan Coverage

Percent of Paid Employees with Employer-sponsored Pension Plan, Extended Health Plan and Dental Plan

Characteristics	Employer-sponsored Pension Plan			Extended Health Plan			Dental Plan		
	Total	Males	Females	Total	Males	Females	Total	Males	Females
Canada	55.2	58.2	51.9	63.3	68.6	57.6	58.9	63.9	53.6
Job Related Characteristics									
Weekly Hours									
Under 30	27.8	14.2	30.6	25.7	17.3	27.4	23	15.7	24.5
30 to 49	60.2	62	57.9	69.3	71.9	66.1	64.3	66.5	61.7
50 and Over	51.5	49.5	57.4	64.8	64.5	66	62.4	62.4	62.5
Temporary Workers									
Permanent	58.5	61.5	55.1	67.6	72.7	62	63.1	67.8	57.9
Non-Permanent	24.9	24.3	25.4	23.5	25.9	21.5	20.3	23	18
Union Status									
Unionized	82.8	84.4	80.9	84.3	88.4	79.3	77.3	80.7	73.1
Not Unionized	36.6	39	34.1	49.2	54	44.3	46.5	51.4	41.6
Firm Size									
Under 20	14.1	15.3	13	24.3	28.1	20.6	21.8	24.2	19.5
20-99	41	43.2	38.1	58.7	63	53.3	53	57.3	47.5
100-500	63	63	63.1	72.6	76.4	68.9	65.3	69.1	61.5
Over 500	78.4	83.1	73.2	81.1	87.1	74.4	77.6	83.4	71
Firm Size and Union Status									
Under 20, Non-Union	10.8	11.1	10.5	20.9	23.4	18.6	18.8	20.6	17.1
20-99, Non-Union	29	31.2	26.2	51.8	55.3	47.3	47.1	52	40.8
100-500, Non-Union	44.7	46.5	42.8	60.6	65.3	55.6	57.5	62.3	52.5
Over 500, Non-Union	65.4	70.9	60.3	72.5	79.9	65.5	70.9	78.5	63.8
Under 20, Union	51.4	50.2	53.5	61.9	66.9	53.1	55.5	54	58.3
20-99, Union	70.5	72.2	68.1	75.9	81.7	68.3	67.6	70.2	64.3
100-500, Union	80.9	80.3	81.4	84.3	88.1	80.8	72.8	76.2	69.7
Over 500, Union	88.4	91.1	84.8	87.7	91.7	82.4	82.6	86.7	77.4
Class of Worker									
Public Employee	84.8	90.5	79.5	81	88.2	74.4	73.7	80.3	67.6
Private Employee	47.8	51	44.3	58.9	64.2	53	55.3	60.2	49.7

Percent of Paid Employees with Employer-sponsored Pension Plan, Extended Health Plan and Dental Plan

Characteristics	Employer-sponsored Pension Plan			Extended Health Plan			Dental Plan		
	Total	Males	Females	Total	Males	Females	Total	Males	Females
Class of Worker and Union Status									
Public, Non-Union	59.4	73.3	47.2	58.8	73.3	46	53.5	67	41.7
Private, Non-Union	35	36.8	33.2	48.5	52.8	44.2	46.1	50.5	41.6
Public, Union	90.6	94.4	87	86.1	91.6	81	78.3	83.3	73.7
Private, Union	77.6	79	75.6	83.1	86.7	77.8	76.6	79.4	72.7
Job Tenure									
1-6 Months	21.7	22.8	20.6	26.8	30.9	22.8	24.1	27.4	20.9
7-12 Months	29	29.6	28.1	42.4	43.9	40.2	38.3	40.9	34.6
1-5 Years	42.4	45.5	39.3	54.7	61.5	48.2	52.2	58.2	46.5
6-10 Years	61.3	62.7	60	71.2	76	66.8	66.2	69.3	63.3
11-20 Years	76.9	79.4	73.9	81.4	85.2	76.8	77.4	81.5	72.5
Over 20 Years	87.2	89	84.3	89	92	84.1	78.7	83.9	70.1
Industry									
Agriculture	13.2	N/A	N/A	22.9	24.5	N/A	22.2	22.5	N/A
Other Primary	63.3	63.9	60.5	72	73.6	65.2	70.5	72.2	63.1
Manufacturing	61.6	65.3	52.6	75.3	78.5	67.6	69.8	73.6	60.8
Construction	33.4	34.8	N/A	46.5	46.7	45.4	43.6	44.1	40.3
Transportation	56.8	59.1	48	66.6	68.2	60.5	63.2	64.8	57.3
Communications	74.1	70.7	79.3	78.6	75.1	83.9	78.3	77.2	79.9
Utilities	83.2	83.7	81.5	84.9	83.7	89.2	78.3	76.3	85
Trade	34.9	39.8	29.3	48.4	57.1	38.5	45	51.6	37.6
Finance	70.1	69.8	70.3	75.6	76.8	75	75.1	74.9	75.2
Community Services	69	76.6	66.1	67.7	77.1	64.2	60.9	67.2	58.6
Business and Personal Services	25.5	31.2	21.4	39.8	48.4	33.8	37.4	47.8	30.1
Miscellaneous Services	26.5	28.1	24.9	43.5	47.5	39.7	38.1	43.2	33.1
Public Administration	86.3	91.2	80.3	85	89.5	79.4	78.5	81.2	75.1
Occupation									
Artistic	37.5	40.4	34.1	47.9	49.3	46.2	45	47.3	42.2
Clerical	54.8	68.9	51.4	61.7	73.7	58.8	59	71.7	55.9
Construction	47.2	47.5	N/A	53.9	54.3	N/A	52.5	52.9	N/A
Fabricating	53	55.1	44	67.4	69.8	57.7	60.6	64.2	45.5
Machining	60.8	60.7	62.2	75.2	74	N/A	69	67.7	N/A
Managers and Other Administrators	64.8	66.7	N/A	78.7	82.9	74.3	73.7	76.3	70.8

Brenda Lipsett and Mark Reesor

Characteristics	Employer-sponsored Pension Plan			Extended Health Plan			Dental Plan		
	Total	Males	Females	Total	Males	Females	Total	Males	Females
Material Handling	52.5	56.7	N/A	60.7	62.7	52.7	54.1	56	46.4
Medicine	68.1	70	67.7	67.1	72.3	66.1	63.8	69.4	62.8
Natural, Social Science and Religion	68.5	68.5	68.5	77	79.4	73	73.6	76.4	69.2
Other Crafts	67.8	74.2	N/A	78.2	84.1	N/A	70.5	78	N/A
Primary	37.4	41.9	N/A	43.8	48	N/A	42	46.5	N/A
Processing	60.4	68.7	31.3	68.5	76.1	41.9	65.4	72.9	39
Sales	36.2	42.9	30.3	47.6	59.1	37.4	44.8	54.3	36.4
Service	37.1	50.2	25.6	41.3	55.2	29.1	38	51.5	26
Teaching	79.5	85.4	76.7	75.7	85.3	71.2	63.5	68.2	61.2
Transportation	43.4	43.6	N/A	55.3	56.2	N/A	51.9	52.9	N/A
Personal Characteristics									
Age									
15-24	23.9	23.4	24.3	34.6	35.1	34.1	32.5	32.9	32.2
25-34	51.4	51.4	51.5	62.4	65.1	59.3	59.2	61.4	56.6
35-44	62.5	67.1	57.7	68.9	75.4	62.2	64.9	71	58.5
45-54	64.6	70.3	58.7	70.3	78.8	61.7	63.9	71.5	56.1
55-69	56	62.7	46.9	63.7	72	52.7	55.7	65.3	42.8
Education									
0-8 Years	40.2	43.8	33.5	48.3	52.9	39.8	38.3	43.3	29.3
Some Secondary	45.5	49.9	38.7	54.2	61.9	42.4	48.4	55.4	38
Graduated High School	49.6	52.9	46.4	58.2	63.9	52.6	55.8	61.8	50
Some Post-Secondary	51.4	53.9	48.9	62.1	63.6	60.6	60	62.4	57.5
Post-Secondary Certificate or Diploma	57	60	53.9	65.1	70.3	59.8	60.6	65.6	55.5
University Degree	70.5	74	66.8	76.5	82.9	69.9	71.1	76.6	65.5
Marital Status									
Married	58.7	63.3	53.6	66	73.7	57.6	61.5	68.9	53.4
Single, Never Married	43.1	42.6	43.8	54.1	53.9	54.5	50.7	49.5	52.2
Widowed, Separated/Divorced	60	64.9	56.8	66.9	71	64.1	61.1	66.2	57.7
Presence of Dependents									
At Least One Child	55.7	60	51.2	62.5	69.9	54.9	58.5	65.3	51.4
No Children	54.6	56.1	52.8	64.4	67	61.3	59.5	62.1	56.6

Percent of Paid Employees with Employer-sponsored Pension Plan, Extended Health Plan and Dental Plan

Characteristics	Employer-sponsored Pension Plan			Extended Health Plan			Dental Plan		
	Total	Males	Females	Total	Males	Females	Total	Males	Females
Marital Status and Presence of Dependents Combined									
Married With At Least One Child	60.4	65.1	55	66.8	75.2	57.1	62.4	70.5	53.2
Married No Children	55.2	59.5	51.1	64.4	70.5	58.7	59.5	65.5	53.9
Single With At Least One Child	24.3	22.4	26.1	33.5	30.7	36.2	31.5	28.6	34.4
Single No Children	51.1	49.6	53.4	62.9	62	64.4	58.9	56.8	61.9
Widowed, Separated, Divorced With At Least One Child	55.4	63	53.7	63.9	71.8	62.1	59.8	61.7	59.4
Widowed, Separated, Divorced Without Children	63.2	65.3	60.7	68.9	70.9	66.6	61.9	67.3	55.5
Province									
Newfoundland	58.9	62.6	55.1	63.8	68.8	58.4	56.8	60.7	52.7
Prince Edward Island	52.1	51.5	52.7	58.4	59.8	57	51.8	53.9	49.7
Nova Scotia	50.8	55	46.1	62.2	67.9	55.9	53.3	60	45.9
New Brunswick	48.8	53.8	43.6	57.7	63.1	52	53.4	57.6	48.9
Quebec	55.2	55.9	54.3	64.5	69.1	59.5	45.2	47.7	42.4
Ontario	57.6	61.5	53.4	66.6	72.2	60.4	66.2	72.2	59.5
Manitoba	60.9	63	58.7	63	67.7	57.7	62.9	69.3	55.9
Saskatchewan	57.1	59.1	55.2	47.8	53.8	42.3	61.3	64.3	58.6
Alberta	51.1	53.6	48.3	57.6	62.1	52.6	60	64.8	54.7
British Columbia	50.5	55.6	45.3	60.3	65.8	54.7	63.5	69.6	57.3
Wages									
Hourly Wage									
0.00-8.99	13.4	14.3	12.9	19.9	22.6	18.5	16.4	19.2	14.9
9.00-11.99	33	26.4	37.9	45.5	43.2	47.2	41.2	37.2	44.1
12.00-15.99	55.9	50.8	60.5	68.7	66.4	70.8	63.2	59.5	66.4
16.00-20.99	76.5	74.5	79.1	81.7	82.4	80.9	77.2	77.8	76.3
21.00 and Over	83.3	83.9	82.1	87.4	91.3	79.8	83.2	86.9	75.9
Missing	55.2	57.9	51.7	63.4	67.4	58	59.3	63.6	53.6

Source: HRDC calculations based on the 1995 Survey of Work Arrangements, Statistics Canada.

Brenda Lipsett and Mark Reesor

A.2: Percent of Married Employees by Entitlement to Workplace Benefit Coverage and Work Arrangement

A.2 Table 1: Percent of Married Employees by Entitlement to Employer-sponsored Pension Plan Coverage and Work Arrangement

Both Genders

Worker Type	No Coverage	Possible Coverage	Own Job Coverage	Total
Permanent-Full-Time	23%	12%	65%	100%
Permanent-Part-Time	39%	27%	34%	100%
Temporary-Full-Time	42%	25%	34%	100%
Temporary-Part-Time	50%	31%	19%	100%
All Worker Types	27%	15%	58%	100%

Males

Worker Type	No Coverage	Possible Coverage	Own Job Coverage	Total
Permanent-Full-Time	23%	10%	67%	100%
Permanent-Part-Time	53%	24%	23%	100%
Temporary-Full-Time	44%	22%	34%	100%
Temporary-Part-Time	72%	N/A	N/A	100%
All Worker Types	25%	11%	63%	100%

Females

Worker Type	No Coverage	Possible Coverage	Own Job Coverage	Total
Permanent-Full-Time	23%	14%	63%	100%
Permanent-Part-Time	37%	27%	35%	100%
Temporary-Full-Time	38%	28%	33%	100%
Temporary-Part-Time	45%	34%	21%	100%
All Worker Types	28%	19%	53%	100%

Source: HRDC calculations based on the 1995 Survey of Work Arrangements, Statistics Canada.

A.2 Table 2: Percent of Married Employees by Entitlement to Employer-sponsored Health Plan Coverage and Work Arrangement

Both Genders

Worker Type	No Coverage	Possible Coverage	Own Job Coverage	Total
Permanent-Full-Time	14%	11%	75%	100%
Permanent-Part-Time	33%	35%	32%	100%
Temporary-Full-Time	36%	30%	34%	100%
Temporary-Part-Time	45%	40%	15%	100%
All Worker Types	18%	16%	66%	100%

Males

Worker Type	No Coverage	Possible Coverage	Own Job Coverage	Total
Permanent-Full-Time	14%	8%	78%	100%
Permanent-Part-Time	47%	27%	26%	100%
Temporary-Full-Time	38%	25%	37%	100%
Temporary-Part-Time	72%	N/A	N/A	100%
All Worker Types	17%	10%	73%	100%

Females

Worker Type	No Coverage	Possible Coverage	Own Job Coverage	Total
Permanent-Full-Time	15%	15%	70%	100%
Permanent-Part-Time	31%	36%	33%	100%
Temporary-Full-Time	32%	37%	31%	100%
Temporary-Part-Time	40%	44%	16%	100%
All Worker Types	21%	22%	58%	100%

Source: HRDC calculations based on the 1995 Survey of Work Arrangements, Statistics Canada.

Brenda Lipsett and Mark Reesor

Both Genders

Worker Type	No Coverage	Possible Coverage	Own Job Coverage	Total
Permanent-Full-Time	19%	11%	70%	100%
Permanent-Part-Time	37%	33%	30%	100%
Temporary-Full-Time	40%	29%	32%	100%
Temporary-Part-Time	49%	40%	11%	100%
All Worker Types	23%	16%	61%	100%

Males

Worker Type	No Coverage	Possible Coverage	Own Job Coverage	Total
Permanent-Full-Time	19%	9%	72%	100%
Permanent-Part-Time	51%	26%	22%	100%
Temporary-Full-Time	41%	24%	35%	100%
Temporary-Part-Time	67%	N/A	N/A	100%
All Worker Types	21%	10%	68%	100%

Females

Worker Type	No Coverage	Possible Coverage	Own Job Coverage	Total
Permanent-Full-Time	19%	15%	66%	100%
Permanent-Part-Time	36%	34%	30%	100%
Temporary-Full-Time	38%	35%	27%	100%
Temporary-Part-Time	46%	43%	12%	100%
All Worker Types	25%	21%	53%	100%

Source: HRDC calculations based on the 1995 Survey of Work Arrangements, Statistics Canada.

A.3 Table 1: Variables Used in the Logistic Regression Models

The following table gives the names and descriptions of the variables used in the logistic regression models.

Group	Description	Variable Name
Job Related Characteristics		
Hours of Work	Less than 30 hrs/week	PARTTIME
	30-49 hrs/week	Base
	50+ hrs/week	LONGTIME
Non-Permanent Workers	Permanent	Base
	Non-permanent	TEMPJOB
Union Status	Unionized	UNION1
	Not unionized	Base
Firm Size	Less than 20 workers	FIRM1
	20-99 workers	FIRM2
	100-500 workers	FIRM3
	Over 500 workers	Base
Class of Worker	Public	GOVTEMP
	Private	Base
Job Tenure	1-6 months	TEN1
	7-12 months	TEN2
	1-5 years	Base
	6-10 years	TEN3
	11-20 years	TEN4 .
	Over 20 years	TEN5
Industry	Agriculture	IND1
	Other primary	IND2
	Manufacturing	IND3
	Construction	IND4
	Transportation	IND5
	Communications	IND6
	Utilities	IND7
	Trade	IND8
	Finance	IND9

Brenda Lipsett and Mark Reesor

Group	Description	Variable Name
	Community services	Base
	Business and personal services	IND10
	Miscellaneous	IND11
	Public administration	IND12
Occupation	Artistic	OCC5
	Clerical	Base
	Construction	OCC12
	Fabricating	OCC11
	Machining	OCC10
	Managers and other administrators	OCC1
	Material handling	OCC14
	Medicine	OCC4
	Natural, social science and religion	OCC2
	Other crafts	OCC15
	Primary	OCC8
	Processing	OCC9
	Sales	OCC6
	Service	OCC7
	Teaching	OCC3
	Transportation	OCC13
Interactions		
Union Status and Firm Size	UNION1*FIRM1	UNFIRM1
	UNION1*FIRM2	UNFIRM2
	UNION1*FIRM3	UNFIRM3
Union Status and Class of Worker	UNION1*GOVTEMP	UNGOVT
Personal Characteristics		
Age Groups	15-24 years	AGE1
	25-34 years	AGE2
	35-44 years	Base
	45-54 years	AGE3
	55-69 years	AGE4

Group	Description	Variable Name
Education	0-8 years	EDU1
	Some secondary	EDU2
	Graduated high school	EDU3
	Some post-secondary	EDU4
	Post-secondary certificate/ diploma	Base
	University degree	EDU5
Marital Status	Married or living common law	Base
	Single, never married	SINGLE
	Widowed, divorced or separated	OTHER
Children	At least one child	Base
	No children	NOCHILD
Province	Newfoundland	NWFLD
	Prince Edward Island	PEI
	Nova Scotia	NOVASC
	New Brunswick	NEWBRUN
	Quebec	QUEBEC
	Ontario	Base
	Manitoba	MANITOBA
	Saskatchewan	SASK
	Alberta	ALBERTA
	British Columbia	BC
Interactions		
Marital Status and Presence of Children	SINGLE*NOCHILD	SINGNOCH
	OTHER*NOCHILD	OTHNOCH
	Wages	
Hourly Wages	$0.00-$8.99 per hour	Base
	$9.00-$11.99 per hour	WAGE1
	$12.00-$15.99 per hour	WAGE2
	$16.00-$20.99 per hour	WAGE3
	$21.00+ per hour	WAGE4
	Refused, not stated, don't know	WAGE5

A.4 Table 1: Results of Males Extended Health Coverage Logistic Regression Model

Variable	Coefficient	Standard Error	Significance Level	Odds Ratio
INTERCPT	0.5277	0.2431	0.0299	1.695
Job Related Characteristics				
PARTTIME	-1.5667	0.1737	0.0001	0.209
LONGTIME	-0.0631	0.0871	0.4686	0.939
TEMPJOB	-1.7624	0.1156	0.0001	0.172
UNION1	0.9404	0.1271	0.0001	2.561
FIRM1	-2.1422	0.1024	0.0001	0.117
FIRM2	-0.7846	0.1033	0.0001	0.456
FIRM3	-0.6059	0.1149	0.0001	0.546
GOVTEMP	0.1016	0.2185	0.642	1.107
UNFIRM1	1.2103	0.2182	0.0001	3.354
UNFIRM2	0.3253	0.1895	0.086	1.384
UNFIRM3	0.4881	0.1874	0.0092	1.629
UNGOVT	-0.1435	0.2242	0.5222	0.866
TEN1	-0.8585	0.0989	0.0001	0.424
TEN2	-0.3684	0.1089	0.0007	0.692
TEN3	0.3287	0.088	0.0002	1.389
TEN4	0.4376	0.097	0.0001	1.549
TEN5	0.7196	0.1407	0.0001	2.054
IND1	0.1563	0.3536	0.6585	1.169
IND2	0.5788	0.257	0.0243	1.784
IND3	0.4586	0.1576	0.0036	1.582
IND4	-0.0726	0.2054	0.7238	0.93
IND5	0.2052	0.1978	0.2995	1.228
IND6	-0.3578	0.2187	0.1018	0.699
IND7	0.0765	0.2867	0.7895	1.08
IND8	0.0935	0.1601	0.5591	1.098
IND9	0.3464	0.2056	0.0921	1.414
IND10	-0.1968	0.1579	0.2126	0.821
IND11	0.1533	0.2369	0.5175	1.166
IND12	0.3369	0.2146	0.1165	1.401
OCC1	0.4008	0.1534	0.009	1.493
OCC2	0.2572	0.177	0.1462	1.293
OCC3	0.1771	0.268	0.5087	1.194
OCC4	-0.6312	0.262	0.016	0.532
OCC5	-0.4409	0.2544	0.0831	0.643
OCC6	-0.0362	0.1648	0.8262	0.964

Variable	Coefficient	Standard Error	Significance Level	Odds Ratio
OCC7	-0.348	0.1648	0.0347	0.706
OCC8	-0.6124	0.2782	0.0277	0.542
OCC9	-0.3979	0.1937	0.0399	0.672
OCC10	-0.0571	0.2149	0.7906	0.945
OCC11	-0.2658	0.1531	0.0824	0.767
OCC12	-0.288	0.1948	0.1393	0.75
OCC13	-0.4345	0.1818	0.0169	0.648
OCC14	-0.1658	0.2019	0.4116	0.847
OCC15	-0.0671	0.2858	0.8143	0.935
Personal Characteristics				
AGE1	-0.0802	0.1306	0.5393	0.923
AGE2	-0.00109	0.0808	0.9893	0.999
AGE3	0.0534	0.0971	0.5821	1.055
AGE4	0.0322	0.1334	0.8091	1.033
EDU1	-0.6793	0.1454	0.0001	0.507
EDU2	-0.2126	0.0968	0.0281	0.808
EDU3	-0.0193	0.0853	0.8209	0.981
EDU4	-0.1811	0.119	0.1279	0.834
EDU5	0.2824	0.1052	0.0072	1.326
SINGLE	-0.4161	0.1491	0.0053	0.66
OTHER	-0.2286	0.2886	0.4284	0.796
NOCHILD	-0.00398	0.0828	0.9617	0.996
SINGNOCH	0.5609	0.1693	0.0009	1.752
OTHNOCH	0.1136	0.3271	0.7283	1.12
NWFLD	0.3295	0.2708	0.2236	1.39
PEI	0.3836	0.4951	0.4385	1.468
NOVASC	0.3757	0.186	0.0434	1.456
NEWBRUN	0.2684	0.206	0.1926	1.308
QUEBEC	-0.1827	0.0809	0.0239	0.833
ALBERTA	-0.1892	0.1049	0.0713	0.828
MANITOBA	-0.0447	0.1641	0.7854	0.956
SASK	-0.9294	0.1809	0.0001	0.395
BC	-0.4024	0.0994	0.0001	0.669
Wages				
WAGE1	0.5468	0.1288	0.0001	1.728
WAGE2	1.0139	0.1282	0.0001	2.756
WAGE3	1.3555	0.1382	0.0001	3.879
WAGE4	1.7403	0.1522	0.0001	5.699
WAGE5	0.8695	0.1222	0.0001	2.386

Brenda Lipsett and Mark Reesor

A.4 Table 2: Results of Females Extended Health Coverage Logistic Regression Model

Variable	Coefficient	Standard Error	Significance Level	Odds Ratio
INTERCPT	0.1737	0.1719	0.3123	1.19
Job Related Characteristics				
PARTTIME	-1.3901	0.0771	0.0001	0.249
LONGTIME	0.00168	0.1383	0.9903	1.002
TEMPJOB	-1.8669	0.1098	0.0001	0.155
UNION1	0.5386	0.1183	0.0001	1.714
FIRM1	-2.1604	0.0973	0.0001	0.115
FIRM2	-0.7447	0.1036	0.0001	0.475
FIRM3	-0.4213	0.1093	0.0001	0.656
GOVTEMP	-0.4985	0.1697	0.0033	0.607
UNFIRM1	0.8967	0.2466	0.0003	2.451
UNFIRM2	0.3428	0.1815	0.059	1.409
UNFIRM3	0.5135	0.1629	0.0016	1.671
UNGOVT	0.2654	0.1858	0.1531	1.304
TEN1	-0.6382	0.1021	0.0001	0.528
TEN2	-0.119	0.1256	0.3433	0.888
TEN3	0.3742	0.0804	0.0001	1.454
TEN4	0.6282	0.0937	0.0001	1.874
TEN5	0.8095	0.1388	0.0001	2.247
IND1	-0.1593	0.4543	0.7258	0.853
IND2	-0.2069	0.3309	0.5317	0.813
IND3	0.4419	0.1457	0.0024	1.556
IND4	0.2934	0.2643	0.267	1.341
IND5	0.2346	0.2513	0.3506	1.264
IND6	0.4582	0.2487	0.0654	1.581
IND7	1.198	0.4943	0.0154	3.314
IND8	-0.2804	0.1223	0.0219	0.756
IND9	0.3799	0.1396	0.0065	1.462
IND10	-0.339	0.1152	0.0033	0.713
IND11	-0.0507	0.2054	0.8052	0.951
IND12	0.3116	0.1674	0.0627	1.366
OCC1	0.3416	0.0965	0.0004	1.407
OCC2	0.1587	0.1515	0.2948	1.172
OCC3	0.2133	0.1577	0.1761	1.238
OCC4	-0.448	0.1273	0.0004	0.639
OCC5	-0.3033	0.2412	0.2087	0.738
OCC6	-0.3459	0.1206	0.0041	0.708

Variable	Coefficient	Standard Error	Significance Level	Odds Ratio
OCC7	-0.5692	0.1144	0.0001	0.566
OCC8	-0.1288	0.5592	0.8178	0.879
OCC9	-1.0987	0.2471	0.0001	0.333
OCC10	2.0008	1.0379	0.0539	7.395
OCC11	-0.4733	0.1945	0.0149	0.623
OCC12	-0.9807	0.8706	0.26	0.375
OCC13	-1.0009	0.3648	0.0061	0.368
OCC14	-0.1981	0.312	0.5254	0.82
OCC15	0.1773	0.3941	0.6528	1.194
Personal Characteristics				
AGE1	-0.1466	0.1216	0.228	0.864
AGE2	0.0415	0.078	0.595	1.042
AGE3	-0.212	0.0857	0.0134	0.809
AGE4	-0.3753	0.1385	0.0067	0.687
EDU1	-0.3291	0.1836	0.073	0.72
EDU2	-0.23	0.1096	0.0359	0.795
EDU3	-0.1754	0.0812	0.0307	0.839
EDU4	0.1455	0.1133	0.199	1.157
EDU5	0.138	0.0946	0.1444	1.148
SINGLE	0.0831	0.1383	0.5478	1.087
OTHER	0.0745	0.1343	0.579	1.077
NOCHILD	0.1805	0.0786	0.0216	1.198
SINGNOCH	0.113	0.1669	0.4985	1.12
OTHNOCH	-0.00196	0.2054	0.9924	0.998
NWFLD	0.6981	0.2671	0.009	2.01
PEI	0.5943	0.4825	0.2181	1.812
NOVASC	0.4835	0.1755	0.0059	1.622
NEWBRUN	0.2685	0.1994	0.178	1.308
QUEBEC	0.087	0.0779	0.264	1.091
ALBERTA	-0.0613	0.1052	0.5601	0.941
MANITOBA	0.1255	0.1601	0.4329	1.134
SASK	-0.9202	0.1695	0.0001	0.398
BC	-0.0264	0.0937	0.7781	0.974
Wages				
WAGE1	0.8404	0.1043	0.0001	2.317
WAGE2	1.3923	0.1103	0.0001	4.024
WAGE3	1.6017	0.1283	0.0001	4.961
WAGE4	1.5548	0.1448	0.0001	4.734
WAGE5	1.0787	0.1057	0.0001	2.941

Brenda Lipsett and Mark Reesor

A.4 Table 3: Results of Males Dental Coverage Logistic Regression Model

Variable	Coefficient	Standard Error	Significance Level	Odds Ratio
INTERCPT	0.8345	0.2362	0.0004	2.304
Job Related Characteristics				
PARTTIME	-1.4597	0.1784	0.0001	0.232
LONGTIME	0.0222	0.0852	0.7944	1.022
TEMPJOB	-1.4216	0.1148	0.0001	0.241
UNION1	0.7567	0.1162	0.0001	2.131
FIRM1	-2.4145	0.1043	0.0001	0.089
FIRM2	-0.9324	0.1031	0.0001	0.394
FIRM3	-0.6972	0.1121	0.0001	0.498
GOVTEMP	-0.072	0.1976	0.7154	0.931
UNFIRM1	1.2795	0.2095	0.0001	3.595
UNFIRM2	0.2133	0.1708	0.2115	1.238
UNFIRM3	0.1593	0.1619	0.325	1.173
UNGOVT	-0.1281	0.1969	0.5154	0.88
TEN1	-1.0379	0.1011	0.0001	0.354
TEN2	-0.4615	0.1094	0.0001	0.63
TEN3	0.1525	0.0849	0.0724	1.165
TEN4	0.4658	0.0928	0.0001	1.593
TEN5	0.3861	0.118	0.0011	1.471
IND1	0.179	0.3568	0.6159	1.196
IND2	0.6252	0.2448	0.0106	1.869
IND3	0.7097	0.1457	0.0001	2.033
IND4	0.0728	0.195	0.7089	1.076
IND5	0.4717	0.1858	0.0111	1.603
IND6	0.1597	0.2144	0.4565	1.173
IND7	0.0548	0.2552	0.83	1.056
IND8	0.2878	0.1509	0.0566	1.333
IND9	0.6248	0.1947	0.0013	1.868
IND10	0.1521	0.1494	0.3087	1.164
IND11	0.3181	0.2357	0.1771	1.375
IND12	0.1597	0.1774	0.3679	1.173
OCC1	-0.0284	0.1458	0.8453	0.972
OCC2	0.1467	0.1692	0.386	1.158
OCC3	-0.875	0.2261	0.0001	0.417
OCC4	-0.1862	0.2479	0.4527	0.83
OCC5	-0.4328	0.2546	0.0891	0.649
OCC6	-0.2975	0.1629	0.0679	0.743

Variable	Coefficient	Standard Error	Significance Level	Odds Ratio
OCC7	-0.4511	0.1577	0.0042	0.637
OCC8	-0.55	0.2697	0.0414	0.577
OCC9	-0.4256	0.1884	0.0239	0.653
OCC10	-0.4469	0.2041	0.0285	0.64
OCC11	-0.5136	0.1473	0.0005	0.598
OCC12	-0.2856	0.1879	0.1286	0.752
OCC13	-0.5517	0.1763	0.0018	0.576
OCC14	-0.5061	0.1935	0.0089	0.603
OCC15	-0.2056	0.2568	0.4234	0.814
Personal Characteristics				
AGE1	-0.1331	0.1303	0.3071	0.875
AGE2	0.0206	0.0777	0.7912	1.021
AGE3	-0.1345	0.0891	0.131	0.874
AGE4	-0.0627	0.124	0.6131	0.939
EDU1	-0.6937	0.1409	0.0001	0.5
EDU2	-0.3667	0.0929	0.0001	0.693
EDU3	-0.0145	0.0826	0.8604	0.986
EDU4	-0.1262	0.1161	0.2769	0.881
EDU5	0.1972	0.0982	0.0446	1.218
SINGLE	-0.4774	0.1522	0.0017	0.62
OTHER	-0.4692	0.2549	0.0657	0.626
NOCHILD	-0.0119	0.0782	0.8791	0.988
SINGNOCH	0.4814	0.1705	0.0047	1.618
OTHNOCH	0.359	0.2937	0.2216	1.432
NWFLD	-0.317	0.2459	0.1973	0.728
PEI	-0.0895	0.4712	0.8493	0.914
NOVASC	-0.2526	0.173	0.1444	0.777
NEWBRUN	-0.2242	0.1965	0.2538	0.799
QUEBEC	-1.6542	0.0764	0.0001	0.191
ALBERTA	0.000353	0.1048	0.9973	1
MANITOBA	0.1041	0.1633	0.5238	1.11
SASK	0.0131	0.1865	0.944	1.013
BC	-0.0752	0.0991	0.4479	0.928
Wages				
WAGE1	0.5366	0.1346	0.0001	1.71
WAGE2	1.0118	0.1306	0.0001	2.751
WAGE3	1.4081	0.1384	0.0001	4.088
WAGE4	1.7568	0.1471	0.0001	5.794
WAGE5	1.0305	0.1261	0.0001	2.803

Brenda Lipsett and Mark Reesor

A.4 Table 4: Results of Females Dental Coverage Logistic Regression Model

Variable	Coefficient	Standard Error	Significance Level	Odds Ratio
INTERCPT	0.1845	0.173	0.286	1.203
Job Related Characteristics				
PARTTIME	-1.364	0.0777	0.0001	0.256
LONGTIME	0.0258	0.1317	0.8448	1.026
TEMPJOB	-1.7789	0.112	0.0001	0.169
UNION1	0.5845	0.1137	0.0001	1.794
FIRM1	-2.1493	0.0984	0.0001	0.117
FIRM2	-0.9406	0.1049	0.0001	0.39
FIRM3	-0.4211	0.1087	0.0001	0.656
GOVTEMP	-0.6826	0.1652	0.0001	0.505
UNFIRM1	1.4834	0.2513	0.0001	4.408
UNFIRM2	0.5472	0.1773	0.002	1.728
UNFIRM3	0.1641	0.1522	0.2808	1.178
UNGOVT	0.0869	0.1792	0.628	1.091
TEN1	-0.6798	0.1053	0.0001	0.507
TEN2	-0.4752	0.1293	0.0002	0.622
TEN3	0.2797	0.0805	0.0005	1.323
TEN4	0.4444	0.0915	0.0001	1.56
TEN5	0.1055	0.1216	0.3858	1.111
IND1	0.1291	0.439	0.7687	1.138
IND2	-0.1783	0.3222	0.5799	0.837
IND3	0.3873	0.1418	0.0063	1.473
IND4	0.1972	0.2716	0.4677	1.218
IND5	0.3859	0.2526	0.1265	1.471
IND6	0.3478	0.2315	0.133	1.416
IND7	1.1739	0.4413	0.0078	3.235
IND8	-0.1521	0.1217	0.2113	0.859
IND9	0.5772	0.138	0.0001	1.781
IND10	-0.4203	0.1146	0.0002	0.657
IND11	-0.3824	0.2118	0.0709	0.682
IND12	0.4093	0.1547	0.0081	1.506
OCC1	0.2252	0.0939	0.0165	1.253
OCC2	0.0798	0.145	0.582	1.083
OCC3	-0.1718	0.1484	0.2471	0.842
OCC4	-0.351	0.1232	0.0044	0.704
OCC5	-0.3607	0.2359	0.1262	0.697
OCC6	-0.4023	0.1216	0.0009	0.669

Women and Men's Entitlement to Workplace Benefits

Variable	Coefficient	Standard Error	Significance Level	Odds Ratio
OCC7	-0.6358	0.1157	0.0001	0.53
OCC8	-0.8704	0.5535	0.1159	0.419
OCC9	-0.961	0.2482	0.0001	0.383
OCC10	1.5803	0.9055	0.081	4.856
OCC11	-0.7613	0.1931	0.0001	0.467
OCC12	-1.2781	0.8875	0.1498	0.279
OCC13	-1.2862	0.3668	0.0005	0.276
OCC14	-0.4893	0.3117	0.1164	0.613
OCC15	-0.4112	0.3814	0.281	0.663
Personal Characteristics				
AGE1	-0.1813	0.1237	0.1427	0.834
AGE2	0.0447	0.077	0.5618	1.046
AGE3	-0.1984	0.0826	0.0163	0.82
AGE4	-0.5883	0.132	0.0001	0.555
EDU1	-0.3892	0.1917	0.0423	0.678
EDU2	-0.128	0.1092	0.2413	0.88
EDU3	-0.1658	0.08	0.0381	0.847
EDU4	0.1004	0.1112	0.3667	1.106
EDU5	0.1305	0.0912	0.1523	1.139
SINGLE	0.1542	0.1405	0.2725	1.167
OTHER	0.1821	0.1294	0.1593	1.2
NOCHILD	0.1749	0.0765	0.0222	1.191
SINGNOCH	0.1403	0.1675	0.4023	1.151
OTHNOCH	-0.4266	0.1932	0.0273	0.653
NWFLD	0.2553	0.255	0.3167	1.291
PEI	0.0946	0.4586	0.8366	1.099
NOVASC	-0.1601	0.1709	0.3488	0.852
NEWBRUN	0.1527	0.1956	0.435	1.165
QUEBEC	-1.0354	0.0757	0.0001	0.355
ALBERTA	0.1607	0.1047	0.1249	1.174
MANITOBA	0.0818	0.1588	0.6066	1.085
SASK	0.4779	0.1776	0.0071	1.613
BC	0.2022	0.0938	0.0311	1.224
Wages				
WAGE1	1.0179	0.1088	0.0001	2.767
WAGE2	1.581	0.1137	0.0001	4.86
WAGE3	1.8495	0.1287	0.0001	6.356
WAGE4	1.8864	0.1438	0.0001	6.596
WAGE5	1.307	0.1102	0.0001	3.695

Brenda Lipsett and Mark Reesor

A.4 Table 5: ESPP, Results of Males Logistic Regression Model

Variable	Coefficient	Standard Error	Significance Level	Odds Ratio
INTERCPT	1.002	0.2472	0.0001	2.724
Job Related Characteristics				
PARTTIME	-1.5322	0.1933	0.0001	0.216
LONGTIME	-0.2437	0.086	0.0046	0.784
TEMPJOB	-1.3751	0.1255	0.0001	0.253
UNION1	1.0699	0.1129	0.0001	2.915
FIRM1	-2.4694	0.1086	0.0001	0.085
FIRM2	-1.2775	0.0971	0.0001	0.279
FIRM3	-0.9222	0.103	0.0001	0.398
GOVTEMP	0.4772	0.2207	0.0306	1.612
UNFIRM1	1.0013	0.2104	0.0001	2.722
UNFIRM2	0.4767	0.1715	0.0054	1.611
UNFIRM3	0.2599	0.1646	0.1143	1.297
UNGOVT	0.2217	0.2284	0.3317	1.248
TEN1	-0.7301	0.1073	0.0001	0.482
TEN2	-0.3948	0.1152	0.0006	0.674
TEN3	0.3287	0.084	0.0001	1.389
TEN4	0.7707	0.0925	0.0001	2.161
TEN5	1.0595	0.1308	0.0001	2.885
IND1	-0.6398	0.3891	0.1001	0.527
IND2	-0.2999	0.2373	0.2063	0.741
IND3	-0.273	0.1537	0.0757	0.761
IND4	-0.7512	0.2077	0.0003	0.472
IND5	-0.2377	0.2015	0.2381	0.788
IND6	-0.6717	0.221	0.0024	0.511
IND7	-0.111	0.2958	0.7074	0.895
IND8	-0.6497	0.1596	0.0001	0.522
IND9	0.0596	0.1966	0.762	1.061
IND10	-1.0141	0.1598	0.0001	0.363
IND11	-0.9444	0.2483	0.0001	0.389
IND12	0.1404	0.2352	0.5506	1.151
OCC1	-0.3603	0.15	0.0163	0.697
OCC2	-0.267	0.1722	0.121	0.766
OCC3	-0.3592	0.2764	0.1937	0.698
OCC4	-0.9706	0.2666	0.0003	0.379
OCC5	-0.9691	0.2645	0.0002	0.379
OCC6	-0.4797	0.1657	0.0038	0.619
OCC7	-0.4687	0.1721	0.0065	0.626

Variable	Coefficient	Standard Error	Significance Level	Odds Ratio
OCC8	-0.5238	0.2778	0.0594	0.592
OCC9	-0.41	0.1902	0.0311	0.664
OCC10	-0.4167	0.2052	0.0423	0.659
OCC11	-0.8018	0.153	0.0001	0.449
OCC12	-0.3976	0.2013	0.0483	0.672
OCC13	-1.0215	0.1908	0.0001	0.36
OCC14	-0.1017	0.2012	0.613	0.903
OCC15	-0.7655	0.2624	0.0035	0.465
Personal Characteristics				
AGE1	-0.243	0.138	0.0782	0.784
AGE2	-0.1382	0.0789	0.0798	0.871
AGE3	-0.1877	0.0931	0.0437	0.829
AGE4	-0.2881	0.1316	0.0286	0.75
EDU1	-0.6334	0.1481	0.0001	0.531
EDU2	-0.3413	0.0973	0.0005	0.711
EDU3	-0.1175	0.085	0.1671	0.889
EDU4	-0.1096	0.1178	0.3521	0.896
EDU5	0.2277	0.0985	0.0208	1.256
SINGLE	-0.2258	0.1632	0.1665	0.798
OTHER	-0.2039	0.278	0.4633	0.816
NOCHILD	0.0176	0.0808	0.828	1.018
SINGNOCH	0.2824	0.1816	0.1198	1.326
OTHNOCH	0.3632	0.3184	0.254	1.438
NWFLD	0.2498	0.2676	0.3505	1.284
PEI	0.3474	0.5133	0.4985	1.415
NOVASC	-0.0451	0.1847	0.807	0.956
NEWBRUN	0.2391	0.206	0.2458	1.27
QUEBEC	-0.4162	0.0785	0.0001	0.66
ALBERTA	0.1125	0.1066	0.2911	1.119
MANITOBA	0.3853	0.1661	0.0204	1.47
SASK	0.2659	0.1941	0.1707	1.305
BC	-0.2727	0.1004	0.0066	0.761
Wages				
WAGE1	0.2506	0.1488	0.0922	1.285
WAGE2	0.7034	0.1418	0.0001	2.021
WAGE3	1.2567	0.148	0.0001	3.514
WAGE4	1.424	0.1555	0.0001	4.154
WAGE5	0.9729	0.1376	0.0001	2.646

Brenda Lipsett and Mark Reesor

A.4 Table 6: ESPP, Results of Females Logistic Regression Model

Variable	Coefficient	Standard Error	Significance Level	Odds Ratio
INTERCPT	0.3405	0.1787	0.0567	1.406
Job Related Characteristics				
PARTTIME	-1.0375	0.0817	0.0001	0.354
LONGTIME	-0.1864	0.1425	0.1908	0.83
TEMPJOB	-1.4191	0.1112	0.0001	0.242
UNION1	0.636	0.1137	0.0001	1.889
FIRM1	-2.5375	0.1048	0.0001	0.079
FIRM2	-1.4643	0.105	0.0001	0.231
FIRM3	-0.6791	0.1039	0.0001	0.507
GOVTEMP	0.00923	0.163	0.9548	1.009
UNGOVT	0.324	0.181	0.0734	1.383
UNFIRM1	1.2949	0.2498	0.0001	3.651
UNFIRM2	0.8549	0.1805	0.0001	2.351
UNFIRM3	0.537	0.1597	0.0008	1.711
TEN1	-0.6063	0.1097	0.0001	0.545
TEN2	-0.3126	0.1329	0.0186·	0.732
TEN3	0.3758	0.0816	0.0001	1.456
TEN4	0.7542	0.0947	0.0001	2.126
TEN5	1.2209	0.1451	0.0001	3.39
IND1	-0.8283	0.5435	0.1275	0.437
IND2	-0.2643	0.3183	0.4063	0.768
IND3	-0.187	0.1414	0.1858	0.829
IND4	-0.5156	0.2863	0.0717	0.597
IND5	-0.3818	0.2459	0.1206	0.683
IND6	-0.1886	0.2294	0.4109	0.828
IND7	-0.2408	0.4136	0.5604	0.786
IND8	-0.7509	0.1269	0.0001	0.472
IND9	0.2636	0.1375	0.0553	1.302
IND10	-0.8846	0.1209	0.0001	0.413
IND11	-0.7426	0.2216	0.0008	0.476
IND12	-0.0428	0.1726	0.8043	0.958
OCC1	0.0875	0.0952	0.358	1.091
OCC2	0.268	0.1496	0.0731	1.307
OCC3	0.2765	0.1651	0.0939	1.319
OCC4	-0.418	0.1323	0.0016	0.658
OCC5	-0.3075	0.2573	0.232	0.735
OCC6	-0.2172	0.1243	0.0806	0.805
OCC7	-0.5334	0.1223	0.0001	0.587

Variable	Coefficient	Standard Error	Significance Level	Odds Ratio
OCC8	-0.3339	0.6065	0.582	0.716
OCC9	-0.9721	0.2611	0.0002	0.378
OCC10	-0.6144	0.5821	0.2913	0.541
OCC11	-0.6384	0.1925	0.0009	0.528
OCC12	-0.2117	0.9227	0.8185	0.809
OCC13	-1.0169	0.3449	0.0032	0.362
OCC14	-1.0607	0.3117	0.0007	0.346
OCC15	0.0619	0.3873	0.8731	1.064
Personal Characteristics				
AGE1	-0.045	0.128	0.7251	0.956
AGE2	0.0463	0.0789	0.5569	1.047
AGE3	-0.161	0.0884	0.0686	0.851
AGE4	-0.4273	0.1418	0.0026	0.652
EDU1	-0.0723	0.1911	0.7052	0.93
EDU2	0.1508	0.1139	0.1855	1.163
EDU3	-0.0485	0.0835	0.5616	0.953
EDU4	-0.00417	0.1141	0.9709	0.996
EDU5	0.0415	0.0956	0.6642	1.042
SINGLE	-0.496	0.1452	0.0006	0.609
OTHER	-0.3936	0.1372	0.0041	0.675
NOCHILD	-0.1211	0.0804	0.1321	0.886
SINGNOCH	0.4686	0.1742	0.0072	1.598
OTHNOCH	0.4865	0.2073	0.0189	1.627
NWFLD	0.6217	0.2711	0.0218	1.862
PEI	0.5425	0.5076	0.2852	1.72
NOVASC	0.0843	0.1828	0.6447	1.088
NEWBRUN	-0.1105	0.2068	0.593	0.895
QUEBEC	0.0816	0.0796	0.3053	1.085
ALBERTA	0.0157	0.1092	0.8858	1.016
MANITOBA	0.5067	0.1654	0.0022	1.66
SASK	0.4606	0.1825	0.0116	1.585
BC	-0.2651	0.0973	0.0065	0.767
Wages				
WAGE1	0.6924	0.1142	0.0001	1.998
WAGE2	0.9425	0.1168	0.0001	2.566
WAGE3	1.5294	0.1333	0.0001	4.615
WAGE4	1.7543	0.1521	0.0001	5.78
WAGE5	0.967	0.115	0.0001	2.63

Brenda Lipsett and Mark Reesor

References

Ascah, L. (1995), "Public Pension Theory for the Real World", in G. Harcourt, A. Roncagila and R. Rowley (eds.), *Income and Employment in Theory and Practice* (New York: St. Martin's Press).

Banting, K. and R. Boadway, eds. (1997), *Reform of Retirement Income Policy, International and Canadian Perspectives* (Kingston: School of Policy Studies, Queen's University).

Bodie, Z. and O.S. Mitchell (1996), "Pension Security in an Aging World", in Z. Bodie, O.S. Mitchell and J. Turner (eds.), *Securing Employer-Based Pensions* (Philadelphia: The Pension Research Council and University of Pennsylvania Press).

Canadian Press (1996), "Royal Extends Work Benefits to Part-Timers", *Ottawa Citizen*, April 4.

Currie, J. and R. Chaykowski (1995), "Male Jobs, Female Jobs, and Gender Gaps in Benefits Coverage in Canada", *Research in Labor Economics*, Vol. 14 (Greenwich, CT: JAI Press), 171-192.

Ehrenberg, R.G. and R.S. Smith (1994), *Modern Labour Economics: Theory and Public Policy*, 5th ed. (Toronto: HarperCollins College Publishers).

Freeman, R. and R. Medoff (1984), *What Do Unions Do?* (New York: Basic Books).

Frenken, H. (1991), "The Pension Carrot: Incentives to Early Retirement", *Perspectives on Labour and Income, Quarterly*, Cat. No. 75-001E (Ottawa: Statistics Canada), 18-27.

_____ (1996), "The Impact of Changes in the Canada Pension Plan on Private Pensions", *Canadian Business Economics* 4(4), 65-72.

Hipple, S. and J. Stewart (1996), "Earnings and Benefits of Contingent and Noncontingent Workers", *The Monthly Labor Review* (October) (Washington: Bureau of Labor Statistics), 46-54.

Hosmer, D. and S. Lemeshow (1989), *Applied Logistic Regression* (New York: John Wiley & Sons).

Johnson, R.E. (1996), *Flexible Benefits: A How-To Guide* (Brookfield, WI: International Foundation of Employee Benefit Plans).

Krahn, H. (1992), *Quality of Work in the Service Sector,* General Social Survey Analysis Series, Cat. No. 11-612E, No. 6 (Ottawa: Statistics Canada).

The Labor Secretariat of the Commission for Labor Cooperation (1996), "North American Labor Markets: A Comparative Profile, 1984-1995 Preliminary Findings", *Bulletin of the Commission for Labor Cooperation*, Special Edition, 1(2).

Lipsett, B., A. Harris and M. Reesor (1997), "The Provision of Employer Sponsored Benefits", unpublished analytical note (Ottawa: Applied Research Branch, Human Resources Development Canada),

Lipsett, B. and M. Reesor (1997a), "Flexible Work Arrangements: Evidence from the 1991 and 1995 Survey of Work Arrangements", Research Paper R-97-10E (Ottawa: Applied Research Branch, Human Resources Development Canada).

_____ (1997b), "Employer-sponsored Pension Plans — Who Benefits?", Working Paper W-97-2E (Ottawa: Applied Research Branch, Human Resources Development Canada).

Lowe, G.S. (1991), "Retirement Attitudes, Plans and Behaviour", *Perspectives on Labour and Income, Quarterly*, Cat. No. 75-001E (Ottawa: Statistics Canada), 9-17.

Luchak, A.A. (1997), "Pensions and Job Search: Survey Evidence from Unionized Workers in Canada", *Journal of Labor Research* 18(2), 333-349.

Morissette, R. (1991), "Are Jobs in Large Firms Better Jobs?", *Perspectives on Labour and Income, Quarterly*, Cat. No. 75-001E (Ottawa: Statistics Canada), 40-50.

Pesando, J.E. (1992), "The Economic Effects of Private Pensions", in *Private Pensions and Public Policy*, OECD Social Policy Studies No. 9 (Paris: OECD).

Picot, G. and R. Dupuy (1996), "Job Creation by Company Size Class: Concentration and Persistence of Job Gain and Losses in Canadian Companies", Research Paper #93 (Ottawa: Analytical Studies Branch, Statistics Canada).

Polivka, A.E. (1996), "Contingent and Alternative Work Arrangements, Defined", *The Monthly Labor Review* (Washington: Bureau of Labor Statistics), 3-9.

Reesor, M. and B. Lipsett (1997), "Families and Non-Wage Benefits", unpublished analytical note (Ottawa: Applied Research Branch, Human Resources Development Canada).

_____ (1998), "Employer-sponsored Health and Dental Plans — Who is Insured?", Working Paper W-98-2E (Ottawa: Applied Research Branch, Human Resources Development Canada).

Scofea, L.A. (1994), "The Development and Growth of Employer-Provided Health Insurance", *The Monthly Labor Review* (March) (Washington: Bureau of Labor Statistics).

Statistics Canada (1996a), *Pension Plans in Canada, Statistical Highlights and Key Tables, January 1, 1995*, Cat. No. 74-401-SPB (Ottawa: Statistics Canada).

_____ (1996b), *Canada's Retirement Income Programs: A Statistical Overview*, Cat. No. 74-507-XPB (Ottawa: Statistics Canada).

_____ (1997), *Pension Plans in Canada, January 1*, Cat. No. 74-401-XPB (Ottawa: Statistics Canada).

Wiatrowski, W.J. (1990), "Family Related Benefits in the Workplace", *The Monthly Labor Review* (March) (Washington: Bureau of Labor Statistics).

Technological Change, Organizational Change and Skill Requirements: Impacts on Women in the Workforce

Gordon Betcherman, Darren Lauzon and Norm Leckie

Introduction

Over the past decade, new technologies and organizational practices have transformed many aspects of work. One important dimension concerns the implications of these changes for the composition of labour demand. According to conventional wisdom and indeed much of the empirical evidence, technological and organizational change are shifting demand in favour of skilled labour (OECD, 1996). While this may be the aggregate effect, it seems likely that these skill-bias trends are not homogeneous and that they vary for different segments of the labour force. If this is the case, this may help explain observed variations in employment outcomes.

One important issue for researchers and policymakers is how men and women may be affected differentially by technological and organizational change. It is well known that there are gender differences in terms of the occupations, industries, and types of firms and jobs in which they work.

The authors wish to thank the Applied Research Branch of Human Resources Development Canada for sponsoring this research and Statistics Canada for allowing us to make use of the data from the Workplace Employee Survey.

Given the uneven patterns of technological and organizational change, this might suggest that the exposure of men and women to these changes may differ along with their skill impacts. However, if there are differences, the expected direction is not obvious.

On the one hand, consider the declining male-female wage differentials. A neoclassical perspective would suggest that this was evidence of greater growth in the marginal productivity of female workers compared to male workers. This might lead to the expectation that the upward skill bias which has been observed to accompany technological and organizational change may be stronger for women than for men. If this were indeed the case, then it would be consistent with evidence that suggests that women may have greater relative exposure to technological and organizational change and that they may experience more favourable skill (and wage) gains as a result of these changes.

On the other hand, more critical institutional and sociological theories of the labour market, such as segmentation theories or feminist perspectives on work, would lead one to the opposite expectation. That is, that while technological and organizational change may be productivity- and skill-enhancing, there is a "political" dimension to these innovations and that the power and status of the employee will have a lot to do with their eventual implications. Since the female labour force is disproportionately in non-standard jobs and in "secondary" occupations and industries, according to this line of reason we would expect women to have less exposure to technological and organizational change that would improve their skills and their opportunities to accumulate human capital.

This paper reports on a quantitative analysis that compares the experiences of female and male employees with organizational and technological change. In particular, we examine the following three questions:

1. Are there differences between women and men in terms of their exposure to technological and organizational change?
2. Do the skill impacts of technological and organizational change differ between men and women?[1]
3. How does access to training opportunities differ between men and women in the wake of technological change?

---

[1]The question of the skill impacts of technological change receives more detailed analysis in a companion paper prepared by the authors. See Lauzon, Betcherman and Leckie (1998).

Our analysis is based on the Workplace and Employee Survey (WES) conducted on a pilot basis by Statistics Canada in 1995. The WES is a particularly useful survey for this study on a number of counts. First, it is a very wide-ranging survey which gathered information not only on the core items of technological and organizational change, skill impacts and skill acquisition, but also on a host of relevant contextual factors. Moreover, the WES is a linked employer-employee survey with data collected from about 750 establishments and from almost 2,000 workers employed in these organizations. This linked nature of the database offers significant advantages for addressing the questions of interest in our research. While earlier studies on the implications of technological or organizational change rest on only partial and/or incomplete evidence drawn from *either* establishment or household surveys, the WES data cover both the nature of the technological and organizational changes within the establishment *and* employee assessments of skill impacts and skill acquisition. This linked evidence can provide a more complete picture.[2]

The next section reviews the relevant literature with a focus on the existing Canadian research. In the third section, we turn to methodology, describing the Workplace and Employee Survey and discussing the key variables on which our empirical analysis is based. That analysis is the subject of the fourth section, which presents our evidence on the three questions driving our research. The short final section summarizes our findings.

Literature Review

In this section, we briefly review the empirical Canadian research on the three issues that are considered in our study — the diffusion of technological change and organizational change, their skill impacts and related training.

---

[2]However, the WES database has been generated by a pilot survey and, as such, does not have the sample coverage or the "track record" on content and procedure that would be expected from established production surveys.

Diffusion of Technological and Organizational Change

Research on the diffusion of new technologies has typically focused on computer-based technologies (CBTs). The analysis has been based on both establishment and household surveys. One example of the former has been the Working with Technology Survey (WWTS) which has been carried out three times since the mid-1980s.[3] Each time, respondents were asked to estimate the proportion of their employees working directly with computer-based technologies. The mean estimates for the three waves together illustrate the diffusion of CBTs — 13% in 1985, 37% in 1991 and 43% in 1994. The same question included in the 1995 Ekos Workplace Training Survey yielded an estimate of 46%.

Another source of evidence is the General Social Survey (GSS), a Statistics Canada survey, which asked about computer use in the workplace twice, first in 1989 and then again in 1994. Although the GSS is a household survey, its findings closely track those found by the WWTS. In 1989, 33% of workers reported using a computer at work and by 1994 this figure had increased to 48%. The results also demonstrated that over these years, on-the-job computer use became more intensive, both in terms of the amount of time employees used their computer and the range of activities involved (Lowe, 1996).

These and other studies have found that the diffusion of CBTs tends to be greatest in "dynamic" services (e.g., information and distribution services), in large establishments, in non-union establishments and where competition is intense and has an international component.[4]

Both the WWTS and the GSS have found that women have had higher rates of computer use than men. The WWTS estimates in 1985, 1991 and 1994 for women and men were, respectively, 17% vs. 12%, 51% vs. 37% and 57% vs. 39%. Corresponding GSS figures were 38% vs. 32% in 1989 and 52% vs. 45% in 1994. As Lowe (1996) points out, the higher rates for women primarily reflect their employment concentration in occupations where computer use is more widespread (e.g., clerical).

---

[3]The WWTS was carried out in 1985, 1991 and 1995. Results of the most recent wave are reported in McMullen (1996).

[4]See, as well, Baldwin, Diverty and Johnson (1995) and Baldwin, Diverty and Sabourin (1995).

There is less empirical evidence on the diffusion of organizational change. The concept itself is a broad and fluid one and there is not really a consensus among researchers about how it should be operationalized. It typically refers to changes in the organizational structure and/or in the organization of work, and can involve changes that are either internally- or externally-focused. The fundamental thrust of these changes has been to enhance organizational flexibility (OECD, 1996).

In North America, surveys on organizational change have tended to focus on the adoption of so-called "high-performance" practices. These generally refer to a set of complementary practices including flat organizational hierarchies, fluid job designs, team-based structures, employee involvement, broadly-based training and variable pay systems. Far less is known about other types of organizational change such as downsizing, re-engineering and outsourcing. Given that these practices may well account for the majority of organizational change, it is evident that our knowledge in the area is only piecemeal.

North American evidence suggests that roughly one in four establishments have adopted high-performance practices. For example, from the Human Resource Practices Survey (HRPS) which covered four major sectors, Betcherman *et al.* (1994) found that the high-performance model (of which they identified two variants) had been adopted by about 30% of participating establishments. These establishments represented about 46% of the employment among firms with at least 40 employees in the industries covered. This figure should be treated cautiously because of sample exclusions (i.e., sectors not surveyed, small establishments); because this calculation does not consider the exposure of high-performance practices within establishments; and because not all types of organizational change were included.

In general, research in Canada and elsewhere has found two very important correlates of organizational change (Government of Canada/ OECD, 1997). The first is firm size, with diffusion rates highest in large organizations. The second is technological change. Organizational changes, both in terms of internal processes and relations with external markets, often have been initiated as new technology has been introduced and has penetrated deeply within enterprises. It is often this combination of technological and organizational change that exerts the most effect on skills.

Skill Impacts

Over the years, there has been a great deal of interest in the aggregate skill effect of technological change. The conventional wisdom is one of "up-skilling" — that increasingly sophisticated technologies and work processes require increasingly skilled workers (e.g., Bell, 1973). However, a more critical "deskilling" perspective argues that technology routinizes and systematizes work and eliminates individual discretion (e.g., Braverman, 1974). A host of methodological obstacles have made it difficult to settle empirically this debate.

To begin, "skill" is a concept that is difficult to operationalize. It is multidimensional, incorporating both technical requirements (know-how, abilities, etc.) and social roles (responsibility, autonomy, etc.). Furthermore, when we talk about skill impacts in an upskilling/deskilling context — which has been the focus of much of the debate — it is important to understand that these impacts come via two channels: first, through changes in the particular work that an individual does in his/her job and, second, through the job creation/destruction process which alters the composition of employment. Finally, the skill impact of a change in technology (or a new organizational practice) is not necessarily determinate but can depend on how it is imple-mented; there are many examples where a given technology has had very different implications in different organizational settings.

On balance, the data seem to support the upskilling hypothesis more than the deskilling. This evidence comes from various sources: occupational employment trends; widening educational wage differentials; and more qual-itative survey and case study evidence incorporating manager and employee assessments of the skill effects of new technology and new organizational practices.[5]

The primary focus of this work has tended to be on the skill bias of technological change. This is true of how analysts have interpreted occu-pational and wage data and also in terms of the micro data on manager and worker assessments. McMullen (1996) found, for example, that managers reported an overall upskilling impact of CBT both in terms of how it altered the occupational composition (eliminating lower-skilled occupations and creating higher-skilled ones) and in terms of how the skill requirements of

---

[5]The Canadian evidence is synthesized in Betcherman, McMullen and Davidman (1998).

specific jobs were upgraded. The General Social Survey data, collected from workers, leads to the same conclusion. In 1989, over 60% reported that their skill requirements had increased because of computers and this figure had risen to over 70% in the 1994 survey (Lowe, 1996).

While there has been less focus on the impacts of organizational change, the OECD (1996) has concluded that evidence from a number of countries indicates that flexible work systems are also skill-biased upwards, both in terms of technical and social skill requirements. Again, it is difficult to sort out the independent effects of organizational and technological change because of the interconnection between the two.

Turning to gender differences, there is not a lot of direct evidence. The narrowing wage differentials between men and women are consistent with the notion that the skill upgrading is happening more rapidly for women than for men (even if there are other perhaps more direct explanatory factors).[6] In an analysis of occupational employment trends by gender over 1971-91, Leckie (1996) concluded that, while women remained overrepresented in lower-skill occupations, the gap in terms of skill requirements had narrowed appreciably over that period. Finally, the GSS evidence on the upskilling effects of CBT was the same for men and women (Lowe, 1996).

Training Activities

Our specific interest in training focuses on the question of how employees accumulate the skills called for by new technology and, more pointedly, on whether the skills acquisition process differs for women than for men.[7] While there is a substantial literature on training, there is little on the particular issue of training in response to technological change and less on gender differences.

---

[6]These include increasing hours, greater tenure and experience, and a decrease in occupational segmentation.

[7]Here we are focusing on technological change and not organizational change. This is because the WES data can only directly address this training question as it pertains to technology. Given the interdependence, however, it seems likely that the results pertaining to technology may also apply to organizational change.

A profile of training activity has emerged from both household- and establishment-based surveys. As a general rule, participation in training increases with the worker's human capital (i.e., education, literacy). It also rises with age through the prime-age group, before declining for older workers. Training and firm size have also been positively correlated.

The evidence on gender has not always been consistent. Overall, the balance of evidence does seem to point to males getting somewhat more job-related training, especially when it is sponsored by the employer (see de Broucker, 1997; Kapsalis, 1997). When variables such as industry and occupation are controlled for through econometric modelling, however, gender either becomes insignificant or women are shown to have a slightly greater probability of receiving job-related training, including employer sponsored activity (de Broucker, 1997). This suggests that any female disadvantage in training stems from the types of jobs they tend to occupy.

Technology-driven training accounts for an important share of the overall training effort so these results may well reflect the narrower issue of how workers learn new skills required by technological change. However, few studies specifically address this aspect of training, especially considering the gender dimension. One exception is the Working with Technology Survey analysis (McMullen, 1996). This study found that a considerable share of formal technology-driven training involves learning software applications (40% of training courses, 34% of training person-days). Here, too, there were no significant differences between men and women with the amount of formal training roughly equal for the two groups.[8]

Data and Methodology

The Workplace and Employee Survey Pilot

The Workplace and Employee Survey (WES) arose out of a growing interest in complementing the "supply-side" information collected from workers in

---

[8]It should be noted that virtually all studies on training, including the ones cited here, consider the formal dimension only. Some surveys, including the WWTS, indicate that informal learning accounts for the majority of all training (including training in response to new technology). However, these informal activities are difficult to capture quantitatively.

the standard household surveys with "demand-side" information captured through the workplace. The WES, essentially two surveys, was developed jointly by Statistics Canada and Human Resources Development Canada. The complex design of the survey and the sampling and collection process necessitated a pilot run which was conducted by Statistics Canada (with some additional funding support from Industry Canada) in winter/spring of 1996.

The pilot project was designed to test, among other things, the potential of the questionnaires to collect the data required to answer questions of interest to researchers and policy analysts. Two questionnaires were delivered: one to establishments drawn from select industry, region and size strata, and one to workers randomly sampled from these establishments. The data are not representative of the Canadian economy as a whole, but of the selected industry/region combinations. These "sub-strata" were, however, representative of both goods and service producing parts of the economy, being drawn from a wide range of primary, manufacturing and service sectors in several provinces.

The establishment surveys were conducted by personal interview while the worker surveys were conducted by telephone interview. Of the expected 1,000 establishments and 5,000 workers in the original pilot sample, the final database contains 750 establishments and about 2,000 workers. The low response rate from workers is partly an artifact of how employees were sampled.[9] The methodology and the major findings of the pilot study are presented in an overview report by Statistics Canada and Human Resources Development Canada (1998).

---

[9]Statistics Canada did not directly approach workers. Establishments provided Statistics Canada with employee lists, a sample of up to six employees was drawn, and contact information was to be delivered to the selected employees by their establishments. Employees returned the signed consent letters to Statistics Canada (either agreeing or not agreeing to participate in the survey) and Statistics Canada interviewed those agreeing to participate. The low response rate was due mostly to establishments being unable to distribute the consent letters to employees rather than employees refusing to participate in the survey. A detailed discussion of this complex survey is beyond the scope of this paper. More detail is presented in Krebs *et al.* (1998).

Survey Questions of Interest

Before examining the results of the analysis on the three questions dealt with in this paper, we discuss in this section the relevant survey questions on technological and organizational change, skills and training. In the following section, we discuss the methodologies used to address them.

Exposure of Workers to Technological and Organizational Change. Three questions on the establishment survey asked about the adoption of new technologies in the three years preceding the survey. The questions asked about the introduction of significantly new hardware or software, other computer-assisted technologies, and other non-computer-related technologies. Information on the costs of these technologies was collected. There were also questions about innovation. Establishments in the goods sector were asked if they had developed a new product or process innovation, and establishments in the service industries were asked if they had developed a new service or a change in the delivery of an existing service. Since both technology adoption and innovation in goods and services are a part of technological change, we included data from each of these questions in our analysis.

The questions on significantly new hardware or software and other computer-assisted technologies were combined into one category: computer-based technologies. An establishment was a "CBT adopter" if it responded "yes" to one or both of these. An establishment was a "technology adopter" if it adopted CBT or another, non-computer-related technology, or both.

However, there was a wide range in the costs of the technologies adopted by establishments: from as low as $60 to as high as several million. Early analysis showed a distinct difference between adopting higher-cost technologies and adopting lower-cost technologies on the probability that workers reported an increase in skill requirements. After experimenting with a dollar cut-off, we settled on a further distinction between establishments adopting technologies that cost $100,000 or more, and those where new technologies cost less than this.[10] Product and process innovations were combined into a

---

[10]The experiments involved running regressions on the probability of reporting changes in skill requirements conditional on working for a technology adopter with two variables, a "cheap" technology adopter and an "expensive" technology adopter. The regressions involved increasing the cut-off between "cheap" and "expensive" in $1,000 increments from $10,000 to $100,000. While a cut-off as low as $20,000 resulted in a significantly positive effect on the

single innovation indicator: an establishment was an "innovator" if it reported introducing either in the three years preceding the survey date.

We also wanted to examine technological change from the perspective of workers using data from the employee questionnaire. While there are no questions that deal directly with technological *change* on the worker questionnaire, there are questions on the use of technologies, particularly computer use. There are also questions that ask about how computer users learned to use the application they use the most, and on whose time — the company's or the worker's own time — that learning took place.[11] Picot (1998) goes into greater detail on the WES training and computer-use data than we do here, so we limit our analysis to gender differences in computer use and how computer users learn their applications.

Concerning organizational changes, one question on the establishment survey asked whether establishments had introduced any of the 13 specific organizational changes in the three years preceding the survey. Another asked which of the organizational changes that had been introduced was most significant in terms of the number of employees effected. In a previous paper (Ekos Research Associates, 1998), two of the authors grouped establishments into one of three groups on the basis of a cluster analysis of answers to the first question. The three clusters were labelled Flex I, Flex II and Stand-pat. These were distinguished by the relative adoption rates of each of the 13 organizational changes. Establishments in the Flex I cluster tended to have a relatively high rate of adoption of almost all the changes relative to firms in the Flex II and especially Stand-pat clusters. Firms in the Flex II cluster tended to focus relatively more on downsizing and delayering and relatively less on flexible staffing innovations such as the use of part-time or temporary employees or the use of flexible working time. Stand-pat establishments did relatively less of everything.

Previous work by the authors has shown that establishments tended to report that downsizing or re-engineering were the most significant organiza-

---

probability of reporting an increase in skill requirements when there were no other controls in the model, the cut-off had to be increased for this effect to remain statistically significant as more controls were added. More detail on this issue is reported in Lauzon, Betcherman and Leckie (1998).

[11]There are similar questions on other technologies not covered by the computer-use question. However, the quality of data derived from these questions was too suspect to be included.

tional changes (Statistics Canada and Human Resources Development Canada, 1998; and Ekos Research Associates, 1998). Taking this into account, we also constructed an indicator variable based on the most significant changes undertaken: downsizing, re-engineering, other changes and no change.

Skill Measures. The WES employee questionnaire asks workers directly how they perceive their skill requirements and how the technical complexity of their jobs have changed. Workers could report that either had increased, decreased, or remained the same. Though perhaps a more qualitative assessment of the skill-biased nature of technological change than that used in some previous studies, this approach does give us insight into how workers themselves perceive change rather than using their employers' perceptions or labour market indicators.[12]

Training Measures. While a number of questions on both the worker and establishment components of WES deal with training, we focus here on learning directly associated with the use of computers. In particular, computer-users were asked about the applications they use and which they use most often. With respect to the application they use most often, they were also asked what was the most important method of learning that application. Workers could report self-learning, employer-paid formal training, self-paid formal training, informal training, university or community college courses, or other methods. Workers were then asked whether they learned more on their own time, on company time or about equally on both.

Multivariate Analysis

One of the biggest advantages of WES is the amount of data collected from both workers and their establishments. Thus it is possible to control for any number of factors that might also explain differences in the exposure of men and women to technological and organizational change, or how they perceive

---

[12]The consideration of wage-trend data would have been a useful addition to this analysis on the assumption, for example, that wage increases would accompany skills upgrading. However, we did not include wage measures primarily because of quality concerns with the WES wage data.

Gordon Betcherman, Darren Lauzon and Norm Leckie

the impact of that change, or how they learn to use computers. We employ binary logistic regression models to examine whether differences established in simple cross-tabulations remain when other important factors are controlled for.[13]

The binary logit probabilities take the forms:

$$P(1|b,x) = \frac{e^{b'x}}{1+e^{b'x}}$$

$$P(0|b,x) = \frac{1}{1+e^{b'x}}$$

where P_1 and P_0 are the probabilities of a binary variable y taking on the values of 1 (= increase) and 0 (= not an increase), respectively; x is a vector of worker and establishment characteristics; and b are the unknown parameters of the model. Our goal is to estimate the b and hence the conditional probabilities P_1 and P_0. In the analysis that follows, the b are estimated by a maximum likelihood algorithm and P_1 and P_0 are evaluated at the means of x except those "x" under consideration. For example, if we are interested in the probability of a worker reporting increased skill requirements conditional on working for a recent innovator, all "x" variables are set to the sample mean except the indicator for innovation, which is set to 1. Any b not significantly different from zero (0) at the 10% level are set to zero (0) in the probability computations, given that the estimations indicated that the respective variable exerts a statistically insignificant impact on the probability of the event in question occurring.

---

[13]In an earlier version of this paper, our logistic regressions to describe skill requirement trends took a multinominal form (i.e., to model the differences between men and women in the probability that they report an increase, a decrease, or no change in skill requirements). Given the small proportion actually reporting a decrease, we were unable to get reliable estimates of the proportion reporting decreased skill requirements, especially for women. In this version, then, we have combined the "decrease" and "no change" categories and estimated binary logistic regressions to model the probability of reporting or not reporting "increased" skill requirements.

In Table 1, we provide a list of the control variables used in the econometric equations, along with the sample means and proportions for women and men and the source of the variables (workplace or employee survey). The respective proportions for the variables in question — skill requirements, technical complexity, technological change and organizational change — appear in subsequent tables.

Analysis

Exposure to Technological and Organizational Change

The first issue we address is the differences between women and men in terms of their exposure to technological and organizational change. We examine first the incidence of technological change and innovation in establishments where women and men are employed (Table 2). The results indicate that men are more likely than women to be employed in establishments that introduced technology, whether that be "expensive" (costing $100,000 or more) or cheap technology (costing less than $100,000). Cross-tabulations controlling for establishment size (not shown) indicate that the link between gender and technological change holds in all size categories. On the other hand, the second panel of Table 2 indicates little difference between men and women in terms of the incidence of innovation in the establishments where they work, with no clear link to establishment size (not shown).

Table 3 indicates little variation between men and women in terms of their exposure to organizational change. The first panel shows that women and men exhibit similar tendencies in terms of which clusters their establishments fit into. The only difference of any significance is that women are somewhat more likely to be employed in establishments in the Flex II cluster (i.e., in establishments that have introduced organizational changes other than flexible staffing arrangements such as temporary and part-time work). This may seem somewhat surprising since female workers are over-represented in these types of employment arrangements; however, it should be noted that the cluster assignments are based on a flow concept (i.e., a *change* in an organizational practice) rather than a stock concept.

Table 1: Control Variables Used in Multivariate Analyses: Definition, Weighted Percentages/Means for Men and Women*, and Employee or Workplace Survey Source, WES 1996

Variable Definition	Mean/Percentage Share		Survey Source
	Women	Men	
Tenure of worker (mean weeks since started job)	281	317	Employee
Education of Worker (% distribution)			
Non-postsecondary**	27.3	28.6	Employee
Non-university postsecondary	50.4	47.6	Employee
University completion (degree)	21.9	23.8	Employee
Occupation of Worker (% distribution)			
Managers	29.4	23.8	Employee
Professionals	12.6	6.3	Employee
Clerical	37.4	28.2	Employee
"Other" occupation**	20.6	41.7	Employee
Part-time workers (mean % working < 30 hours/week)	16.1	4.1	Employee
Average hourly earnings ($)	14.63	19.18	Employee
Size of establishment (mean number of employees)	2,510	2,613	Workplace
Industry of Establishment (% distribution)			
Forestry	1.8	5.7	Workplace
Natural-resource based manufacturing**	6.2	6.8	Workplace
Scale-based manufacturing	7.0	18.5	Workplace
Product-differentiated manufacturing	6.1	6.3	Workplace
Science-based manufacturing	8.1	8.6	Workplace
Construction industry	2.6	8.3	Workplace
Communications services	13.0	14.5	Workplace
Transportation services	6.8	14.6	Workplace
Retail services	15.0	4.1	Workplace
Real estate services	6.4	1.9	Workplace
Financial services	13.8	5.5	Workplace
Health and education services	13.2	5.2	Workplace

Note: * The weighted proportion of the sample that is female is 44.8%.
  ** Indicates reference variables that were omitted from econometric equations.

Technological and Organizational Change and Skill Requirements *117*

Table 2: Percentage Distribution of Men and Women Employees According to Technology Adoption and Innovation in their Respective Establishment[1]

	Men	Women	All Employees
Technology Adopters			
"Expensive" technology (>= $100,000)	36.0	32.2	33.6
"Cheap" technology (< $100,000)	37.1	30.5	35.0
Non-adopters	26.9	37.3	31.6
Total	**100.0**	**100.0**	**100.0**
Innovator			
Yes	53.8	55.4	54.5
No	46.2	44.6	45.5
Total	**100.0**	**100.0**	**100.0**

Note: 1. Differences between men and women are not necessarily statistically significant.
Source: Calculations by the authors based on weighted employee data from Statistics Canada (1996).

In the second panel of Table 3, we examine exposure by gender to organizational change, operationalized as the *most significant* organizational change introduced in the survey reference period. Once again, there were no major differences.[14]

---

[14]There were some gender differences, however, when we looked at different establishment size categories. In small establishments (less than 20 employees), men were more likely to work in establishments that re-engineered; in medium-size ones (20-99 employees), women were more likely to work in those that have downsized, and in large establishments (100 or more employees), men were more likely to work in establishments reporting downsizing.

Table 3: Percentage Distribution of Men and Women Employees According to Organizational Change in Their Respective Establishment[1]

Organization Change	Men	Women	All Employees
Organizational Change Cluster[2]			
Flex II	30.2	36.8	35.2
Flex I	31.9	29.4	30.8
Stand Pat	37.9	35.4	32.4
Total	**100.0**	**100.0**	**100.0**
Most Significant Organizational Change			
Downsizing	32.4	33.2	32.7
Re-engineering	25.8	28.3	26.9
Other change	32.4	28.0	30.4
No change	9.5	10.5	9.9
Total	**100.0**	**100.0**	**100.0**

Notes: 1. Differences between men and women are not necessarily statistically significant.
2. For explanation, see text.
Source: Calculations by the authors based on weighted employee data from Statistics Canada (1996).

The results discussed so far do not control for other factors that can affect the likelihood of working for a recent technology adopter or for an establishment that undertook a certain kind of organizational change. Recall that previous studies have showed a difference in the composition of employment between technology adopters and non-adopters, the former using a higher proportion of highly educated workers, and workers in higher-skilled occupations. Previous work by the authors and others with this database has also shown that technology adoption rates vary with size and industry. Therefore, it is necessary to control for these and other factors. Our logistic regressions, discussed in an earlier section, do this and Table 4 shows the estimated probabilities that men and women work for various kinds of

Table 4: Percentage Probability[1] that Men and Women are Employed in an Establishment with Different Technological and Organizational Change Characteristics

	Men	Women
Technological Change Adopter		
"Expensive" technology adopter (>= $100,000)	35.6	35.6
"Cheap" technology adopter (< $100,000)	31.4	31.4
Non-adopter	33.0	33.0
Total	**100.0**	**100.0**
Innovator		
Yes	66.8	66.8
No	33.2	33.2
Total	**100.0**	**0.0**
Organizational Change Cluster[2]		
Flex II	16.3	16.3
Flex I	35.0	35.0
Stand Pat	48.7	48.7
Total	**100.0**	**100.0**
Most Significant Organizational Change		
Downsizing	33.3	42.2
Re-engineering	28.0	28.0
Other change	35.7	27.4
No change	3.1	2.4
Total	**100.0**	**100.0**

Notes: 1. Probabilities computed based on results from logistic regressions, where the probability of being in an organization with changes in technology and organization is regressed on sex, controlling for tenure, education, occupation, part-time status, wage, establishment size and industry. Parameters that were not significant at the 10% level or lower were set to zero for the computation of the probabilities, as the respective variable exerts a statistically insignificant impact on the probability.

2. For explanation, see text.

Source: Calculations by the authors based on weighted employee data from Statistics Canada (1996).

Gordon Betcherman, Darren Lauzon and Norm Leckie

establishments. When one controls for age, education, tenure, occupation, wage, part-time status, size and industry there is no significant difference between men and women in their likelihood of working for either a technology adopter or innovator.[15] There is also no difference in their respective likelihoods of working for an establishment that is in one of the three organizational change clusters. There are, however, differences in the probability of working in establishments that have undertaken certain significant organizational changes. Women are more likely to have worked for an establishment reporting downsizing, and less likely to work for an establishment that reported organizational changes other than downsizing or re-engineering.

Skill Impacts

The second research question we address concerns the links between gender, changes in skill requirements and technological and organizational change. We start by looking at differences in skill and technical complexity reported by men and women, independent of organizational technological change (Table 5). First, observe that, both by the skill requirements indicator and by the technical complexity one, the WES data strongly support an upskilling thesis. In terms of the skill requirement measure, 48.1% of employees indicated that requirements had increased since they started in their current job while only 6.5% reported a decrease. The upskilling story is even stronger according to the technological complexity indicator with 60.7% reporting increases and just 0.6% reporting decreases. The table also shows that there are no major distinctions between men and women in these assessments. The only difference, albeit slight, concerns technical complexity where men are somewhat more likely to report increases whereas women are more likely to report that there has been little change.

One other point from Table 5 concerns the incidence of employees who report increases in *both* the skill requirements and technical complexity of their job. It could be argued that the intersection of these two measures may

---

[15]It should be pointed out that the wage variable is actual wages and therefore correlated with the other explanatory variables entered. Ideally, instead of actual wages, predicted wages should have been entered, thus eliminating the endogeneity in the model.

Table 5: Percentage Distribution of Men and Women Employees by Reported Change in Skill Requirements and Technical Complexity[1]

	Men	Women	All
Change in Skill Requirements			
Increased	45.4	45.4	45.4
Remained the same	49.5	46.4	48.1
Decreased	5.1	8.3	6.5
Total	**100.0**	**100.0**	**100.0**
Change in Technical Complexity			
Increased	64.2	56.4	60.7
Remained the same	35.5	42.6	38.7
Decreased	0.4	1.0	0.6
Total	**100.0**	**100.0**	**100.0**
Percentage with increase in both skill requirements and technical complexity	35.4	29.5	32.8

Note: 1.   Differences between men and women are not necessarily statistically significant.
Source: Calculations by the authors based on weighted employee data from Statistics Canada (1996).

be the most complete indicator of upskilling available in the WES data. Overall, about one-third of employees reported upgrading along both measures. Note that the incidence was slightly higher for women than for men.

We now turn to the role played by occupation in gender-skill patterns. In Table 6a, we observe more distinct differences in skill changes between men and women when occupational groups are considered than when aggregate comparisons are made. Men are more likely to report skill increases in the managerial and trades-dominated "other" occupational groups, while women are more likely to report skill increases in professional and clerical occupations. For skill decreases, the reverse is true in the managerial

Gordon Betcherman, Darren Lauzon and Norm Leckie

Table 6a: Percentage Distribution of Men and Women Employees in Occupation Groups by Reported Change in Skill Requirements[1]

| | Percentage Distribution by Change in Skill Requirements | | | |
	Increased	Remained the Same	Decreased	Total
Managers				
Men	65.6	32.4	2.0	100.0
Women	55.8	34.3	9.9	100.0
All	61.1	33.3	5.6	100.0
Professional				
Men	25.9	69.2	4.9	100.0
Women	33.5	55.0	11.4	100.0
All	30.3	61.1	8.6	100.0
Clerical				
Men	40.5	47.9	11.7	100.0
Women	51.4	39.8	8.8	100.0
All	49.5	41.2	9.3	100.0
Other				
Men	38.4	55.7	6.0	100.0
Women	27.4	68.8	3.8	100.0
All	35.8	58.8	5.5	100.0
Overall	**45.4**	**48.1**	**6.5**	**100.0**

Note: 1. Differences between men and women are not necessarily statistically significant.
Source: Calculations by the authors based on weighted employee data from Statistics Canada (1996).

and clerical categories but not in the professional and other occupational categories, where women are (still) more likely to report decreases (despite being more likely to report skill increases). Note the relatively high incidence of decreased skill requirements for female professionals and male clerks.

In Table 6b, we present the analogous results for technical complexity. These indicate that men are more likely to report technical complexity increases than women in all occupational categories and the differences are large in all but the professional category. Conversely, women are substantially more likely to report no complexity change in all occupational groups, except again for professionals, where there are few gender differences. Incidences of complexity decrease are negligible and similar across the board.

We now examine the link between skill and technological/organizational changes. The first two panels of Table 7a indicate similar skill-change patterns among the employees of adopters and non-adopters of technology (computer-based or all). However, as the first two rows of the second panel indicate, the amount spent on the technology clearly matters. Employees in "expensive" technology adopters (spending $100,000 and more) are twice as likely to report skill increases as employees in "cheap" technology adopters (less than $100,000). In fact, employees in cheap technology firms are less likely to report a skill increase than those in firms reporting no technological change. For those reporting no skill change, the reverse is true: the likelihood of no skill change in expensive adopters is twice as high as it is for cheap adopters. The incidence of upskilling is also positively associated with employment in "innovator" establishments.

Turning to organizational change, the fourth panel of Table 7a indicates that employees in Flex II cluster establishments are more likely to report skill increases and less likely to report no change than in the other two clusters. The fifth panel shows that when organizational change is operationalized as individual changes versus no change, there is more upskilling reported by employees where change has occurred, especially where the change has been either re-engineering or downsizing. Finally, while employees in downsizing establishments had a higher-than-average probability of reporting upskilling, they also had a relatively high incidence of decreased skill requirements (12.4%).

In Table 7b, we compare technical complexity patterns between adopters and non-adopters of technological/organizational change in the same way as we did for skill requirements. The broad patterns are quite similar. As was

Table 6b: Percentage Distribution of Men and Women Employees in Occupation Groups by Reported Change in Technical Complexity[1]

| | Percentage Distribution by Change in Technical Complexity | | | |
	Increased	Remained the Same	Decreased	Total
Managers				
Men	76.1	23.7	0.3	100.0
Women	55.6	43.0	1.4	100.0
All	66.7	32.5	0.8	100.0
Professional				
Men	73.2	26.4	0.5	100.0
Women	69.4	30.6	0.0	100.0
All	71.0	28.8	0.2	100.0
Clerical				
Men	80.7	18.1	1.2	100.0
Women	67.0	32.6	0.4	100.0
All	69.4	30.1	0.5	100.0
Other				
Men	55.8	43.9	0.3	100.0
Women	33.7	64.4	1.9	100.0
All	50.5	48.8	0.7	100.0
Overall	**60.7**	**38.7**	**0.7**	**100.0**

Note: 1. Differences between men and women are not necessarily statistically significant.
Source: Calculations by the authors based on weighted employee data from Statistics Canada (1996).

Table 7a: Percentage Distribution of Employees in Establishments, Defined by Technological and Organizational Change, by Reported Change in Skill Requirements[1]

	Percentage Distribution by Change in Skill Requirements			
	Increased	*Remained the Same*	*Decreased*	*Total*
Computer-Based Technology Adopter				
Yes	44.6	47.8	7.6	100.0
No	46.8	48.6	4.6	100.0
Technology Adopter				
"Expensive" adopters[2]	55.1	37.1	7.8	100.0
"Cheap" adopters[2]	27.7	57.3	6.7	100.0
All adopters	45.4	47.4	7.3	100.0
Non-adopters	45.4	49.6	5.0	100.0
Innovator				
Yes	48.4	44.9	6.8	100.0
No	41.8	52.0	6.3	100.0
Organizational Change Cluster[3]				
Flex II	47.1	45.9	7.2	100.0
Flex I	41.0	53.5	5.5	100.0
Stand Pat	37.0	56.2	6.8	100.0
Most Significant Organizational Change				
Downsizing	47.7	39.8	12.4	100.0
Re-engineering	49.4	45.7	5.0	100.0
Other change	42.9	53.9	3.2	100.0
No change	34.4	64.0	1.6	100.0
Overall	**45.4**	**48.1**	**6.5**	**100.0**

Notes: 1. Differences are not necessarily statistically significant.
2. Establishments that spend more than and less than or equal to $100,000 on technology, respectively.
3. For explanation, see text.

Source: Calculations by the authors based on weighted employee data from Statistics Canada (1996).

Gordon Betcherman, Darren Lauzon and Norm Leckie

Table 7b: Percentage Distribution of Employees in Establishments, Defined by Technological and Organizational Change, by Reported Change in Technical Complexity[1]

| | Percentage Distribution by Change in Technical Complexity | | | |
	Increased	Remained the Same	Decreased	Total
Computer-Based Technology Adopter				
Yes	62.2	37.1	0.7	100.0
No	58.0	41.6	0.6	100.0
Technology Adopter				
"Expensive" adopters[2]	70.4	28.8	0.8	100.0
"Cheap" adopters[2]	54.2	45.3	0.5	100.0
All adopters	62.2	37.2	0.6	100.0
Non-adopters	57.5	41.9	0.7	100.0
Innovator				
Yes	64.2	35.3	0.5	100.0
No	56.5	42.7	0.8	100.0
Organizational Change Cluster[3]				
Flex II	68.6	31.3	0.2	100.0
Flex I	57.0	41.9	1.1	100.0
Stand Pat	57.4	42.0	0.6	100.0
Most Significant Organizational Change				
Downsizing	68.5	31.2	0.4	100.0
Re-engineering	67.7	31.3	1.0	100.0
Other change	52.6	46.9	0.5	100.0
No change	40.7	58.3	1.1	100.0
Overall	**60.7**	**38.7**	**0.7**	**100.0**

Notes: 1. Differences between men and women are not necessarily statistically significant.
2. Establishments that spent more than and less than or equal to $100,000 on technology, respectively.
3. For explanation, see text.
Source: Calculations by the authors based on weighted employee data from Statistics Canada (1996).

the case with the skill requirements measure, the incidence of increased technical complexity is associated with major technology adoption and innovation. However, while differences did not exist between adopters and non-adopters using the earlier measure, all variants of technology are associated with technical complexity increases. For organizational change, the skill trends are similar to those observed in Table 7a: particularly high complexity increases among employees in establishments that are in the Flex II cluster and that have downsized or re-engineered, compared to employees in establishments that have undergone no organizational change.

In Tables 8a and 8b, we introduce gender into the analysis. To keep our presentation of the results manageable, we limit these tables to employees in firms that have introduced technological or organizational change and focus on any differences by gender. We observe almost identical incidences of skill increases among men and women among computer- and all-technology adopters; however, in innovating firms women are somewhat more likely than men to report a skill increase (Table 8a). No matter how the samples are dissected, women are more likely to report skill declines (although the percentages remain small) and men no change in skill requirements. As for organizational change, we observe similar patterns of skill increase for men and women in establishments that have introduced no change or "other" change. Men are more likely to report skill increases in downsized establishments, while women are more likely to report skill increases in re-engineered ones. Of note is that women are over three times as likely as men to report skill decreases in establishments that have downsized. In fact, the 19.9% proportion reporting a skill decrease is the highest for any sub-sample.

Turning to the technical complexity measure, men are more likely than women to report increases in establishments that have introduced CBTs, any technology, and where innovation has occurred (Table 8b). As for organizational change, men are more likely than women to report technical complexity increases in establishments undergoing downsizing or, to a greater extent, other organizational change. Conversely, women are more likely to report complexity increases in establishments that have introduced no organizational change.

Once again, the data presented so far do not control for other worker and establishment characteristics that could explain answers to the skill requirements and technical complexity questions. For example, the skill requirements question refers to change since the worker started the job and the

Gordon Betcherman, Darren Lauzon and Norm Leckie

Table 8a: Percentage Distribution of Men and Women Employees in Establishments Defined by Technological Change and Organizational Change by Reported Change in Skill Requirements[1]

| | Percentage Distribution by Change in Skill Requirements | | | |
	Increased	Remained the Same	Decreased	Total
Technology				
Computer-Based Technology Adopters				
Men	44.3	49.8	5.9	100.0
Women	44.9	45.2	10.0	100.0
All	44.6	47.8	7.6	100.0
All Technology Adopters				
Men	45.0	49.3	5.7	100.0
Women	45.9	44.6	9.5	100.0
All	45.4	47.4	7.3	100.0
Innovators				
Men	46.0	49.0	5.0	100.0
Women	51.2	39.9	8.8	100.0
All	48.4	44.9	6.8	100.0
Organizational Change				
Downsized Establishments				
Men	50.5	43.3	6.2	100.0
Women	44.4	35.7	19.9	100.0
All	47.7	39.8	12.4	100.0
Re-Engineered Establishments				
Men	46.2	47.1	6.7	100.0
Women	52.9	44.1	3.0	100.0
All	49.4	45.7	5.0	100.0
Establishments with Other Change				
Men	43.2	53.3	3.5	100.0
Women	42.4	54.8	2.8	100.0
All	42.9	53.9	3.2	100.0
Establishments with No Change				
Men	32.9	64.3	2.8	100.0
Women	36.2	63.6	0.2	100.0
All	34.4	64.0	1.6	100.0
Overall	**45.4**	**48.1**	**6.5**	**100.0**

Note: 1. Differences between men and women are not necessarily statistically significant.
Source: Calculations by the authors based on weighted employee data from Statistics Canada (1996).

Technological and Organizational Change and Skill Requirements 129

Table 8b: Percentage Distribution of Men and Women Employees in Establishments Defined by Technological Change and Organizational Change, by Reported Change in Technical Complexity[1]

	Percentage Distribution by Change in Technical Complexity			
	Increased	Remained the Same	Decreased	Total
Technology				
Computer-Based Technology Adopters				
Men	65.4	34.4	0.2	100.0
Women	57.8	40.9	1.3	100.0
All	62.2	37.1	0.7	100.0
All Technology Adopters				
Men	64.5	35.3	0.2	100.0
Women	58.9	39.9	1.2	100.0
All	62.2	37.2	0.6	100.0
Innovators				
Men	68.3	31.5	0.2	100.0
Women	59.3	39.9	0.8	100.0
All	64.2	35.3	0.5	100.0
Organizational Change				
Downsized Establishments				
Men	73.7	26.2	0.1	100.0
Women	62.2	37.2	0.6	100.0
All	68.5	31.2	0.4	100.0
Re-Engineered Establishments				
Men	68.6	31.0	0.4	100.0
Women	66.7	31.7	1.7	100.0
All	67.7	31.3	1.0	100.0
Establishments with Other Change				
Men	60.1	39.6	0.2	100.0
Women	41.9	57.2	0.9	100.0
All	52.6	46.9	0.5	100.0
Establishments with No Change				
Men	33.2	65.2	1.6	100.0
Women	49.0	50.5	0.5	100.0
All	40.7	58.3	1.1	100.0
Overall	60.7	38.7	0.7	100.0

Note: 1. Differences between men and women are not necessarily statistically significant.
Source: Calculations by the authors based on weighted employee data from Statistics Canada (1996).

Gordon Betcherman, Darren Lauzon and Norm Leckie

technical complexity question refers to change since the worker was hired. Certainly, *ceteris paribus*, longer-tenure workers will be more likely to report change than will shorter-tenured workers. Similarly, "initial" conditions matter. That is, highly skilled workers may be less likely to report an increase because they are already highly skilled. They may, in fact, be more likely to report a decrease. Establishment size matters because technology introduced into a small establishment is more likely to affect the workers sampled in that establishment than in a larger establishment (since the chance of sampling an "affected" worker decreases with the size of the establishment). Finally, skill effects might vary by industry as different sectors use different technologies for different goals.[16]

To control these other factors, we ran binary logistic regressions separately for men and women in which the probability of increased skill requirement and technical complexity is explained in terms of technological change, innovation and the control variables. (Note that no change and decreased skill requirements or technical complexity are collapsed into one category). The results indicate that men were more likely than women to report increased skill requirements and technical complexity than women (Tables 9a and 9b). Both men and women were more likely to report increased skill requirements if they worked for an "expensive" technology adopter (Table 9a); for men, however, the difference was greater.

Women were more likely to report increased skill requirements if they worked for an innovator than if they did not, but men were more likely to report increased skill requirements if they worked for a non-innovator. Even considering establishment size levels different from the average size of innovators in which men in the sample worked, the probability of a man working for an innovator does not rise much higher than that of non-innovators, and then only in the smallest establishments (81.4% in the small establishments with 20 employees compared to 76.6% for non-innovators).

Men were also more likely to report increased technical complexity in their jobs than women (Table 9b). The difference, however, was very small between men and women working for expensive technology adopters (2.8 percentage points). Once again the probability that a man reported increased

---

[16]We interact size and technology adoption and innovation in the regressions. We do this for two reasons. The first is that a $100,000 technology investment in a small establishment is almost certainly qualitatively different from one in a large establishment. Second, early examination of the data showed that there was a greater likelihood of being an innovator if establishments were larger.

Table 9a: Percentage Probability[1] that Men and Women Employees Reported Changes in Skill Requirements in Establishments Undergoing Technological Change and Innovation

	Men		Women	
	Increased	*No Change or Decreased*	*Increased*	*Decreased*
Technology Adopters				
"Expensive" technology[2]	81.8	18.2	64.5	36.5
"Cheap" technology[2]	58.8	41.2	49.6	50.4
Non-adopter	72.1	27.9	49.6	50.4
Innovation and Size				
Large innovator[3]	78.4	21.6	58.2	42.8
Medium-size innovator[3]	81.0	19.0	58.2	42.8
Small innovator[3]	81.4	18.5	58.2	42.8
Innovator	65.1	34.9	58.2	42.8
Non-innovator	79.6	23.4	42.2	57.8

Notes:
1. Probability computed from logistic regressions, separate for men and women, where the probability of reporting an increase in skill requirements is regressed on technology variables, controlling for tenure, education, occupation, part-time status, wage (natural log), establishment size and industry. The two technology controls (<$100,000 and $100,000 and over) and the innovator control are interacted with the employment size variable. Parameters not significant at the 10% level are set to zero for the computations, as the respective variable exerts a statistically insignificant impact on the probability.
2. Establishments that spent more than and less than or equal to $100,000 on technology, respectively.
3. Large = 500 employees, medium-size = 100 employees, and small = 20 employees.

Source: Calculations by the authors based on weighted employee data from Statistics Canada (1996).

Gordon Betcherman, Darren Lauzon and Norm Leckie

Table 9b: Percentage Probability[1] that Men and Women Employees Reported Changes in Technical Complexity in Establishments Undergoing Technological Change and Innovation

| | Men | | Women | |
	Increased	No Change or Decreased	Increased	Decreased
Technology Adopters				
"Expensive" technology[2]	54.4	45.6	51.8	48.4
"Cheap" technology[2]	54.4	46.6	28.7	71.3
Non-adopter	54.4	46.6	38.3	81.7
Innovation and Size				
Large innovator[3]	75.0	25.0	29.0	71.0
Medium-size innovator[3]	78.3	21.7	29.0	71.0
Small innovator[3]	78.9	21.1	29.0	71.0
Innovator	58.3	41.7	29.0	71.0
Non-innovator	72.8	27.2	29.0	71.0

Notes:
1. Probability computed from logistic regressions, separate for men and women, where the probability of reporting an increase in complexity is regressed on technology variables, controlling for tenure, education, occupation, part-time status, wage (natural log), establishment size and industry. The two technology controls (<$100,000 and $100,000 and over) and the innovator control are interacted with the employment size variable. Parameters not significant at the 10% level are set to zero for the computations, as the respective variable exerts a statistically insignificant impact on the probability.
2. Establishments that spent more than and less than or equal to $100,000 on technology, respectively.
3. Large = 500 employees, medium-size = 100 employees, and small = 20 employees.

Source: Calculations by the authors based on weighted employee data from Statistics Canada (1996).

technical complexity was higher among establishments that did not recently innovate than those that did; a higher percentage point difference, in fact, than for skill requirements. But unlike the case for skill requirements, establishment size does have a larger effect. Looking even at the larger establishments (500 employees), the probabilities of reporting increased technical complexity are considerably higher than for men working in non-innovating establishments.

Thus, after controlling for other factors explaining the likelihood of reporting increased skill requirements or technical complexity, men were more likely than women to report such increases, even comparing men and women working for technology adopters, non-adopters, innovators and non-innovators. Both men and women working for "expensive" technology adopters were more likely than their counterparts working for "cheaper" technology adopters or non-adopters to report increased skill requirements/ technical complexity. However, while women working for innovators were more likely to report increased skill requirements than their counterparts in non-innovating establishments, the reverse was true for men.

Training Activities

The third question we have addressed concerns how employees learn the new skills called for by computer-based technology.[17] Two data issues should be reiterated. First, in contrast to the earlier segments of our analysis, the measure of technology here comes from the employee survey (i.e., whether the employee uses CBT) rather than from the employer survey (which would indicate only whether the organization itself had experienced technological change). While the employee survey, then, offers more direct evidence of how CBT affects the work of the particular employee, it yields a measure of technology that pertains to the *use* of technology rather than a technological *change*. Ultimately, our particular focus is on whether there are differences between how men and women learn the skills required by computer use on the job. We examine two particular aspects of this learning process — which is the most important method of acquiring these skills and on whose time this learning takes place.

Before turning to these measures, we begin by looking at whether there are differences between men and women in terms of computer use. Overall, the WES data indicate that two out of three employees use computers in their work (Figure 1). This figure is higher than the percentages found in other

---

[17]As noted earlier, this segment of the analysis was limited to training in the wake of technological change because the WES did not offer direct evidence on training for organizational change.

Figure 1: Distribution of Men and Women by Incidence of Computer Use

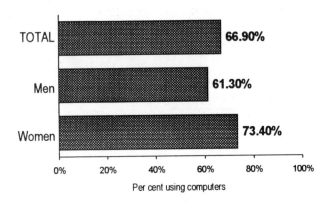

Source: Based on data from the Workplace Employee Survey.

surveys (e.g., GSS, WWTS).[18] As Figure 1 indicates, female employees are more likely to report that they use some sort of computer in their work. This gender difference is consistent with what earlier surveys have found and most probably reflects the fact that women are more likely to be in occupations with high rates of computer use.

Table 10 describes how computer users learn the skills required for the application they use the most. The left-hand side of the table considers all computer users and shows that much of this learning happens informally. The most frequently cited method was self-learning, followed by informal training, and then employer-sponsored formal training. The results suggest that male and female employees do not differ a great deal. Informal methods (either informal training or self-learning) are cited by about two-thirds of

---

[18]These surveys found just under 50%. This probably reflects differences in the samples. It is true that the WES is the most recent of these surveys; however, it was conducted at most two years after the others and the limited evidence that does exist suggests that diffusion paths are not that steep.

Technological and Organizational Change and Skill Requirements 135

Table 10: Percentage Distribution of Men and Women Computer Users According to the Most Important Way they Learned How to Use the Computer Application they Use the Most[1]

Method of Learning	All Computer Users			Computer Users Whose Technical Complexity Increased		
	Men	Women	All	Men	Women	All
Employer-paid formal training	23.0	26.7	24.9	22.0	22.9	22.4
Self-paid formal training	7.1	1.9	4.5	8.2	1.6	4.8
University/community college courses	2.6	4.4	3.5	2.8	4.0	3.0
Self-learning	41.0	33.2	37.1	41.1	36.6	35.8
Informal training	26.3	33.5	29.8	25.9	34.8	27.4
Total	100.0	100.0	100.0	100.0	100.0	100.0
Sample size (000s)			1,752			1,310

Note: 1. Differences between men and women are not necessarily statistically significant.
Source: Calculations by the authors based on weighted employee data from Statistics Canada (1996).

both groups.[19] From a policy point-of-view, it is particularly relevant to see whether there are differences in access to formal training paid by the employer. The WES data suggest there are no major differences, with women having a slightly higher incidence rate.[20]

We also examined how learning took place for those computer users who had identified that the technical complexity of their job had increased. This

---

[19]As the table indicates, males were more likely to report self-learning while females had higher incidences of informal training. The distinctions between these two categories, while undoubtedly real, are nonetheless blurry. Thus we have tended to consider them together as informal learning.

[20]The WES data do not allow us to consider the intensity of training, such as duration.

group is of particular interest in that we can expect that new skill needs have arisen in the wake of CBT. These results are shown on the right-hand side of Table 10 and are basically similar to those reported for all users. Informal methods predominate for both genders. In terms of employer-sponsored formal training, the slight advantage for females when all computer users were considered disappears when only those reporting increasing technical complexity are included.

Table 11 focuses in on another aspect of the human capital investment question — has the computer-driven learning taken place primarily on the employer's or employee's time? As the left-hand panel shows, learning is most likely to occur on company time or through a relatively even mixture of company and employee time. These time distributions are almost identical for men and women. When we look only at users who have also reported that the technical complexity of their job has increased, there were no sizable gender differences.

While Table 10 showed that women are marginally more likely to receive employer-sponsored training than men, Table 12 indicates that when we control for age, tenure, education, occupation, part-time status, size and industry, we see this difference increasing substantially. Fully 30.9% of women computer users receive employer-sponsored training compared to 9.5% of men.

Table 11: Percentage Distribution of Men and Women Computer Users According to on Whose Time they Learned How to Use the Computer Application they Use the Most[1]

On Whose Time	All Computer Users			Computer Users Whose Technical Complexity Increased		
	Men	Women	All	Men	Women	All
More on company time	54.9	54.9	54.9	57.7	56.9	57.3
More on own time	13.9	13.6	13.7	14.7	13.7	14.2
About equally on company and own time	31.2	31.6	31.4	27.6	29.4	28.4
Total	100.0	100.0	100.0	100.0	100.0	100.0

Note: 1. Differences between men and women are not necessarily statistically significant.
Source: Calculations by the authors based on weighted employee data from Statistics Canada (1996).

Table 12: Percentage Probability[1] that Men and Women Computer Users Receive Employer-Paid Training to Learn How to Use the Computer Application that they Use the Most

	Men	Women
Employer-paid training	9.5	30.9
No employer-paid training	90.5	69.1

Note: 1. Probability computations based on logistic regressions where, for males and females separately, the probability of receiving the training is regressed on age, education, occupation, wage, part-time status, establishment size and industry. Parameters not significant at the 10% level were set to zero for the computation, as the respective variable exerts a statistically insignificant impact on the probability.

Source: Calculations by the authors based on weighted employee data from Statistics Canada (1996).

Conclusion

Different perspectives on the labour market can lead to very different expectations of how the experiences with technological and organizational change might differ between men and women. A neoclassical perspective might anticipate that these sorts of innovations, which are acknowledged in the aggregate to have an upward skill bias, might lead to relatively greater benefits for women than men and that this might be an explanation for the declining male-female wage differentials. Alternatively, more institutional or feminist perspectives that focus on the secondary labour market situation of women might lead to conclusions that technological and organizational change is having a more positive impact on men than women.

In this paper, we have used new micro data from the Workplace and Employee Survey pilot to analyze how technological and organizational change affects men and women. The comparative advantage of these data for addressing this issue stems from the linked nature of the survey which covers a wide range of relevant information drawn from linked employee-establishment records. However, these are pilot data that are based, in a sense, on an experimental survey design and on a relatively small and segmented sample.

Below we summarize our findings with respect to the three particular issues we have examined: (i) exposure to technological and organizational change; (ii) the effects of these changes on skill; and (iii) ways in which employees accumulate the human capital required by technological change.

1. The descriptive evidence indicates that, on the one hand, there is very little difference between men and women in terms of being employed in different organizational change environments. On the other hand, women are somewhat less likely than men to be employed in establishments that have experienced technological change (regardless of the particular indicator). However, once basic establishment and worker characteristics were controlled for, there were no statistically significant gender differences with respect to technological change. *In the final analysis, then, the WES data indicate that exposure to technological and organizational change is similar for men and women.*

2. In the aggregate, the evidence from the WES strongly supports an upskilling perspective, regardless of whether a general or a technical conceptualization of "skill" is used. Moreover, the descriptive data suggest that technological and organizational change is playing a role in this upskilling. *The analysis indicates that, in the context of technological and organizational change, there are no gender differences in skill requirement trends, but men do report a somewhat higher incidence of increases in technological complexity.* This finding appears to contradict somewhat the extant literature, which indicates a narrowing of (Leckie, 1996), or at worst no change in (Lowe, 1996), the complexity gap of the jobs that men and women occupy.

3. Employees who are computer users report a primary reliance on informal training methods, like self-learning, to acquire the skills required by technology. *The patterns are quite similar for men and for women at the descriptive analysis stage.* The multivariate analysis indicates, however, that once controls are introduced, women become more likely than men to acquire skills through formal employer-paid training. The fact that simple training rates are very similar but the rates that control for other factors are higher for men suggests that men more often have personal characteristics or job characteristics that are associated with training access.This reflects past findings from the literature (e.g., Betcherman, Leckie and McMullen, 1997).

What can we conclude from our investigation? At the most general level, the WES data show no important gender differences in terms of exposure to technological and organizational change; the impacts of the changes on skill requirements; and the methods used to meet these new skill imperatives. At this level, then, the WES data do not support hypotheses that these forms of innovation are having differential effects on women and men.

Still, the apparent gender neutrality of technological, organizational and skill changes does not mean that this is the case at a deeper level within the organization. Truly understanding the impacts of change on workers requires more than just measuring incidence at the organization level, but obtaining information on the breadth and depth of diffusion *within* organizations. As McMullen (1996) has pointed out, the ongoing deepening of the use of computer-based technologies within organizations is resulting in an upgrading of the skill mix within those organizations. As organizations differ in the extent to which technological and organizational change is diffused within the organization, skill impacts could differ as well. Thus, it is important to investigate the changes and impacts of the changes on workers at the sub-organization level, that is, in different jobs and contexts, since at this level changes may be occurring that are not gender-neutral. Moreover, just because technological and organizational change appear to be advancing with gender neutrality *to date*, it is quite possible that in the future changes will occur that may have differential outcomes for the two genders.

Finally, our analysis dealt only with organizations that have already adopted new technologies and organizational practices. We still must look at differential gender access to workplaces that have either implemented, or are implementing, technological and organizational change. If there is differential access to technologies, then there may be differential access to any benefits and costly outcomes as well. Though, as we showed, the broad organizational context shows relatively equitable access within organizations that have implemented change, it may well be that one sex is systematically working in the establishments that use specific types of technology or that employ them in different ways, and thus may be experiencing greater benefits or costs than the other sex. While the broad industry and occupation variables that we introduced into the models were able to control somewhat for these differences, further work is needed on this question.

References

Baldwin, J., B. Diverty and J. Johnson (1995), "Success, Innovation, Technology, and Human Resource Strategies", paper prepared for the OECD conference on "The Effects of Technology and Innovation on Firm Performance and Employment", Washington.

Baldwin, J., B. Diverty and D. Sabourin (1995), *Technology Use and Industrial Transformation: Empirical Perspectives,* Research Paper Series No. 75 (Ottawa: Analytical Studies Branch, Statistics Canada).

Bell, D. (1973), *The Coming of Post-Industrial Society* (New York: Basic Books).

Betcherman, G., K. McMullen, N. Leckie and C. Caron (1994), *The Canadian Workplace in Transition* (Kingston: IRC Press, Queen's University).

Betcherman, G., N. Leckie and K. McMullen (1997), *Developing Skills in the Canadian Workplace: The Results of the Ekos Workplace Training Survey* (Ottawa: Canadian Policy Research Networks).

Betcherman, G., K. McMullen and K. Davidman (1998), *Training for the New Economy* (Ottawa: Canadian Policy Research Networks).

Braverman, H. (1974), *Labour and Monopoly Capital* (New York: Monthly Review Press).

de Broucker, P. (1997), "Job-Related Education and Training: Who Has Access?" Statistics Canada Cat. No. 81-008-XPE, *Education Quarterly Review* 4(1).

Ekos Research Associates Inc. (1998), "Using WES Data to Study Organizational Change: Final Report", unpublished paper prepared for Statistics Canada, Ottawa.

Government of Canada/OECD (1997), *Changing Workplace Strategies: Achieving Better Outcomes for Enterprises, Workers and Society,* summary report of a conference sponsored by Human Resources Development Canada and the Organization for Economic Cooperation and Development, Ottawa.

Kapsalis, C. (1997), *Employee Training: An International Perspective* (Ottawa: Statistics Canada and Human Resources Development Canada).

Krebs, H., Z. Patak, G. Picot and T. Wannell (1998), "The Workplace and Employee Survey: Methodological Challenges and Pilot Results", unpublished paper, Statistics Canada, Ottawa.

Lauzon, D., G. Betcherman and N. Leckie (1998), "Technology Adoption and Workers' Perceptions of Changes in Skill Requirements and Technical Complexity: Evidence from the 1996 Workplace and Employee Survey Pilot", paper prepared for the International Symposium on Linked Employer-Employee Data, Arlington, VA.

Leckie, N. (1996), "On Skill Requirement Trends in Canada, 1971-1991", unpublished paper, Canadian Policy Research Networks, Ottawa.

Lowe, G.S. (1996), "The Use and Impact of Computers in the Canadian Workplace, *1989-1994*", paper prepared for the Centre for Information Technology Innovation (Ottawa: Industry Canada).

McMullen, K. (1996), *Skill and Employment Effects of Computer-Based Technology* (Ottawa: Canadian Policy Research Networks).

Organization for Economic Cooperation and Development, OECD (1996), *Technology, Productivity, and Job Creation* (Paris: OCED).

Picot, G. (1998), "Computer Technologies, Training and International Competition: Preliminary Results from the Pilot Workplace and Employee Survey", unpublished paper, Statistics Canada, Ottawa.

Statistics Canada (1996), *Workplace Employee Survey* (WES) (Ottawa: Statistics Canada).

Statistics Canada and Human Resources Development Canada (1998), *The Evolving Workplace: Findings from the Pilot Workplace and Employee Survey*, Cat. No. 71-583-XPE (Ottawa: Statistics Canada).

The Effect of Computer Skills and Training on Salaries: A Study of Male and Female Industrial Relations and Human Resource Management Professionals

Caroline L. Weber and Işik Urla Zeytinoğlu

Introduction

Rapidly changing technologies, especially computer technology, drive concomitant changes in demand for labour market skills. The rapid changes may result in wage premiums for those at the higher end of the skills distribution. Meanwhile, for low-skilled workers labour market conditions seem to be deteriorating (OECD, 1997). Most of the research evidence examining the relationship between labour market skills and income polarization is based

This project was completed with financial support from Queen's University-ARC; the Social Science and Humanities Research Council; and the School of Business at Queen's. We would like to thank the participants, and especially our discussant, Anil Verma, who attended the "Women & Work" conference, sponsored by CWRN and the John Deutsch Institute, for their helpful comments and suggestions. We would also like to thank Katayoun Bagher, F. Cameron Fraser, Liann Joanette, Genevieve Lamorie and Stacey Anderson for expert research assistance and unflagging spirits.

on U.S. data. In a recent Canadian study, Boothby and Gingras (1998) showed no evidence of deterioration of labour market conditions for low-skilled workers in Canada in general, although there was some evidence that there has been a decline in access to the labour market and employment for low-skilled workers aged 55 and over. While they also discussed the effects of computer technology on the work of women and men, no definitive conclusions were provided.

There is some concern that the high demand for and low supply of computer skills may contribute to the polarization of individual earnings in society (Bound and Johnston, 1992; Picot, 1997), and polarization between female and male earnings, although the causes of polarization have been difficult to identify (Morissette, 1995). Krueger (1993) estimated that workers using computers on the job earned between 10 and 15% more than workers who were not using computers. If this is true, then skills attainment and access to training for these skills would also be a policy concern, especially if identifiable groups within a society are excluded from or have less access to opportunities to develop or enhance computer skills.

The difficulty in any discussion of the causes of increased polarization of earnings is that we generally have only gross measures of various human capital attributes to work with. With respect to education and training, usually only a measure of years of education or highest degree obtained is available; other explanatory variables, such as the academic field of study, or measures of additional training or course work are generally not available. Similarly, labour market experience, when available, has usually been measured as total (or overall) labour market experience (and often, it is only an estimate and a proxy, created by subtracting years of education from age). Also, labour market experience is not differentiated by the types of jobs held, nor does it capture the effects of periods of unemployment or part-time or contract work because these measures are unavailable in typical data sets. Only a few studies (from the United States) have been able to include these types of variables in their studies (see, e.g., Solberg and Laughlin, 1995; or Loury, 1997).

The purposes of this paper are to examine the effects of computer skills and training on salaries of male and female industrial relations and human resource management professionals, and to investigate whether there are gender differences in the acquisition of computer skills and training. We use a data set comprised of male and female industrial relations (IR) and human resource management (HR) professionals over the period 1962-91. This time

Caroline L. Weber and Işik Urla Zeytinoğlu

period also coincides with tremendous changes in computer information technology and its usage.

By focusing on one narrowly defined occupational category, we can minimize the effects of omitted variable bias (Gunderson, 1992), and thus we can more precisely isolate the effects of computer skills and training on career outcomes. IR and HR professionals are an appropriate occupational category for a study of the relationships between gender differences in skills, training and career outcomes since the occupation has been fairly integrated with respect to gender (see Table 1). Occupational segregation is often cited as a major source of gender differences in pay (Solberg and Laughlin, 1995).

Table 1: National and Provincial Gender Composition of IR/HR Occupations

Region and Year	1136 - Personnel and IR Managers [a]	1174 - Personnel and Related Officers[b]
Ontario		
1986 - Total	10, 980	14,855
1986 - Percent Female	39 %	56 %
1991 - Total	16,035	19,675
1991 - Percent Female	46 %	54 %
Canada		
1986 - Total	31,105	36,850
1986 - Percent Female	36 %	54 %
1991 - Total	44,010	43,880
1991 - Percent Female	42 %	57 %

Notes: a. Includes employee relations, industrial relations, and labour relations managers.
b. Includes analysts, counsellors, interviewers, and employee representatives, in addition to "officers".

Source: Statistics Canada Census Data, based on 1980 Standard Occupational Classification, Cat. No. 93-327, Table 1.

The data for this study come from 1,055 resumes which were submitted to the Toronto office of the Technical Service Council (TSC) from IR/HR professionals over the period 1962 through 1991. Since 1927, the TSC had functioned as a placement centre, matching professionals with employers all across Canada. The mandate of the TSC, from its inception, was to encourage Canadian professionals in the fields of science, engineering and management, to remain in Canada by facilitating their job searches and helping them to locate and contact appropriate Canadian employers.[1]

The resumes contain an abundance of detail not usually available with public data. In addition to the salary information provided on most of the resumes (for the last job held) or on an information sheet completed by the TSC, there is complete information about education (degrees, institutions and majors), employment histories (job titles, description of duties and place of employment), professional development activities (such as professional memberships and certificates obtained), and additional skills and abilities. Of particular relevance for this project, individuals tend to describe the types of computer skills they have and list courses they have taken in addition to any formal degree or diploma programs. If particular types of computer skills are an important determinant of salaries, then we expect to find a positive correlation between specific reported computer skills and salaries in this data set.

In the next section we briefly review the research literature on the relationships between gender and salaries, computer technology, and the use of computer technology by IR and HR professionals. We then describe our data source and variables, and the methods used to analyze the data. The final sections present our results and conclusions based on our findings.

Literature Review

In our review of the research literature, we first focus on the dependent variable of salary, and then continue with the literature that discusses the effects of technology — particularly computers — on career outcomes.

---

[1]In August 1994, The Technical Service Council (TSC) closed its doors for the last time, and the bank of resumes was donated to Caroline Weber to be used in research.

The Gender Wage Gap

There is a vast amount of research, begun in the 1970s, documenting and examining the persistent existence of a wage gap between male and female earnings (e.g., Corcoran and Duncan, 1979; Malkiel and Malkiel, 1973; Mincer and Polachek, 1974; Oaxaca, 1973). However, most of this work resorts to the use of proxies or truncation of the data set (Robb, 1978) of some sort, either for education or unemployment or work experience, since detailed information about these human capital variables is lacking from most data sets. The problem is so pervasive that some authors (e.g., Nakamura and Nakamura, 1985) have suggested methods for modeling information such as employment history. Other training or skills, such as computer skills, which are more difficult constructs to measure, are rarely if ever incorporated in the analyses.

More currently, there is evidence that the "gender gap" in earnings is narrowing in the United States (Blau and Kahn, 1994; Loury, 1997). Managerial and professional occupations in particular show evidence of the same trend in the United States (Gerhart and Milkovich, 1989; Jacobs, 1992), although the pattern is not so consistent in other countries (for a study from Sweden and the banking industry there, see Acker, 1991).

Studies show that women in managerial and most professional occupations are well represented in middle and entry level positions, but that few reach the senior level (Almey, 1995; Davidson and Burke, 1994; Denton and Zeytinoğlu, 1993; Konrad and Cannings, 1994; Vinnicombe and Colwill, 1995). In the IR/HR profession, as shown above in Table 1, there are more women in the lower levels of the occupation, although the women are reasonably well represented in the managerial levels.

The few studies in Canada using macro-level data (Robb, 1978; Gunderson, 1979; Holmes, 1976; Shapiro and Stelcner, 1987) and those based on single-employer data sets (Cannings, 1988; Cannings and Montmarquette, 1991; Nadeau, Walsh and Wetton, 1993) provide further evidence about the gender wage gap in Canada. Recent Statistics Canada reports show that in the mid-1990s a substantial gender wage gap still exists, although there does seem to be a narrowing of the gap (Almey, 1995). The reduction of the gender wage gap is attributed to women's increased investment in human capital (education and training), as well as men's reduced labour force participation due to job loss in the traditional manufacturing sectors, and the movement of men into the lower paying service sector.

As the literature suggests, there are many factors that can affect wage attainment. Human capital variables of investment in education and training (Becker, 1964) are well-researched factors that affect career outcomes in general, and salaries in particular. Individuals with more work experience and with higher levels of education are expected to earn more.

In this analysis, in addition to the usual human capital variables (experience and formal education), we include measures of computer skills and training. Just as the gender wage gap is changing over time, one might expect that the determinants of salaries are not static, fixed elements, but rather change over time in response to a dynamic environment. An examination of the role of computer skills in wage determination and the gender wage gap, and perhaps how this role has changed over time, is important since rapidly changing computer technologies are the revolutionizing force of our times.

Gender and Computer Technology

Theorizing about the effects of computer technology on the work of men and women predicts either positive or negative effects for women, depending on the theory, with no substantiating evidence either way. The volume edited by Davidson and Cooper (1987) presented both arguments: that male advantages with respect to technological training and knowledge would exacerbate gender segregation of the workforce, and that "women's" jobs would be deskilled and eliminated; or that the shortage of workers with computer skills would make discriminatory behaviour and occupational segregation so costly that employers would make greater efforts to encourage and facilitate the acquisition of computer skills by females as well as males. These two views are repeated in "un-gendered" debates about the effects of technology on labour. Long summarizes the debate by saying that there are "pessimists" and "optimists" who, while they see different outcomes resulting from the implementation of computer technology, share a belief in "technological determinacy" (1987, p. 6).

The existing research evidence regarding gender differences in the effects of new technology on occupations has focused primarily on the textile industry (Crewe, 1991; Truman and Keating, 1988; Walsh, 1991) and clerical occupations (several of the articles in the volume edited by Davidson and Cooper, 1987; Liff, 1990). Truman and Keating (1988), in their study of the UK clothing industry, concluded that work was being deskilled and

Caroline L. Weber and Işik Urla Zeytinoğlu

feminized and that jobs were being lost due to the introduction of new technologies. Crewe (1991) reinforced this conclusion with her study of large textile mills in West Yorkshire, but also presented evidence that the gender wage gap amongst textile workers had remained relatively stable over the period 1983 to 1988 (female to male earnings ratios of about 65%). Walsh's (1991) study of a UK textile company suggests that "unskilled" females were used to replace "skilled" males in specific jobs, as the result of technological innovation. Gender differences within typesetting trades have also been examined. As typesetting has been changed by technology to resemble a more clerical occupation (Edvardsson, 1994; Roos, 1990), wages have declined and women have replaced men.

The effects of new technology on gender differences in career outcomes have not been studied in general for professional occupations except perhaps, computer professionals. Hodson and Hagan (1988) interviewed 48 employees in 22 high-tech companies in a southwestern city in the United States. They content analyzed and coded their interview data in order to perform a systematic analysis of their qualitative data. While they see no pattern of gender differences in any of their results, they re-interpret the effect of technology on jobs as "skill disruption", as opposed to deskilling or skill upgrading. They describe a pattern of skill transformation in which previous skills that are not applicable to the current job are lost and replaced by new skills acquired through on-the-job training (Hodson and Hagan, 1988, p. 122).

Donato (1990) compared employment and salaries from U.S. Census data for men and women in two computer occupations (computer systems analysts and scientists, and operations and systems researchers and analysts) for the period 1970-80. While women comprise a small percentage of these occupational categories, their representation grew over the period of study, almost doubling for the computer systems analysts and scientists (from 13.6% female in 1970 to 22.5% female in 1980), and more than doubling for the operations and systems researchers and analysts (from 11.1% in 1970 to 27.7% in 1980). Donato attributes the increase in employment of females to a number of factors, especially the increasing fragmentation of tasks and the increasing numbers of women in higher education and in more fields of study.[2] Women in these occupations earned on average 72% of men's

---

[2]Donato provides statistics showing that the numbers of women being awarded degrees in computer science was three-to-five times higher between 1970 and 1980, across different degree programs.

earnings, but it is clear from Donato's breakdown by industry that a considerable proportion of this gap is due to segregation by industry.

Since the pervasiveness of computer technology is a relatively recent phenomenon, the effects of computer skills and the presence of computer technology in the workplace, and whether or not these effects are different for men and women, has not been fully assessed. In Canada, McMullen (1996) reports the results of her research on working with technology. She has gender composition of the participating establishments by broad (2-digit) occupational categories, but the only results reported by gender are with respect to training. For the establishments in this sample, we learn that for the types of training that are most often offered, women receive proportionately more training than men for software applications (48.1% versus 41.7%), about the same for professional/technical skills (16.9% versus 15.8%), and less than men in the "other" category (orientation and computerized cash registers; 20% versus 25%). McMullen's (1996) review of the research literature on the diffusion of computer technologies and their skill effects makes no mention of gender.

Part of the discussion about the effects of computer technology on gender differences in labour market outcomes hinges on the presumption that there will be increasing occupational segregation. Since we are examining only one occupation, we are unable to test this hypothesis. However, we will be able to examine whether women demonstrate similar acquisition of training as men in this occupation, and whether there are different returns to this training for men and women. Ultimately, whether employers are paying a premium for computer skills, and whether they are willing to pay that premium to men as well as to women, should show up in salaries.

Although different researchers present different ideas about the ultimate effects of computer technology on labour market outcomes, there seems to be a fairly consistent belief that those who are able to acquire computer skills will be the "winners" in the labour market. With the exception of Krueger's (1993) study, no other data exist to substantiate the prediction that individuals with computer skills will earn more. It may instead be that the acquisition of computer skills allows individuals to retain jobs and maintain employment, rather than increasing salaries.

Caroline L. Weber and Işik Urla Zeytinoğlu

Computer Technology and IR/HR Professionals

Another advantage of limiting our study to one occupation is that we can more accurately examine the impact of computer technology on one occupation, and thus more precisely predict how particular computer skills might affect salaries. IR/HR is an occupation in which the use of computers is primarily for human resource information systems (HRIS, which could take forms ranging from spreadsheet applications to database management), presentation preparations and word processing. This more narrow and explicit use of computer technology should facilitate an examination of the effects of technological change on the occupation. We therefore review what is known about the use of computers in the field of IR/HR.

Beutell and Walker (1991) describe the changes in human resource information systems from the 1970s to the mid- to late-1980s. In the early to mid-1970s, mainframe computer systems were the reason for the growth in the use of computerized payroll systems that were centrally developed and maintained by data processing departments in corporations. The late 1970s and early 1980s witnessed the development of database management, allowing for more flexibility and variety in the use and applications of data. This increasing flexibility, coupled with a growing sense of frustration with the computer experts who designed and maintained systems but did not have any knowledge of the IR/HR field, led to the creation of new positions of human resources information systems analysts and data administrators. Finally, in the mid-1980s, the further development of the personal computer, coupled with the introduction of local area networks, created more decentralization and again further increased flexibility.

However, as Beutell and Walker (1991, p. 6-170) point out, the huge potential of the new technology has not yet manifested itself; they feel this is due to the "complexity of the technology and the nature of the HRIS data". A Towers Perrin survey (as cited in Milkovich and Boudreau, 1994, pp. 266-267) of international HR managers and other experts asked respondents to identify the four greatest impediments to reaching the full potential of HRIS. The top four reasons were: insufficient resource/budgets; lack of availability of applications; system designers' lack of HR knowledge; and maintaining confidentiality of personal information; thus confirming Beutell and Walker's observations. The next four reasons though were: insufficient numbers of users, rapid rates of technological change, lack of training for HRIS users, and poor quality of data, suggesting that the failure of HRIS to reach its potential may in part be due to a training gap. IR/HR professionals do not usually come from engineering or basic sciences backgrounds, and would not generally be described as technophiles. Furthermore, IR/HR programs historically often did not include computer training for spreadsheets or database management, or, more specifically, HRIS training. While the use and applications of HRIS grew from the 1970s to the 1990s, skills and training in computer applications and HRIS remained scarce amongst IR/HR professionals, and we could therefore expect to see a premium paid for these types of analytical skills for the time period of our study. However, since word processing and presentation software skills are characterized as clerical, which is low paid (compared to professionals), we would not expect to see a premium paid for these skills.

Methodology

Data Source and Collection Process

The 1,055 resumes which were submitted to the Toronto office of the Technical Service Council from IR/HR professionals over the period 1962 through 1991 provide the data for this paper. Anonymity of individuals was protected as only the first author and her designated research assistants had access to the original resumes to prepare the data set. At the initial stage of the research, the resumes from the IR/HR professionals were coded into two files: a career history file, which stores each job (and employment "gap") reported by each applicant as one record (hence there are multiple records for each applicant); and an education and background file, which stores all pertinent education, training and skills information (one record for each applicant).

Variables

The *dependent variable* of LN Salary is the log of last salary recorded in the resume multiplied by the Consumer Price Index (CPI) to get constant 1986 dollars. *Independent variables* include individual characteristics (gender and human capital variables of formal education, certificates and professional memberships, computer skills and training, and labour market experience), job characteristics and environment or control variables. The names of the variables and how they were operationalized are presented in Table 2. For

Table 2: Variables and Descriptions

Variable Name	Description	N
Last Salary (1986$)	Last annual salary recorded in application file (sometimes this information is on the resume, and other times it is recorded on the TSC interviewer's form), multiplied by the CPI in order to get constant 1986 dollars.	631
Gender	"1" if female, based on name or other information referring to gender of applicant	943
High School, College, University, Graduate School (Degrees)	Indicator variables; "1" if degree obtained, 0 otherwise	954
Certificates	Number of professional certificates indicated on resume	954
Professional Memberships	Number of professional memberships indicated on resume	954
Number of Courses	Count of number of courses outside formal degree program listed/described on resume	954
Statistical/Analytical Courses	If academic field for courses indicates computer science, then value is "Number of courses"; else zero	954
Typing/WP Courses	If academic field for courses indicates word processing/presentation software, then value is "Number of courses"; else zero	954
Statistical/Analytical Skills	"1" if resume states applicant has computer skills (programming skills, ability to use different statistical packages including spreadsheets, or ability to use database managers)	954
Typing/WP Skills	"1" if resume states applicant has typing or word processing skills	954
Full-time Experience (in months)	Sum experience for all jobs that were not contract or part-time	783
Number of Employers	Sum number of times resume indicates applicant changed employers	954
Number of Jobs	Sum number of jobs indicated on resume	961
Contract Experience (in months)	Sum experience for all jobs that were contract	950
Number of Contract Jobs	Sum number of contract jobs indicated on resume	954

Variable Name	Description	N
Part-time Experience (in months)	Sum experience for all jobs that were part-time	951
Number of Part-time Jobs	Sum number of part-time jobs indicated on resume	954
Total Employment Gap (in months)	Sum of periods of unaccounted time in the career history (sometimes described on the resume as "unemployed", other times simply not referred to)	954
Number of Gaps	Sum number of employment gaps indicated on resume	954
HR, IR or Both[3]	Whether individual's last position dealt only with non-union, union, or "both" (union and non-union) matters and employees. Coded as IR=0, HR=1, and Both=2, and recoded into separate dummy variables.	954
Occupation Level	Level of occupational hierarchy represented by job, using NOC codes. Coded as 1 (analyst/clerical) if Last NOC > 1300; 2 (supervisory) if Last NOC > 1200 and < 1300; 3 (consultants/"professionals") if Last NOC > 1100 and < 1200; 4 (managerial) if Last NOC > 100 and < 1000; 5 (executive) if Last NOC < 20.	942
Year	Last year of contact with the TSC	954
Industries (Resources, Construction, Manufacturing, Transp/Comm/Util, Wholesale, Retail, Financial, Services, Health, Education & Other, Public Admin.	Indicator variables created for 11 industry categories	954

---

[3]We would especially like to thank Tom Courchene and Anil Verma for suggesting that we add this variable to our data set.

most of the variables, information is available for 954 of the original 1,055 resumes.[4] The unfortunate exception is the salary for the last job held, for which there are only 631 observations.

Since our focus is on computer skills and training, we explain these independent variables in further detail. As discussed above, the computer skills used by IR/HR professionals consist primarily of spreadsheet and database management applications, and word processing or presentation software. Since the two types of skills are different, and statistical or analytical skills are viewed as more complex and thus more highly valued, we coded the computer skills that are listed on the resumes as dummy variables for two different types of skills: programming skills (either applications software programming or computer language software programming), and word processing or presentation software skills. Additional training or courses have also been recorded by coding the number of courses described and the related academic field that best describes the courses. In this way, we can identify additional training in computers (again, differentiating between analytical or statistical training and word processing training) and separate it from all other types of training. Since the changes in computer technology in this profession are characterized by decades, we constructed decade dummy variables and crossed them with the computer training and skills variables to examine the interaction effects.

The Regression Equation

In the regression analyses we estimate a general salary equation of the form

$$\ln (W) = \beta X + \gamma V + \zeta Z + e$$

where W represents salaries, e is the error term, X is a vector of individual characteristics including the demographic variable gender as well as human capital variables (formal education, certificates and professional member-

---

[4]We lose about 100 individuals who submitted resumes as new graduates, with no labour market experience; and calculating full-time experience by job is impossible in instances when only organizational tenure is available on the resume. Although we could use an organization-based calculation, rather than a job-based one, we are so limited by salary observations that this different calculation is unnecessary.

ships, computer skills and training and labour market experience), V is a vector of job characteristics of the last job reported on the resumes (such as whether the job entails only human resource or union responsibilities or both and occupational level of the job) and Z is a vector of environment or control variables (year and industry).

Analysis

We examine descriptive statistics and the results of difference of means tests (t-tests) to investigate whether there are gender differences in access to or acquisition of training in this sample. We use ordinary least squares regression techniques to investigate the relationship between wages, computer skills and training and gender. We use a gender dummy variable for analysis of the whole sample, and when that variable is significant, we separate the sample and run separate analyses on the male and female subjects.

Results

Characteristics of the Sample

Descriptive statistics for the sample are presented in Table 3. Average annual salary for this sample, in 1986 dollars, is $40,694. Almost one-third of this sample is female. This is a well-educated population: almost all of these people report having high school diplomas and 67% hold a university degree. Individuals in this sample tend to report taking on average about four courses in addition to their formal degree training, but only a small number of these courses are computer-related and small percentages of the sample indicate that they have different types of computer skills. The average of about 12 and one-half years of full-time labour market experience reflects employment with an average of four different organizations, comprised of five or six different jobs. While there is low reporting of contract and part-time employment experience, on average, each of these individuals reveals one period of unaccounted labour market time, or an employment "gap". Differentiating between IR and HR environments, we observe that almost half of the sample reports that their last job did not deal with a union, while only 10% report working with a union and 27% were in positions with

Table 3: Descriptive Statistics
(Full sample)

Variable Name	Mean or Percent (std. dev.)	Minimum	Maximum
Dependent Variable			
Last Salary (1986$)	40,694 (16,794)	9,247	241,361
LN(Last Salary)	10.55 (0.36)	9.13	12.39
Individual Characteristics			
Gender (1=female)	31 %	0	1
High School	99 %	0	1
College	23 %	0	1
University	67 %	0	1
Graduate School	19 %	0	1
Certificates	0.44 (0.85)	0	7
Professional Memberships	0.9 (1.51)	0	25
Number of Courses	4.37 (4.61)	0	36
Statistical/Analytical Courses	0.28 (1.79)	0	36
Typing/WP Courses	0.04 (.68)	0	15
Statistical/Analytical Skills	10 %	0	1
Typing/WP Skills	20 %	0	1
Full-time Experience (months)	150.72 (99.80)	1	491
Number of Employers	3.96 (2.12)	1	13
Number of Jobs	5.61 (2.76)	0	18
Contract Experience (months)	2.21 (8.97)	0	98
Number of Contract Jobs	0.19 (0.57)	0	5
Part-time Experience (months)	2.90 (14.95)	0	226
Number of Part-time Jobs	0.13 (0.50)	0	5

Variable Name	Mean or Percent (std. dev.)	Minimum	Maximum
Total Employment Gap (in months)	14.55 (29.65)	0	288
Number of Gaps	0.92 (1.01)	0	5
Only HR Responsibilities	49 %	0	1
Only IR Responsibilities	10 %	0	1
Both HR & IR Responsibilities	27 %	0	1
Occupation Level	3 (1.2)	1	5
Environment/ Control Variables			
Year[a]	1986	1962	1991
Industry:			
Resources	3 %	0	1
Construction	1 %	0	1
Manufacturing	32 %	0	1
Transportation/ Communication/ Utilities	6 %	0	1
Wholesale	1 %	0	1
Retail	3 %	0	1
Financial	7 %	0	1
Services	16 %	0	1
Health	3 %	0	1
Education & Other Services	6 %	0	1
Public Administration	7 %	0	1

Note: a. For purposes of analysis, "Year" has been recoded as a continuous variable starting at t=1 for Year=1961, and continuing up to t=31. For ease of interpretation in this table of descriptive statistics, Year is presented in its original form.

Caroline L. Weber and Işık Urla Zeytinoğlu

responsibilities for both union and non-union employees. The average occupational attainment level for this sample is at about the middle of the occupational hierarchy, in positions that would usually be described as internal (or external) consultants and professionals. Most of the sample reports a last job that was either in the manufacturing (32%) or service industry (16%).

Gender Differences

Using t-tests, we examined the differences in the means of all variables by gender. The results are presented in Table 4. Not surprisingly, women exhibit average annual earnings that are much less than men's: women are earning an average of 77% of what men are earning in this sample. Males report graduate degrees more often than the females, and more professional memberships, while women report more professional certificates.

Of interest for this paper is that women in this sample indicate more often than men that they have statistical/analytical computer skills (17% versus 7%), as well as word processing skills (40% versus 11%). Men and women report about equally the number of additional courses taken in statistical or analytical computer skills (about one course for all, on average), and in word processing or presentation software (close to zero) that they have taken. Since these were not statistically significant, they are not reported in Table 4.

Women generally are exhibiting less, and perhaps inferior, labour market experience compared with the men in this sample, as demonstrated by the differences in full-time and part-time work experience, and in employment "gaps".[5] The last jobs held by males in this sample are at a higher level of the occupational hierarchy than the last jobs held by women.

---

[5]Furthermore, women in this sample on average report about two more months of part-time experience than men (2.28 for men versus 4.39 for women) and about four more months of unexplained absence from the labour market (13.37 for men versus 17.51 for women), although neither of these differences reach acceptable levels of significance (t = -1.85, p = 0.65 for part-time exper- ience, and t = -1.93, p = .054 for employment gaps).

Table 4: Difference of Means Tests (T-tests)
Characteristics By Gender
Significant Differences Only

Variable Name	Males	Females	T value
Last Salary	43,518	33,683	6.85***
Graduate School	21 %	15 %	2.38*
Professional Memberships	1.02	0.66	4.14***
Certificates	0.4	0.54	- 2.33*
Statistical/Analytical Skills	7 %	17 %	- 4.16***
Typing/WP Skills	11 %	40 %	- 9.06***
Full-time Experience (in months)	169.98	108.04	9.34***
Number of Employers	4.17	3.5	4.71***
Number of Part-time Jobs	0.1	0.2	- 2.41*
Number of Employment Gaps	0.87	1.03	- 2.27*
Only HR Responsibilities	44 %	61 %	- 4.97***
Only IR Responsibilities	14 %	4 %	- 5.57***
Both HR& IR Responsibilities	31 %	17 %	- 5.02***
Occupation Level	3.2	2.5	7.96***
Year	1985.5	1986.6	- 3.89***

Notes: * p < .05; ** p < .01; *** p < .001

Caroline L. Weber and Işik Urla Zeytinoğlu

Significant differences between men and women are observed in the types of jobs last held. Both men and women are most likely to be found in positions with no union-related responsibilities. Women, however, are more likely than men to be found in non-union positions, while men are more likely than women to be found in positions with only union-related responsibilities, or with both union and non-union responsibilities. The difference in the "Year" variable indicates that the distribution of men and women applying to the TSC is different over time; women apparently applied more recently than men.

Regression Results

Regression analysis of salary equations are presented in Table 5. Since the gender coefficient was significant, we ran separate male and female equations in order to investigate any possible structural differences in the equations. In general, the results indicate that salaries are increasing over time for this sample. While individuals with university education (either at the undergraduate or graduate level) realize higher salaries, individuals with a college education earn less. Professional Memberships and the acquisition of certificates appear to have no impact on salaries.

The results show only one significant effect of computer skills or training on the salaries of IR/HR professionals, and it is not in the anticipated direction. Individuals reporting statistical or analytical skills seem to earn less in this profession. Separate analyses suggest that women were "penalized" (received lower salaries) when they reported statistical/analytical computer skills. The sign on the coefficient of this variable is still negative in the male equation, but not significant.

Those with more labour market experience and those who change employers more often receive higher salaries, although this latter finding does not hold for women. Contract jobs, part-time jobs and employment gaps generally show no significant relationship with salaries (except for "gaps" in the analysis of the whole sample), although the signs on these variables are almost uniformly negative. We note, however, that the sign on the coefficient for contract jobs is positive in the female equation, suggesting that contract jobs may serve a different role in the salary determination of women as compared with men. Further investigation would require a sample with more contract jobs reported.

Table 5: Regression Results: Effects of Computer Skills and Training and Other Variables on LN(Salary) All and by Gender

(Unstandardized coefficients; Standard Errors in parentheses)

Variable	All	Males Only	Females Only
Individual Characteristics			
Gender (1=female)[a, b]	- 0.12*** (0.03)	-----	-----
High School[a]	0.09 (0.22)	0.01 (0.22)	-----
College	- 0.06* (0.03)	- 0.07* (0.03)	- 0.01 (0.05)
University	0.10*** (0.03)	0.10*** (0.03)	0.13* (0.05)
Graduate School	0.07** (0.03)	0.07* (0.03)	0.17* (0.07)
Certificates	- 0.002 (0.01)	- 0.01 (0.02)	0.01 (0.02)
Professional Memberships	0.01 (0.01)	0.01 (0.01)	0.05* (0.02)
Courses	0.0001 (0.003)	0.001 (0.003)	- 0.002 (0.005)
Statistical/Analytical Courses	0.001 (0.01)	- 0.001 (0.006)	- 0.01 (0.02)
Typing/WP Courses[b]	0.01 (0.02)	-----	- 0.002 (0.02)
Statistical/Analytical Skills	- 0.12* (0.05)	- 0.05 (0.07)	- 0.23** (0.08)
Typing/WP Skills	0.02 (0.04)	- 0.002 (0.05)	0.09 (0.06)
Full-time Experience (months)	0.001*** (0.0002)	0.001*** (0.0002)	0.002*** (0.0004)
Number of Employers	0.01* (0.006)	0.01* (0.007)	- 0.003 (0.01)
Number of Contract Jobs	- 0.001 (0.02)	- 0.03 (0.02)	0.07 (0.04)
Number of Part-time Jobs	- 0.04 (0.02)	- 0.03 (0.03)	- 0.03 (0.04)
Number of Gaps	- 0.03* (0.01)	- 0.01 (0.01)	- 0.04 (0.02)
Job Characteristics ("Only IR" omitted category)			
Only HR Responsibilities	0.07* (0.03)	0.02 (0.03)	0.19** (0.06)

Variable	All	Males Only	Females Only
Both HR & IR Responsibilities	0.09** (0.03)	0.06 (0.03)	0.24** (0.08)
Occupation Level	0.12*** (0.01)	0.12*** (0.01)	0.09*** (0.02)
Environment/Control Variables (Resources omitted industry category)			
Year Count	0.01*** (0.002)	0.01** (0.002)	0.01 (0.01)
Construction[a]	0.04 (0.10)	0.04 (0.10)	-----
Manufacturing	0.01 (0.03)	0.003 (0.03)	0.02 (0.07)
Transportation/ Communication/ Utilities	0.07 (0.05)	0.01 (0.06)	0.25** (0.10)
Wholesale	0.04 (0.12)	- 0.43 (0.25)	0.20 (0.15)
Retail	- 0.12 (0.07)	- 0.14 (0.09)	- 0.08 (0.11)
Financial	- 0.003 (0.04)	0.03 (0.06)	0.03 (0.09)
Services	- 0.03 (0.04)	- 0.03 (0.05)	0.01 (0.07)
Health	- 0.10 (0.07)	- 0.09 (0.08)	- 0.11 (0.17)
Education and Other Services	0.01 (0.05)	0.01 (0.06)	0.05 (0.09)
Public Administration	0.002 (0.04)	- 0.03 (0.05)	0.08 (0.09)
Constant	9.59*** (0.23)	9.73*** (0.23)	9.27*** (0.21)
F	21.06***	13.15***	6.28***
Adjusted R^2	0.5	0.44	0.45
N	631	446	180

Notes: * $p < .05$; ** $p < .01$; *** $p < .001$
a. Variable had no variance for women and was omitted from Female wage equation.
b. Variable had no variance for men and was omitted from Male wage equation.

Compared to working in a position with union-related tasks and responsibilities, salaries are higher when there are no union-related tasks reported, or when the job entails both union and non-union-related responsibilities. This is a general pattern in the analysis of the whole sample and the females-only equation, but does not appear to hold true for men. Occupation level demonstrates a consistently large positive and significant relationship with salary. We observe almost no (with only one exception) significant wage differences across industry categories.

In order to further investigate the effects of computer skills and training on salaries, an attempt was made to evaluate the effect of computer skills on salaries over time. The results (Table 6) indicate that only perhaps in the 1970s was anything like a "premium" ever paid for statistical/analytical training and skills in this profession; but this result is not statistically significant and there are only males in the sample reporting this type of training and skills in that time period, so the positive coefficients may only indicate a confound with gender. The results show significant negative effects of statistical and analytical skills on salaries for the 1980s, although the separate analyses by gender again only show a significant negative effect for women in the 1980s. In general, we observe little evidence of significant effects or changes in the effects of computer skills over time.

It may be argued that computer skills matter less, or are reported less frequently, or at least the impact changes, as one progresses up the occupational hierarchy.[6] In order to investigate this possible explanation for our results, we re-ran all (six, as presented in Tables 5 and 6) equations including interaction terms between occupational level and the two types of computer skills and courses. In general, the interaction terms (four of them) were not significant. The only exception is the male equation using only the year count variable (no decade variables): in this equation, occupation level interacted with word processing skills is positive and significant ($B = .11$, s.d. $= .04$, $p < .05$). Again this is a surprising result, since it indicates there are positive returns for men who report word processing skills as they progress up the occupational hierarchy!

---

[6]We would like to thank the participants at the research seminar at Sir Wilfred Laurier University, and the editors of this volume, for this suggestion.

Caroline L. Weber and Işik Urla Zeytinoğlu

Table 6: Regression Results: Effects of Computer Skills and Training and Other Variables on LN(Salary) Over Time All and By Gender

(Unstandardized coefficients; Standard Error in parentheses)

Variable	All	Males Only	Females Only
Individual Characteristics			
Gender (1=female)[a, b]	- 0.11***(0.03)	-----	-----
High School[a]	0.08 (0.22)	- 0.01 (0.22)	-----
College	- 0.06* (0.03)	- 0.08* (0.03)	- 0.002 (0.05)
University	0.10***(0.03)	0.09**(0.03)	0.14* (0.05)
Graduate School	0.07*(0.03)	0.07* (0.03)	0.17* (0.07)
Certificates	0.003 (0.01)	- 0.01 (0.02)	0.01 (0.02)
Professional Memberships	0.01 (0.01)	0.01 (0.01)	0.04 (0.02)
Courses	0.0002 (0.003)	0.001 (0.003)	- 0.002 (0.01)
1970 Statistical/ Analytical Courses[a]	0.006 (0.03)	0.02 (0.03)	-----
1980 Statistical/ Analytical Courses	0.002 (0.01)	0.001 (0.01)	- 0.001 (0.02)
1990 Statistical/ Analytical Courses	- 0.03 (0.02)	- 0.07* (0.03)	- 0.02 (0.04)
1980 Typing/WP Courses[b, c]	- 0.009 (0.02)	-----	- 0.004 (0.02)
1970 Statistical/ Analytical Skills[a]	0.26 (0.28)	0.43 (0.30)	-----
1980 Statistical/ Analytical Skills	- 0.12* (0.06)	- 0.08 (0.08)	- 0.23* (0.09)
1990 Statistical/ Analytical Skills	- 0.21 (0.11)	- 0.16 (0.16)	- 0.22 (0.16)
1970 Typing/WP Skills	- 0.01 (0.12)	- 0.17 (0.17)	0.20 (0.18)
1980 Typing/WP Skills	0.02 (0.04)	- 0.02 (0.06)	0.10 (0.07)
1990 Typing/WP Skills	0.08 (0.09)	0.21 (0.13)	0.02 (0.13)
Full-time Experience (months)	0.001***(0.0002)	0.001***(0.0002)	0.002***(0.0004)
Number of Employers	0.01 (0.01)	0.01** (0.007)	- 0.003 (0.01)
Number of Contract Jobs	- 0.001 (0.02)	- 0.03 (0.02)	0.07 (0.04)

Variable	All	Males Only	Females Only
Number of Part-time Jobs	- 0.04 (0.02)	- 0.03 (0.03)	- 0.03 (0.04)
Number of Gaps	- 0.03*(0.01)	- 0.01 (0.01)	- 0.03 (0.02)
Job Characteristics ("Only IR" omitted category)			
Only HR Responsibilities	0.06*(0.03)	0.02 (0.03)	0.19**(0.06)
Both HR & IR Responsibilities	0.09**(0.03)	0.05 (0.03)	0.23**(0.08)
Occupation Level	0.12***(0.01)	0.12***(0.01)	0.10***(0.02)
Environment/Control Variables ("Resources" omitted category)			
Year	0.01***(0.002)	0.01**(0.003)	0.02*(0.01)
Construction[a]	0.05 (0.10)	0.03 (0.10)	-----
Manufacturing	0.01 (0.03)	0.001 (0.03)	0.02 (0.07)
Transportation/ Communication/ Utilities	0.07 (0.05)	0.01 (0.06)	0.26**(0.10)
Wholesale	0.04 (0.12)	- 0.43 (0.25)	0.18 (0.15)
Retail	- 0.12 (0.07)	- 0.14 (0.09)	- 0.08 (0.11)
Financial	- 0.004 (0.05)	0.02 (0.06)	0.03 (0.09)
Services	- 0.03 (0.04)	- 0.03 (0.05)	0.01 (0.07)
Health	- 0.09 (0.07)	- 0.08 (0.08)	- 0.09 (0.17)
Education & Other Services	- 0.002 (0.05)	0.01 (0.06)	0.06 (0.10)
Public Administration	- 0.0004 (0.04)	- 0.04 (0.05)	0.07 (0.09)
Constant	9.60***(0.23)	9.76***(0.23)	9.17***(0.23)
F	17.68***	11.25***	5.45***
Adjusted R^2	0.5	0.45	0.44
N	631	446	180

Notes: * $p < .05$; ** $p < .01$; *** $p < .001$

a. Variable had no variance for women and was omitted from Female wage equation.

b. Variable had no variance for men and was omitted from Male wage equation.

c. No Typing/Word Processing courses were reported throughout the 1970s and the 1990s in the sample.

Caroline L. Weber and Işik Urla Zeytinoğlu

Conclusions

In this paper we examined the effects of computer skills and training on the salaries of male and female IR/HR professionals, and investigated whether there were gender differences in the acquisition of computer skills and training. We used 1,055 resumes submitted to the Toronto office of the Technical Service Council over the period 1962 through 1991 for our data source. In general, we found no relationship between computer skills and training and salaries for this sample, with the exception of a negative relationship between statistical/analytical skills and salaries for women. When women reported that they had statistical/analytical skills, they earned less. This result fits neither with the gendered theories of the effects of technology (which predict that women with computer skills would either earn more due to demand, or less due to lack of access to skills and training), nor with the ungendered theories which predict either broad upskilling or deskilling. Rather, these results are consistent with the results of the qualitative studies of typesetting and some textile operations, in that when women have access to or acquire computer skills, the technology is used to reinforce within-occupation segregation. Through skill transformation of jobs within the profession (or deskilling of the job), we observe a decline in wages for women as a result of the introduction and use of computers.

There are two ways to interpret our results. The first is that it is a statistical artifact, resulting from a confound between gender and computer skills in this sample (recall that larger percentages of women were reporting computer skills), reflecting something that we do not observe. For example, perhaps men have these skills but simply do not report them on their resumes. Or, perhaps computer skills play a different role for women: maybe computer skills are necessary to facilitate re-entry into the labour market for women who need to leave the labour market for periods of time.

The other possible explanation is that these skills operate with gender to reinforce segregation within the occupation. If computer analysis and applications have come to be viewed as a task for lower levels and "analysts" only, and if these skills are not used at higher occupational levels, then individuals with these skills might find themselves locked into lower paying levels of the occupational hierarchy. Just as the technological developments in typing skills, originally perceived as a high-skill level to be performed by men, came to be later classified as a low-skilled clerical job to be performed by women, so too the more sophisticated computer skills might be in a transition from "elite" to "common" and thus perceived as appropriate for delegation to the female workforce. This interpretation is consistent with the results of other gender-based studies reporting that the more a job is "feminized", the less likely it is that the job will be perceived as professional or skilled by employers and unions.

Prior to the papers presented in this volume, there had been little to no research assessing the impact of computer skills and training on career outcomes. The theorizing generally assumes that computer skills are in high demand and will result in higher wage outcomes for individuals with those skills. While computer *professionals* are in high demand (Weber and Phillip, 1995), the demand level for computer skills across occupations has not been evaluated. The results presented in this paper suggest that there may have been a period of demand and a premium paid for computer skills during the 1970s, with the first introduction of computer technology in this profession but that, over time, as computers became more pervasive and commonplace, the demand for these skills either leveled off or diminished.

While formal education, represented by degrees and diplomas, demonstrates a significant impact on salaries, as is consistent with previous research, courses taken and certificates earned outside a degree program show no significant relationship with salaries in this profession. This result suggests that skills-upgrading or re-training efforts in the form of single courses, in any subject area, do not contribute to increased salaries. It may be that, while formal educational programs vary, there is a greater degree of standardization which allows employers to use the degrees as a signaling device, while the lack of standardization in non-programatic courses and the proliferation of professional "certificates" would make it nearly impossible for employers to interpret the value of that training. Alternatively, employers may expect professionals to continuously upgrade their knowledge and thus do not pay a premium for these activities. Professional development in the form of additional courses and certificates may merely be a requirement for continued employment in the field. The policy implications would be that we cannot expect non-programmatic training to increase salary levels, but that this type of training might help individuals find new jobs or maintain employment.

The evidence presented here suggests that women are not disadvantaged as compared to men with respect to the acquisition of computer skills or access to computer training. In fact, women in this sample report a higher incidence of both analytical and word processing computer training. However, this increased incidence of training does not translate into higher salaries. Betcherman *et al.*, in this volume, using a very different sample, also report that computer skills show no relationship with wages. Taken together, these results might suggest that computer skills now play the same role as a high school diploma in wage determination: required in order to avoid the depths of the unskilled labour market and frequent unemployment, but not sufficient to scale the heights of the professional occupational ladders. Based on the results reported in this paper though, this conclusion would be in error, since men are more successful than women in the labour market in this sample, and yet men also demonstrate consistently significantly lower rates of computer skills and training than women. Clearly then, computer skills are not necessary for men to find employment or get promoted in this field. Instead, we suggest that our results present further evidence that men and women face different labour markets even in the same occupation.

References

Acker, J. (1991), "Thinking About Wages: The Gendered Wage Gap in Swedish Banks", *Gender and Society* 5(3), 390-407.

Almey, M. (1995), "Labour Force Characteristics", *Women in Canada* (Ottawa: Ministry of Industry), 64-70.

Becker, G.S. (1964), *Human Capital: A Theoretical and Empirical Analysis, with Special Reference to Education* (New York: Columbia University Press and the National Bureau of Economic Research).

Beutell, N. and A.J. Walker (1991), "HR Information Systems", in R.S. Schuler and J. Walker (eds.), *Managing HR in the Information Age* (Washington, DC: BNA Books), 6-167 - 6-203.

Blau, F.D. and L.M. Kahn (1994), "Rising Wage Inequality and the U.S. Gender Gap", *The American Economic Review* 84 (May), *Papers and Proceedings*, 23-28.

Boothby, D. and Y. Gingras (1998), "Labour Market Conditions of Low-Skilled Workers in Canada", Draft Research Paper (Ottawa: Applied Research Branch, Strategic Policy Group, Human Resources Development Canada).

Bound, J. and G. Johnston (1992), "Changes in the Structure of Wages in the 1980s: An Evaluation of Alternative Explanations", *American Economic Review* 82 (June), 371-392.

Cannings, K. (1988), "Managerial Promotion: The Effects of Socialization, Specialization, and Gender", *Industrial and Labor Relations Review* 42(1), 77-88.

Cannings, K. and C. Montmarquette (1991), "Managerial Momentum: A Simultaneous Model of the Career Progress of Male and Female Managers", *Industrial and Labor Relations Review* 44(2), 212-228.

Corcoran, M. and G.J. Duncan (1979), "Work History, Labor Force Attachment and Earnings Differences Between Races and Sexes", *Journal of Human Resources* 14 (Winter), 3-20.

Crewe, L. (1991), "New Technologies, Employment Shifts and Gender Divisions within the Textile Industry", *New Technology, Work and Employment* 6(1), 43-53.

Davidson, M.J. and R.J. Burke, eds. (1994), *Women in Management* (London: Paul Chapman Publishing).

Davidson, M.J. and C.L. Cooper (1987), *Women and Information Technology* (Toronto: John Wiley & Sons).

Denton, M. and I.U. Zeytinoğlu (1993), "Perceived Participation in Decision-Making in a University Setting: The Impact of Gender", *Industrial and Labor Relations Review* 46(2), 320-331.

Donato, K.M. (1990), "Programing for Change? The Growing Demand for Women Systems Analysts", in B.F. Reskin and P.A. Roos (eds.), *Job Queues, Gender Queues: Explaining Women's Inroads into Male Occupations* (Philadelphia: Temple University Press), 167-182.

Edvardsson, I.R. (1994), "Skill, Gender and Technical Change in a Nordic Environment: Typesetting in Iceland and Sweden", *New Technology, Work and Employment* 9(1), 30-42.

Gerhart, B.A. and G.T. Milkovich (1989), "Salaries, Salary Growth, and Promotions of Men and Women in a Large Private Firm", in R.T. Michael and H. Hartmann (eds.), *Pay Equity: Empirical Inquiries* (Washington, DC: National Academy Press), 23-43.

Gunderson, M. (1979), "Decomposition of the Male/Female Earnings Differential: Canada 1970", *Canadian Journal of Economics* 12(3), 479-485.

_____ (1992), "Male-Female Wage Differentials and Policy Responses", *Journal of Economic Literature* 27, 46-72.

Hodson, R. and J. Hagan (1988), "Skills and Job Commitment in High Technology Industries in the U.S.", *New Technology, Work and Employment* 3(2), 112-124.

Holmes, R.A. (1976), "Male-Female Earnings Differentials in Canada", *Journal of Human Resources* 11, 109-117.

Jacobs, J.A. (1992), "Women's Entry into Management: Trends in Earnings, Authority, and Values among Salaried Managers", *Administrative Science Quarterly* 37(2), 282-301.

Konrad, A. and K. Cannings (1994), "Of Mommy Tracks and Glass Ceilings: A Case Study of Men's and Women's Careers in Management", *Relations industrielles/Industrial Relations*, 49(2), 303-335.

Krueger, A.B. (1993), "How Computers Have Changed the Wage Structure: Evidence from Microdata, 1984 - 1989", *Quarterly Journal of Economics* 108(1), 33-60.

Liff, S. (1990), "Clerical Workers and Information Technology: Gender Relations and Occupational Change", *New Technology, Work and Employment* 5(1), 44-55.

Long, R.J. (1987), *New Office Information Technology: Human and Managerial Implications* (New York: Croom Helm).

Loury, L.D. (1997), "The Gender Earnings Gap Among College-Educated Workers", *Industrial and Labor Relations Review* 50(4), 580-593.

Malkiel, B. and J. Malkiel (1973), "Male-Female Pay Differentials in Professional Employment", *American Economic Review* 63(4), 693-705.

McMullen, K. (1996), *Skill and Employment Effects of Computer-Based Technology: The Results of Working with Technology, Survey III* (Ottawa: Canadian Policy Research Networks, Inc.).

Milkovich, G.T. and J.W. Boudreau (1994), *Human Resource Management*, 7th ed. (Boston, MA: Irwin).

Mincer, J. and S.W. Polachek (1974), "Family Investments in Human Capital: Earnings of Women", *Journal of Political Economy* 82(2), part II (March-April), S76-S108.

Morissette, R. (1995), "Why Has Inequality in Weekly Earnings Increased in Canada?", Research Paper No. 80 (Ottawa: Analytical Studies Branch, Statistics Canada).

Nadeau, S., W.D. Walsh and C.E. Wetton (1993), "Gender Wage Discrimination: Methodological Issues and Empirical Results for a Canadian Public Sector Employer", *Applied Economics* 25, 227-241.

Nakamura, A. and M. Nakamura (1985), "Dynamic Models of the Labor Force Behavior of Married Women which can be Estimated Using Limited Amounts of Past Information", *Journal of Econometrics* 27, 273-298.

Oaxaca, R. (1973), "Male-Female Wage Differentials in Urban Labor Markets", *International Economic Review* 14(3), 693-709.

OECD (1997), *OECD Economic Outlook*, No. 62 (Paris: Organisation for Economic Cooperation and Development).

Picot, G. (1997), "What is Happening to Earnings Inequality in Canada in the 1990s?" *Canadian Business Economics* 6(1), 65-83.

Robb, R.E. (1978), "Earnings Differentials Between Males and Females in Ontario, 1971", *Canadian Journal of Economics* 11(2), 350-359.

Roos, P.A. (1990), "Hot-Metal to Electronic Composition: Gender, Technology, and Social Change", in B.F. Reskin and P.A. Roos (eds.), *Job Queues, Gender Queues: Explaining Women's Inroads into Male Occupations* (Philadelphia: Temple University Press), 275-298.

Shapiro, D.M. and M. Stelcner (1987), "The Persistence of the Male-Female Earnings Gap in Canada, 1970-1980: The Impact of Equal Pay Laws and

Language Policies", *Canadian Public Policy/Analyse de Politiques* 13(4), 462-476.

Solberg, E. and T. Laughlin (1995), "The Gender Pay Gap, Fringe Benefits, and Occupational Crowding", *Industrial and Labor Relations Review* 48(4), 692-708.

Truman, C. and J. Keating (1988), "Technology, Markets, and the Design of Women's Jobs — The Case of the Clothing Industry", *New Technology, Work and Employment* 3(1), 21-29.

Vinnicombe, S. and N.L. Colwill, eds. (1995), *Women in Management* (London: Prentice-Hall).

Walsh, J. (1991), "Restructuring, Productivity and Workplace Relations: Evidence from the Textile Industry", *New Technology, Work and Employment* 6(2), 124-137.

Weber, C.L. and A. Phillip (1995), *The Supply and Demand of Computer Professionals in Canada: The Results of a National Delphi Study* (Kingston: IRC Press, Queen's University).

The Self-Sufficiency Project: What Have We Learned So Far?

John Greenwood

Introduction

All attempts to reform welfare face a troubling dilemma — how to encourage work and independence while simultaneously alleviating poverty. Programs that transfer income to poor people in order to reduce poverty typically reduce the incentive for recipients to seek and accept employment, particularly if their potential earnings are low.[1] This problem is reflected in the real-life experiences of welfare-dependent families. Because many of those receiving income assistance have low levels of education or limited work experience, they often face starting wages that will pay them less than the amount they receive in welfare benefits. Therefore, they face a stark choice. They can continue their dependence on welfare or they can accept a lower

---

[1]For a general discussion of the incentive effects of transfer systems, see Barth and Greenberg (1971); Kesselman (1969 and 1973); and Masters and Garfinkel (1977). For an analysis of the empirical evidence on two specific forms of income transfer, see Hum and Simpson (1991) and Robins (1985) on negative income tax experiments in Canada and the United States, respectively, and Eissa and Liebman (1996) and Scholz (1996) on the Earned Income Tax Credit in the United States.

income in the work world, at least until their earnings rise with increasing experience and skills.[2] This is the classic "welfare trap".

A related dilemma for policymakers is the conflict in values that a welfare system creates. Income assistance programs typically pay people when they do not work (based historically on the notion that welfare was paid to people who were unable to work) and they apply a financial penalty to the benefits of those who go to work. If program designers were setting out to create a welfare system today, they would probably try to build a system that provided greater rewards for work rather than non-work; such an approach would be more in line with current societal values. Changes in values and attitudes, particularly with respect to who is expected to work, explain much of the current interest in welfare reform initiatives that aim to promote work effort among welfare recipients.[3]

The Self-Sufficiency Project (SSP) was designed to test a program that would attempt to deal with the poverty-dependency trade-off head-on. It was inspired by the question: What would happen if welfare recipients could be assured of increasing their incomes significantly and immediately if they left income assistance for work; in other words, if work really paid more than welfare? To find the answer, SSP is operating a program that supplements the earnings of selected long-term, single-parent income assistance recipients in New Brunswick and British Columbia.

----

[2]For a discussion of the difficulties that single parents experience as income assistance recipients and in their efforts to make the transition from welfare to work, see Bancroft and Vernon (1995).

[3]For example, in the United States, the Personal Responsibility and Work Opportunity Reconciliation Act of 1996 changed the ways in which federal funds can be used within state welfare programs, providing greater flexibility to states in the allocation of resources to employment-related services and imposing a requirement that a large proportion of the welfare caseload participate in work or work-related activities. The "New Deal" agenda introduced by the Labour government in Great Britain includes a Working Family Tax Credit, which will substantially expand the Family Credit program, in an attempt to increase labour force participation by providing in-work benefits to low-income families. Examples of Canadian initiatives include Quebec's Programme d'aide aux parents pour leur revenus de travail (APPORT), Saskatchewan's Earnings Supplement Program, Ontario Works, and the Youth Works and Welfare to Work components of BC Benefits.

The SSP Program Model

The three key elements of the program being tested by SSP are:

- a substantial financial incentive for work relative to non-work;
- a relatively low tax-back rate for those who experience increases in earnings while receiving a supplement (at least relatively low compared to the provisions for disregarding income in the calculation of welfare payments);[4] and
- a full-time work requirement that prevents most people from reducing their work effort in response to the program.

SSP offers monthly cash payments to single parents who have been receiving income assistance for at least a year, on condition that, within one year of being selected for the program, they leave welfare for full-time work of 30 or more hours a week.[5] These earnings supplements are paid directly to the participants on top of their earnings from employment for up to three years, so long as they continue to work full-time and remain off income assistance.[6]

---

[4]Most welfare programs allow recipients to earn a small amount of income without affecting their benefits; the income assistance amount is then reduced on a dollar-for-dollar basis for all earnings in excess of the "disregarded" amount. In New Brunswick, the disregard for single parents is $200 a month. In British Columbia, until April 1996, the disregard was also $200 a month. In addition, single parents in British Columbia were eligible for an "enhanced disregard" equal to 25% of any earnings in excess of $200 a month, which could be claimed for up to 12 out of every 36 months. The basic $200 disregard is no longer available in British Columbia and a 12-month lifetime limit has been placed on the use of the 25% disregard.

[5]Participants are allowed to meet the full-time work requirement by working at more than one job. In addition, work hours are averaged over two-week periods; so a participant who works fewer than 30 hours in one week can compensate by working more than 30 hours in the second week and qualify for full supplementation for both weeks.

[6]For a detailed description of SSP's program model, see Mijanovich and Long (1995).

The supplement is calculated to make up half the difference between what a participant actually earns and an earnings reference level — initially set at $30,000 in New Brunswick and $37,000 in British Columbia.[7] Under this formula, for example, a woman in New Brunswick who worked 35 hours a week at $6 an hour would receive annual earnings of $10,920 and supplement payments of $9,540. Therefore, her total income would be $20,460, almost double what she would receive from working alone. Her supplemented earnings will also be much higher than her welfare entitlement, and the effective marginal tax-back rate of 50% ensures that there is an incentive for her to seek earnings gains during the period of supplement eligibility.

While collecting the earnings supplement, the eligible single parent receives an immediate payoff from work; indeed, in most cases, a recipient's total income will be about twice what she would receive from working or from welfare alone. And, if her earnings increase, she may experience the longer-term benefit of becoming self-sufficient after the three-year supplement period ends.

SSP's earnings supplement program was originally conceived by Human Resources Development Canada (HRDC) as an innovative and potentially fruitful approach to the dual problems of welfare dependency and poverty. However, it is an untested approach; too little is known about how financial incentives affect behaviour to make public policy in this area with any confidence. Moreover, because financial supplements are expensive, it is important to determine, before such a program is implemented on a broad scale, whether temporary earnings supplementation will actually succeed in reducing welfare dependency and increasing financial well-being. Therefore, HRDC decided that the most prudent course of action would be to begin with a demonstration project in order to test the program model and to generate the information necessary to make informed policy decisions.

Putting a large-scale national demonstration in place meant creating a fully operational program that would seek to answer the identified policy questions, contacting a hard-to-reach population that is often distrustful of governments, and explaining a somewhat abstract concept — a formula-based financial incentive — in a manner that overcame scepticism and

---

[7]There have been periodic increases in these reference levels since the project began at the end of 1992 in order to reflect changes that have taken place in average earnings and in income assistance entitlements. The 1998 levels were set at $32,050 in New Brunswick and $37,625 in British Columbia.

provided those who were eligible for supplementation with sufficient information to make an informed choice.

SSP is managed by the Social Research and Demonstration Corporation (SRDC), a Canadian non-profit social policy research organization, but the project is a collaborative effort involving people and organizations with policy, research, data management and operational experience. In addition to HRDC and SRDC, the SSP team includes the provincial income assistance departments in the two provinces where the project is operating — Human Resources Development-New Brunswick and the British Columbia Ministry of Human Resources; Family Services, Saint John and Bernard C. Vinge and Associates, a non-profit and a for-profit service provider, respectively, to staff the project offices; Statistics Canada to collect survey data and administrative records and to create the research files; the Halifax office of SHL Systemhouse Ltd., to develop and maintain the program's computerized management information and supplement payment systems; and the Manpower Demonstration Research Corporation and several academic researchers to assist in the project design and to conduct implementation, impact and benefit-cost research.

SSP is using a random assignment evaluation design to estimate program impacts. Between November 1992 and March 1995, 5,729 people were enrolled in SSP's main study sample.[8] These potential participants were randomly selected from among all income assistance recipients in the study sites who were single parents and who had been receiving IA benefits for at least a year. Of those who agreed to participate in the study and who signed an informed consent and data release form, half were assigned to a program group that was eligible to receive an earnings supplement and half were assigned to a control group.

SSP is collecting information on the employment, welfare receipt and other activities of both program and control group members. Data are being

---

[8]SSP actually comprises three experiments. In addition to the main study discussed here, a separate sample of new applicants for income assistance in British Columbia was enrolled to provide a basis for a study of entry effects, and a sample of long-term welfare recipients in New Brunswick was enrolled in a separate "SSP Plus" program group that was eligible to receive SSP's financial incentive in combination with a package of employment-related services. The results of the entry effects study are reported in Card, Robins and Lin (1997) and Berlin et al. (1998). The first estimates of program impacts on the new applicant group and the SSP Plus group will be published later in 1999.

collected by means of surveys administered at baseline and at 18, 36 and 54 months after random assignment, as well as through the use of administrative records data dealing with the receipt of income assistance and Employment Insurance benefits and income reported to Revenue Canada-Taxation.[9]

This paper summarizes some of the key early findings from the Self-Sufficiency Project.[10] Evidence is presented on SSP's impacts during the first 18 months after random assignment.[11] It is important to remember, however, that participants who were assigned to the program group were allowed up to 12 months to find a job and leave welfare; they can then receive supplement payments for up to three years after qualifying. Therefore, this is an early point at which to assess the effects of the program. The long-term benefits and costs are still unknown. Nevertheless, because of the one-year take-up window, it is possible at this point to assess how effective the SSP offer was in getting people to begin full-time work who otherwise would not have done so. It is also possible to get an early look at SSP's in-program impacts on public transfer payments, incomes, poverty and living conditions.

Major Findings of the Self-Sufficiency Project

To begin, the Self-Sufficiency Project has been successfully implemented. Participation in the project was voluntary but approximately 90% of those who were contacted agreed to take part and 98% of those assigned to the program group received an orientation to SSP. Based on a survey of 700 program group members, the vast majority appeared to understand the nature of the supplement offer and thought they would be financially better off by receiving the supplement. Within the one-year take-up period, 35% of

---

[9]The results presented here are based on 5,288 people. The analysis excludes 40 people who were found, subsequent to random assignment, not to meet the basic eligibility requirements, three participants who formally withdrew from the study, and 398 people from whom 18-month follow-up data could not be obtained.

[10]The complete results can be found in Lin *et al.* (1998).

[11]Preliminary estimates of impacts, based on the roughly one-third of the sample who enrolled during the first year of the project, were previously reported in Card and Robins (1996).

program group members qualified for the supplement by beginning full-time work, leaving income assistance and receiving at least one supplement payment. A significant minority of supplement takers did not maintain continuous full-time employment and thus became temporarily ineligible for supplement payments.[12] In any given month, therefore, the percentage of the program group that was actually receiving an earnings supplement was lower than the take-up rate (in fact, it never exceeded 25%).

About two-thirds of the program group (65%) did not take up the supplement offer, although the majority reported that they thought they would be much better off financially if they went to work full-time with a supplement. The most commonly cited reason (either the main reason or one of the reasons) for not taking advantage of the supplement was the inability to find a job or to get enough hours of work; this was the reason given by 43% of non-takers. The next most frequently cited reasons were personal or family responsibilities (25%) and health problems or disabilities (19%).

SSP's most significant impact on labour market outcomes is that it *doubled* the number of sample members working full-time. As shown in Figure 1, the impact on the full-time employment rate rose steadily during the 12 months following random assignment. During the fifth and sixth quarters after random assignment, which is expected to be the period of maximum impact, SSP had a 15-percentage-point impact on the full-time employment rate (see Table 1).[13] Among program group members, 29.3% were working 30 hours per week or more, compared with 14% of the control group. It

---

[12]As long as participants initiated supplement payments within the 12-month period available to them to do so, they were eligible to receive supplements anytime during the next 36 months that they were working full-time. They could stop and restart employment (and supplement receipt) any number of times within this three-year period.

[13]After the first year, no further program group members can take up the supplement, and some of those who did so previously will lose or leave their employment, while the employment rate of the control group can be expected to rise gradually over time. Therefore a portion of SSP's impact — that associated with speeding up the employment of income assistance recipients who would have gone to work eventually — will dissipate over time.

The Self-Sufficiency Project: What Have We Learned So Far?   *179*

Figure 1: Monthly Full-Time Employment Rates: Program and Control Groups

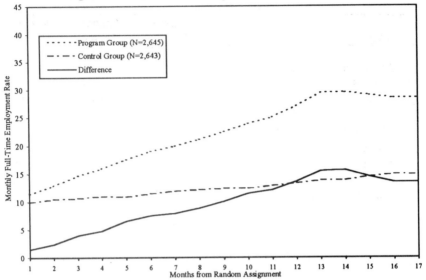

Source: Calculations from 18-month follow-up survey data.

appears that this impact was achieved primarily by inducing people to work full-time who otherwise would not have worked at all.[14]

SSP's impact on full-time employment is smaller than the take-up rate because some of the people receiving the supplement would have gone to work full-time anyway. The difference between the take-up rate and the impact on full-time employment is an estimate of the fraction of sample members who receive "windfall" benefits.[15] For example, in the fifth quarter

---

[14]In the fifth quarter after random assignment, the impact on the percentage of people who did any work at all was 13 percentage points (the overall employment rates of the program and control groups were 41% and 28%, respectively), while the part-time employment rate in the program group was 3.2 percentage points lower than that in the control group (11.7% versus 13.9%).

[15]Windfalls refer to receipt of incentives by people who qualified without actually changing their behaviour. As discussed by Greenberg et al. (1995), any program that offers financial incentives to encourage work effort will make some payments to people who would have gone to work anyway.

John Greenwood

Table 1: SSP Impacts on Employment and Income Assistance Receipt, Quarters 5 and 6 after Random Assignment

Outcome	Program Group	Control Group	Difference (Impact)
Full-time employment rate[a]			
Quarter 5	29.3%	14.0%	15.2 ***
Quarter 6	28.5	14.8	13.7 ***
Part-time employment rate[b]			
Quarter 5	11.7	13.9	-2.2 **
Quarter 6	12.1	15.2	-3.2 ***
Overall employment rate			
Quarter 5	41.0	28.0	13.0 ***
Quarter 6	40.6	30.0	10.6 ***
Percentage receiving Income Assistance			
Quarter 5	70.2	83.2	-13.0 ***
Quarter 6	66.5	80.4	-13.9 ***

Notes: All estimates for quarter 5 are calculated by averaging the estimates for months 13, 14 and 15.

Employment rates for quarter 6 are calculated by averaging the estimates for months 16 and 17.

Percentages receiving Income Assistance in quarter 6 are calculated by averaging the estimates for months 16, 17 and 18.

A two-tailed t-test was applied to differences between the outcomes for the program and control groups. Statistical significance levels are indicated as: * = 10%, ** = 5%; *** = 1%.

Rounding may cause slight discrepancies in sums and differences.

[a] "Full-time employment" is defined as working 30 hours per week in at least one week during the month.

[b] "Part-time employment" is defined as having some employment but no full-time employment during the month.

after random assignment, approximately 40% of the people receiving the supplement could be characterized as windfall recipients. While not directly increasing their employment in response to SSP's supplement offer, these windfall recipients nevertheless experience significant increases in their income and are thus less likely to be poor.

SSP's impact on employment is reflected in increased earnings as well. During the fifth and sixth quarters after random assignment, SSP raised program group members' average earnings (excluding the supplement) by $124 per month and raised their average incomes (including the supplements but net of foregone income assistance payments and the additional income tax paid) by approximately $179 per month. Therefore, each dollar increase in net transfer payments led to more than two dollars in increased earnings and more than three dollars in additional income for sample members. This finding is in sharp contrast to many financial incentive programs that yield less than a one-dollar increase in income for every dollar of program expenditures. Here, there is a three-to-one increase, and most of the extra income results from the increased work effort of the participants.

During the same period, SSP also reduced income assistance receipt among program group members as shown in Figure 2. The percentage who were receiving income assistance was decreased by almost 14 percentage points and SSP reduced income assistance payments by $103 per month per program group member. From a government budget perspective, this reduction in income assistance payments partially offsets the cost of the

Figure 2: Percentage Receiving Income Assistance: Program and Control Groups

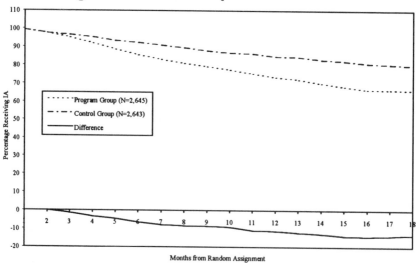

Months from Random Assignment

Source: Calculations from Income Assistance administrative records.

John Greenwood

supplement payments. The net cost of the supplement payments, after subtracting the reduction in income assistance payments and the additional tax revenue generated, was $55 per month per program group member.

The impacts on full-time employment were broad-based, affecting sample members with varying life situations and histories. Table 2 shows estimated impacts for a number of subgroups defined by the program environment, family structure, family background, job readiness and barriers to employment. For each subgroup examined, the estimated impact on the full-time employment rate in quarter 5 was statistically significant and was at least nine percentage points. The impacts tended to be larger, however, for people who were more job-ready and for those who faced fewer barriers to employment. In addition, the impacts estimated for British Columbia and New Brunswick were very similar, despite differences in local labour market conditions, in the characteristics of sample members, and in the benefit levels provided by income assistance and SSP in the two provinces.[16] Thus, SSP was able to produce substantial impacts on full-time employment in more than one provincial setting and the similarity of the impacts in the two provinces may make the findings more generalizable to the rest of Canada.

The additional employment generated by SSP appears to be clustered at wage rates between minimum wage and $2 per hour above (see Table 3). This is not surprising since the people who are only able to find low-wage jobs are those who are least likely to leave welfare for work in the absence of an earnings supplement. This means, however, that in order for work to remain more attractive than welfare after the three-year supplement period ends, supplement takers will have to experience some increases in wage rates, progression in hours of work, an increased preference for work over welfare, or other changes that make it more feasible for them to continue working.

Among sample members who already had a high school diploma or equivalent, SSP had no discernible effects on education and training. Among those who did not have this credential, SSP led to a reduction of three percentage points in the percentage who were taking courses toward a high school credential during the first 18 months after random assignment. However, at this point, SSP has not had any effect on the *attainment* of the credential.

---

[16]The estimated impacts on full-time employment in the fifth quarter after random assignment were 15.3% in New Brunswick and 15.2% in British Columbia.

Table 2: SSP Impacts on Full-Time Employment, by Subgroup, Quarter 5

| | Average Monthly Full-Time Employment Rate | | |
| | Program | Control | Difference |
Status at Baseline	Group	Group	(Impact)
Education and training			
Has high school diploma or equivalent			
Yes	35.9 %	18.8 %	17.1 ***
No	23.6	10.1	13.5 ***
Enrolled in education/training at random assignment			
Yes	36.6	16.4	20.2 ***
No	28.1	13.7	14.4 ***
Employment status at random assignment			
Full-time	64.2	50.8	13.4 ***
Part-time	46.9	23.7	23.2 ***
Not employed, looking for work	32.0	15.1	16.9 ***
Neither employed nor looking for work	20.5	7.0	13.5 ***
Availability of child care			
If got job, could find trustworthy care			
Yes	31.8	14.6	17.2 ***
No	21.9	8.5	13.4 ***
No child care required	28.1	17.6	10.4 ***
Work limitations			
Reported physical condition that limited activity			
Yes	21.3	9.2	12.1 ***
No	31.9	15.7	16.2 ***
Working at random assignment	52.5	33.3	19.2 ***
Not working at random assignment and:			
Couldn't work due to illness/disability	14.7	5.4	9.3 ***
Illness/disability not a reason for not working	25.8	10.2	15.6 ***

Notes: The subgroups are defined according to characteristics at random assignment. Persons answering "don't know" to a particular question that contributed to defining a subgroup are excluded from the analysis of that subgroup.

Average monthly full-time employment rate in quarter 5 is average of the percentages employed full-time in each of months 13-15. "Full-time employment" is defined as working 30 hours or more per week in at least one week during the month.

A two-tailed t-test was applied to differences between the outcomes for the program and control groups. Statistical significance levels are indicated as: * = 10%; ** = 5%; *** = 1%.

Rounding may cause slight discrepancies in sums and differences.

John Greenwood

Table 3: SSP Impacts on the Distribution of Wages in Month 15

Outcome	Program Group	Control Group	Difference (Impact)	Standard Error
Hourly wage rate (% in each category)				
Not working	59.2	71.3	-12.1 ***	(1.3)
Wage unreported[a]	2.0	2.7	-0.7 *	(0.4)
Less than minimum wage[b]	3.2	3.3	-0.2	(0.5)
Minimum to $0.99 above minimum	15.7	6.7	8.9 ***	(0.9)
$1.00 - $1.99 above minimum	8.3	4.8	3.5 ***	(0.7)
$2.00 - $2.99 above minimum	3.5	2.6	0.9 *	(0.5)
$3.00 or more above minimum	8.2	8.6	-0.3	(0.8)
Sample size (total = 5,288)	2,645	2,643		

Notes: A two-tailed t-test was applied to differences between the outcomes for the program and control groups. Statistical significance levels are indicated as: * = 10%; ** = 5%; *** = 1%.
Rounding may cause slight discrepancies in sums and differences.
[a] Sample members in this category were employed during the month but did not report enough information about earnings for the outcome in question to be calculated.
[b] In British Columbia, the minimum wage was $5.50 per hour from the beginning of the random assignment period in November 1992 until April 1993, when it rose to $6.00. In March 1995, it was increased to $6.50 and, in October 1995, it increased again to $7.00 per hour. In New Brunswick the minimum wage was $5.00 per hour from 1992 to 1995. In January 1996, it increased to $5.25 and, in July 1996, it rose again to $5.50.

Source: Calculations from 18-month follow-up survey data.

By raising both the earnings and transfer incomes of program group members, SSP is having a substantial anti-poverty effect during the period of supplement receipt. During the fifth and sixth quarters after random assignment, SSP increased the average income of program group members by $234 per month ($179 per month after taxes). As seen in Table 4, the average family income of program group members was $199 higher at the time of the 18-month follow-up survey and this reduced the fraction with family incomes below Statistics Canada's low-income threshold by 12.4 percentage points, and also reduced the fraction in "extreme poverty" (incomes less than half the low-income threshold) by three percentage points.

A sizable fraction of SSP-generated income gains were spent on basic needs (food, children's clothing and housing) although different groups of families allocated the resources differently. Overall, 19% of the program

Table 4: SSP Impacts on Monthly Income, Poverty, and Expenditures and on Assets at 18-Month Follow-Up Interview

Outcome	Program Group	Control Group	Difference (Impact)
Family income per month	$1,486	$1,286	199 ***
Percentage with low incomes [b]			
Below low-income cut-off	77.5 %	89.8 %	-12.2 ***
Below 50% of low-income cut-off	18.3	21.6	-3.3 ***
Monthly expenditures on			
Food	$413	$389	25 ***
Children's clothing	48	44	4 ***
Rent	470	461	9
Used food bank (last 3 months)	19.1 %	21.1 %	-2.0 *
Asset holdings			
Savings account	50.8 %	46.5 %	4.4 ***
Chequing account	62.4	62.1	0.3
Registered Retirement Savings Plan	2.4	1.2	1.2 ***
Car	26.2	24.6	1.6

Notes: Sample sizes vary for individual measures because of missing values.

A two-tailed t-test was applied to differences between the outcomes for the program and control groups. Statistical significance levels are indicated as: * = 10%; ** = 5%; *** = 1%.

Rounding may cause slight discrepancies in sums and differences.

[a] Family income includes earnings, Income Assistance and SSP payments, and all other sources of individual cash income (tax credits, other transfers, etc.), as well as earnings of other family members.

[b] Calculated by comparing annualized family income with the low-income cut-off defined by Statistics Canada for the sample member's location and family size.

group's additional gross income was spent on food, children's clothing and housing, and the fraction who used food banks was reduced by two percentage points. Families in New Brunswick with more than one child (the most disadvantaged group in the sample) spent 23% of SSP-generated gross income gains on food alone. This rise in food expenditures was accompanied by a ten percentage point drop in the fraction who used food banks and a five-percentage point drop in the fraction who reported not being able to afford needed groceries or food.

SSP also increased program group members' likelihood of holding savings accounts and registered retirement savings plans, suggesting that program group families saved some fraction of the extra income generated by the program.

Policy Implications and Conclusions

These early SSP findings point to several important lessons for policy-makers interested in using financial incentives to encourage welfare recipients to go to work and eventually to achieve economic self-sufficiency.

First, and most important, the results so far show that it is possible to use financial incentives to satisfy three often conflicting goals of welfare reform — namely, to increase work effort, to reduce poverty and to reduce welfare dependence. The early findings from SSP indicate that in the first year and a half of the program, the full-time employment rate is doubled, family income is increased by almost 20%, the gap between the low-income cut-off and family income is reduced by 17%, and dependence on welfare is reduced by 16%. Every additional dollar in transfer expenditures associated with SSP leads to more than three dollars of extra family income, generating a sizable anti-poverty effect. These findings must be tempered by the fact that the SSP supplement is only available for three years, and that these impacts might not be present when the supplement is no longer available. For the results to continue to hold, program participants must experience significant wage and hours progression so that they can become permanently self-sufficient. Of course, some reductions in the impacts are expected as control families follow the natural course of leaving welfare.

Financial incentives can improve living conditions. The early findings indicate that the increased income from SSP is being partially used to increase expenditures on three basic necessities of life: food, clothing and housing. In addition, families are saving some of the additional income through increased contributions to retirement plans and through increased holdings in savings accounts. By improving current and future living conditions, SSP is enhancing the ability of families to eventually become economically self-sufficient.

A financial incentive program can generate broad-based effects. Although only about a third of the recipients offered SSP actually took it up, among those who did, the impacts were broad-based. Substantial impacts were found for virtually every subgroup examined. This suggests that a well-designed financial incentive program can assist a wide spectrum of the welfare population.

Financial incentives are not a quick fix. In the short-run, families who took up the supplement received fairly low wages, most within two dollars of the minimum wage. In addition, some people chose to forego taking courses towards completing high school in order to take advantage of the time-limited supplement offer (although there has so far been no significant impact on the high school completion rate). Finally, because many families are receiving windfall benefits from SSP, total public expenditures are increased. Nonetheless, these short-run costs might be offset by greater benefits in the long-run (after the supplement ends) if families can maintain employment, remain independent of welfare, and resume taking courses towards completion of the high school credential.

In conclusion, program group members have responded to the financial incentives offered by SSP in the manner expected, and the early results are encouraging. If these results hold up over time, they will provide a strong basis for more extensive adoption of strategies designed to "make work pay". Work-based welfare reform is based on two key assumptions. First, there are enough jobs to accommodate those who want to work. Second, people can support themselves and their families by working in those jobs. The declining real wages received by members of some groups (especially low-skilled young males) provides a direct challenge to the second assumption. Furthermore, for women seeking to combine care-giving responsibilities with labour market participation, the problem is even greater. The costs associated with going to work, particularly child-care costs, can be quite high. Earnings must be high enough to cover these costs in order for work to be financially worthwhile. Yet women seeking to leave welfare for work typically find their choices limited to low-wage jobs, at least until they have acquired more experience. Programs to supplement low earnings may be the most effective, and perhaps the only, way to make it financially feasible for many women with children to make the transition from welfare to work.

The SSP program impacts observed during the first 18 months are probably the peak impacts, however. To the extent that the early impacts represent an acceleration of what would have occurred anyway, control group members will begin to "catch up" with program group members, and the impacts will abate somewhat. The extent of the "catch up" will depend on the rate of entry into employment among control group members and how SSP affects the duration and stability of employment among program group members. If SSP reduces the rate of job turnover among program members, then the abatement of impacts may be minimal.

Future reports on this project will analyze SSP's impacts after 36 months and after 54 months. After 36 months, the supplement will be nearing an end for many program group members and many will have begun to adjust to a world without the supplement. After 54 months, everyone will have passed the end of their supplement eligibility period (by at least six months and, in some cases, by as much as 18 months). The estimated impacts at this time will provide the "acid test" for SSP. If SSP is successful in leading to wage and hours progression, or if it permanently changes attitudes towards work, then the impacts of SSP might well extend beyond the three-year supplement period. Future reports will address these longer-term issues and will also include a comprehensive benefit-cost analysis of the program.

References

Bancroft, W. and S. Vernon (1995), *The Struggle for Self-Sufficiency: Participants in the Self-Sufficiency Project Talk About Work, Welfare and Their Futures* (Vancouver: Social Research and Demonstration Corporation).

Barth, M. and D. Greenberg (1971), "Incentive Effects of Some Pure and Mixed Transfer Systems", *Journal of Human Resources* 6 (Spring), 149-170.

Berlin, G., W. Bancroft, D. Card, W. Lin and P. Robins (1998), *Do Work Incentives Have Unintended Consequences? Measuring "Entry Effects" in the Self-Sufficiency Project* (Ottawa: Social Research and Demonstration Corporation).

Card, D. and P. Robins (1996), *Do Financial Incentives Encourage Welfare Recipients to Work? Initial 18-Month Findings from the Self-Sufficiency Project* (Vancouver: Social Research and Demonstration Corporation).

Card, D., P. Robins and W. Lin (1997), "How Important are 'Entry Effects' in Financial Incentive Programs for Welfare Recipients? Experimental Evidence from the Self-Sufficiency Project", SRDC Working Paper (Ottawa: Social Research and Demonstration Corporation).

Eissa, N. and J. Liebman (1996), "Labor Supply Response to the Earned Income Tax Credit", *The Quarterly Review of Economics* (May), 605-637.

Greenberg, D., C. Michalopoulos, P. Robins and R. Wood (1995), "Making Work Pay for Welfare Recipients", *Contemporary Economic Policy* 13(3), 39-52.

Hum, D. and W. Simpson (1991), *Income Maintenance, Work Effort and the Canadian Experiment* (Ottawa: Economic Council of Canada).

Kesselman, J. (1969), "Labor-Supply Effects of Income, Income-Work, and Wage Subsidies", *Journal of Human Resources* 4 (Summer), 111-199.

_____ (1973), "Incentive Effects of Transfer Systems Once Again", *Journal of Human Resources* 8 (Winter), 119-129.

Lin, W., P. Robins, D. Card, K. Harknett and S. Lui-Gurr (1998), *When Financial Incentives Encourage Work: Complete 18-Month Findings from the Self-Sufficiency Project* (Ottawa: Social Research and Demonstration Corporation).

Masters, S. and I. Garfinkel (1977), *Estimating the Labor Supply Effects of Income-Maintenance Alternatives* (New York: Academic Press).

Mijanovich, T. and D. Long (1995), *Creating an Alternative to Welfare: First-Year Findings on the Implementation, Welfare Impacts and Costs of the Self-Sufficiency Project* (Vancouver: Social Research and Demonstration Corporation).

Robins, P. (1985), "A Comparison of Labor Supply Findings from the Four Negative Income Tax Experiments", *Journal of Human Resources* 20, 567-582.

Scholz, J. (1996), "In-Work Benefit in the United States: The Earned Income Tax Credit", *The Economic Journal* 106 (January), 156-169.

The Dynamics of Welfare Participation in Quebec

Jean-Yves Duclos, Bernard Fortin, Guy Lacroix
and Hélène Roberge

Introduction

The main goal of provincial welfare programs in Canada is to guarantee a
basic minimum income for poor individuals and households. Up until
recently, however, some worrying trends in the number of welfare dependent
households and in the level of program spending have emerged. In every
province there has been a dramatic increase in welfare caseloads and in
program expenditures. In Quebec, for instance, between 1980 and 1993,
disbursements rose from $1.860 billion to $3.146 billion (1991 dollars), an

This research was supported by Health and Welfare Canada and by the
Ministère de la solidarité sociale of the Government of Quebec. We are grateful
to Pierre Lanctôt, Jean-Paul Boudraux, Jean St-Gelais, Denis Thiboutot and
Gérald Tremblay for their precious help in accessing and processing the data, and
to Ghyslaine Morin, Suzanne Lévesque, Serge Hamel and Marie-Renée Roy for
their useful comments and advice. We finally wish to thank Nicolas Beaulieu,
Claude Bilodeau, Éric Couture, Patrick Déry, Éric Simard, Christine Soucy and
Jean-François Thibeault for their excellent research assistance. Remaining errors
are ours alone.

increase of nearly 60%. Over the same period, the number of households on assistance grew from 285,174 to 450,675, an increase of 58%.

Not surprisingly, this growth in the costs and in the number of claimants has led most provincial governments to consider reforming their welfare programs. Already, Ontario, British Columbia and Alberta have introduced significant changes; Quebec is also envisaging a major overhaul of its social assistance program, which was already revised in 1989. Despite this political interest in reforms, very few studies have examined the dynamics of participation in welfare in Canada.[1] Evidence on the dynamics of welfare participation is needed particularly for Quebec which, up until 1990, had caseloads higher than that of any other province (including Ontario, which has a population almost 50% larger) and where the per capita welfare spending of $400 was, by 1992, by far the largest in Canada (see *Canada Assistance Plan: Annual Report 1992-93*). We have little or no information, for example, on the flow of beneficiaries into and out of welfare in Quebec, on households likely to experience long or frequent welfare spells, on the average duration of welfare spells, or on the incidence of welfare re-entries. Some claim that lengthy spells on welfare (i.e., defined by the number of consecutive months on welfare) create a dynamic dependence which has the effect of reducing the recipients' chances of exit. Is this true? Moreover, very little is known about the impact of the major reform that occurred in Quebec in 1989.

A deeper knowledge of the dynamics of participation in these programs is, of course, an essential element of a sound understanding of the characteristics and of the effects of the programs, and of any discussion leading to an eventual reform of the system. This paper sheds a little light on some aspects of these important issues by providing a descriptive examination of welfare participation in Quebec. In particular, it presents an analysis of welfare exit and re-entry for different categories of households. Exit rates measure the probability that a household of a particular type will leave assistance in a specific interval (e.g., during the sixth month on assistance),

---

[1]Yet, see Barrett and Cragg (1998). Lacroix (1997) compares the Canadian longitudinal evidence on welfare participation available for Quebec and for British Columbia. Cross-sectional research on the determinants of welfare participation in Canada includes Allen (1993); Charette and Meng (1994); and Dooley (1994). For the U.S. evidence, see Bane and Ellwood (1994) and Moffitt (1992) and, for a comparison of the Canadian and American systems of assistance, Blank and Hanratty (1993).

given that it has remained on welfare until then. Similarly, re-entry rates measure the risk that a household (which has already been in receipt of benefits) returns to welfare during a specific time interval, given that it has remained off social assistance until then. Furthermore, we characterize the average duration of spells on and off welfare for different categories of households. We also derive the distributions of both the starting and the ongoing spells at a given point in time. Finally, this paper examines the overall rate of dependence on social assistance (i.e., the expected proportion of time spent on social assistance) after a household has received it once. This overall rate combines our estimates of both entry and exit rates.

Among other things, the paper thus seeks to answer the following questions:

1. How can one characterize the dynamics of participation in social assistance? For example, do exit rates tend to diminish with the length of welfare spells? Conversely, how do re-entry rates tend to vary with the length of time spent off welfare?
2. Do these dynamics vary with the characteristics of households?
3. Which claimants are at risk for lengthy or frequent welfare spells?
4. What is the relative importance of short and long spells in aggregate welfare budgets?
5. Which socio-economic characteristics seem associated with a high overall rate of welfare dependence?

To answer these questions, we use a representative sample of individuals who had a claim between 1979 and 1993, and made available to us by the Ministère de la solidarité sociale. Our analysis is therefore conditional on participating in welfare at least once over the sample period and does not provide any information on the decision to claim social assistance for the first time over the life cycle. This limitation, also found in Barrett and Cragg (1998), must be kept in mind in what follows. Section two of the paper provides a detailed description of these data. Section three presents the basic statistical tools utilized to characterize the dynamics of participation. These tools are then applied to the data in the fourth section. Finally, the next section provides a synthetic measure of welfare dependence based on the results of the previous section. Our conclusions are in the final section.

Sampling Procedure and Basic Data Description

The data used for this study were drawn from the records of Quebec's Ministère de la solidarité sociale. These files contain information on all individuals who have received welfare benefits at some time between 1979 and 1993.

The size of these administrative records makes a study based on the entire database impractical, so we drew a random sample. Our sampling procedure used the fact that individual files are organized by social insurance numbers (SIN). Thus, each SIN appears exactly once in the files, regardless of the length or frequency of spells. A random draw from a uniform distribution generated a sample of 95,514 cases.[2] It should be noted that for certain individuals the stay on welfare can be considered, for all intents and purposes, permanent. These are individuals whose physical or mental state is such that, for an indeterminate length of time, or even for life, they are unable to work. For obvious reasons, these individuals are excluded from the sample. The final sample is thus comprised of individuals having no handicap or only a minor, intermediate, or temporary physical handicap. Furthermore, they are fit to work.

The sample period runs from January 1979 to December 1993. A window of this size is necessary to analyze lengthy and repeated spells on welfare. The sampling procedure will pick up some spells which were ongoing in January 1979 and some which have not ended in December 1993. In the first case, we have truncation on the left, and in the second, truncation on the right. Truncation on the right does not pose any particular methodological difficulty, but truncation on the left is more delicate. For this reason, spells which were ongoing in January 1979 were followed back as far as January 1975.[3] Spells that were ongoing at that date were simply dropped from the sample. Thus, while the random sample was drawn from welfare records from the period between January 1979 and December 1993, some spells actually begin as early as February 1975.

Tables 1 and 2 present several characteristics of the sample. Since the information is tabulated for the period 1979-93, it provides a portrait of

---

[2]The sampling methodology and sample size are similar to those of Barrett and Cragg (1998).

[3]The administrative records have only been computerized as of 1975.

Table 1: Distribution of Age Groups by Household Type*
(Proportion of the row total)
[Proportion of the column total]

Household	18-24	25-30	31-45	46-55	56+	Total
Couples with children	2003 (0.115) [0.049]	3425 (0.197) [0.228]	8554 (0.492) [0.343]	2297 (0.132) [0.312]	1092 (0.062) [0.150]	17371 (1.00) [0.182]
Childless couples	2079 (0.275) [0.051]	1094 (0.144) [0.073]	1289 (0.170) [0.011]	914 (0.121) [0.124]	2173 (0.287) [0.298]	7549 (1.00) [0.079]
Single-parent families	2297 (0.205) [0.056]	2246 (0.200) [0.149]	5055 (0.452) [0.202]	1115 (0.099) [0.151]	467 (0.041) [0.064]	11180 (1.00) [0.117]
Single persons	34248 (0.579) [0.843]	8223 (0.139) [0.548]	10018 (0.169) [0.402]	3029 (0.051) [0.411]	3545 (0.060) [0.487]	59063 (1.00) [0.620]
Total	40627 (0.426) [1.00]	14988 (0.157) [1.00]	24916 (0.261) [1.00]	7355 (0.077) [1.00]	7277 (0.076) [1.00]	95163 (1.00) [1.00]

Note: * In the case of couples, age applies to the claimant.

welfare recipients over 15 years, and may not be representative of any given year within that period. Table 1 shows a decomposition of households by age groups.[4] The distinction between "couples with children" and "childless couples" is based on the presence or absence of children under the age of 18 in the household during the welfare spell.

---

[4]Household characteristics describe those observed at the beginning of the first spell in the sample period, and pertain to the claimant in the case of couples.

Table 2: Distribution of Age Groups by Level of Education
(Proportion of the row total)
[Proportion of the column total]

Education	18-24	25-30	31-45	46-55	56+	Total
Years of schooling						
< 6	1598	950	3267	2275	3704	11794
	(0.135)	(0.080)	(0.277)	(0.192)	(0.314)	(1.00)
	[0.039]	[0.063]	[0.131]	[0.308]	[0.508]	[0.123]
6 - 11	27144	8583	13978	3986	2992	56683
	(0.478)	(0.151)	(0.246)	(0.070)	(0.052)	(1.00)
	[0.668]	[0.572]	[0.560]	[0.540]	[0.410]	[0.595]
11 - 14	10568	3787	5041	729	426	20551
	(0.514)	(0.184)	(0.245)	(0.035)	(0.020)	(1.00)
	[0.260]	[0.252]	[0.202]	[0.098]	[0.058]	[0.215]
14+	1326	1678	2650	380	168	6202
	(0.213)	(0.270)	(0.427)	(0.061)	(0.027)	(1.00)
	[0.032]	[0.111]	[0.106]	[0.051]	[0.023]	[0.065]
Total	40636	14998	24936	7370	7290	95230
	(0.426)	(0.157)	(0.261)	(0.077)	(0.076)	(1.00)
	[1.00]	[1.00]	[1.00]	[1.00]	[1.00]	[1.00]

Reading row-wise across the rows of the table, we see the distribution of types of households among the different age groups. We notice that nearly half of couples with children are between 31 and 45 years old, and that only 11.5% are between 18 and 24. Childless couples are primarily situated in the 18-24 and the 56+ groups, as one would expect. As to single-parent families, over 45% of them are between 31 and 45 years of age (we do not decompose single-parent families by gender since they are 95% headed by women). Finally, singles are relatively young, since over 58% of them are in the 18-24 age group.

Reading column-wise yields information about the age groups by household type. We observe that single people constitute the largest segment

J.-Y. Duclos, B. Fortin, G. Lacroix and H. Roberge

of all age groups, which is not surprising since they represent 62% of all households in our sample. Similarly, the 18-24 group accounts for over 42% of the entire sample. The second largest group includes individuals 31-45 years old, who make up 26% of the sample.

Table 2 presents the joint distribution of age and education. This data show clearly that younger people tend to be more educated than their elders, reflecting the fact that the level of schooling has generally increased over time. Reading column-wise reveals that individuals in the 18-24, 25-30 and 31-45 age groups are concentrated in the ranges 6-11 and 11-14 years of schooling. Individuals in groups 46-55 and 56+ are concentrated in the <6 and 6-11 years-of-schooling range.

It is also of some interest to examine the level of education of different types of households. Table 3 below shows that the majority of individuals on welfare have between six and eleven years of schooling, i.e., have not completed high school. This is true for all types of households. Couples tend to be more heavily represented in the least educated group (<6 years), but that partly reflects the fact that their average age tends to be higher than that of other types of households.

Methodology

For the purposes of our present study, a welfare *spell* is defined as an uninterrupted sequence of months during which a household receives welfare benefits. Analogously, an off-welfare spell is defined as an uninterrupted sequence of months during which a household does not receive welfare benefits, following at least one month of previous welfare receipt. The principal advantage of using the concept of spells is that the distribution of their durations characterize exhaustively the dynamics of welfare participation.

A useful tool for studying the duration of welfare spells is the *exit rate*. For a household receiving welfare, the exit rate in month t corresponds to the probability that the spell will end in that month, given that it has lasted at least $t-1$ months. It is thus a conditional probability. For some purposes it may be practical to divide the duration of a spell into "windows". Each window encompasses a given number of months. An exit rate can then be interpreted as the probability that a spell ends in window t, given that it was ongoing at the end of window $t-1$. Finally, the unit of observation for estimating exit rates is the spell — a person having more than one spell

Table 3: Distribution of Household Types by Education Level
   (Proportion of the row total)
   [Proportion of the column total]

Education	Childless couples	Couples with children	Single-parent families	Single persons	Total
Years of schooling					
< 6	3296	1848	1339	5335	11818
	(0.279)	(0.156)	(0.184)	(0.451)	(1.00)
	[0.194]	[0.243]	[0.118]	[0.090]	[0.124]
6 - 11	10363	3966	7356	35151	56836
	(0.182)	(0.069)	(0.129)	(0.618)	(1.00)
	[0.612]	[0.523]	[0.652]	[0.594]	[0.598]
11 - 14	2766	1257	2094	14427	20544
	(0.134)	(0.061)	(0.101)	(0.702)	(1.00)
	[0.163]	[0.165]	[0.185]	[0.244]	[0.216]
14+	509	509	492	4225	5735
	(0.088)	(0.088)	(0.085)	(0.736)	(1.00)
	[0.030]	[0.067]	[0.043]	[0.071]	[0.060]
Total	16934	7580	11281	59138	94933
	(0.178)	(0.079)	(0.118)	(0.622)	(1.00)
	[1.00]	[1.00]	[1.00]	[1.00]	[1.00]

between 1979 and 1993 appears as a new observation at the beginning of each new spell.

Derivation of the Exit Rates and of the Associated Distributions

The exit rate $\lambda(t)$ is simply computed as the number of spells ending in the window t, $N(t)$, divided by the number of remaining participants at the

J.-Y. Duclos, B. Fortin, G. Lacroix and H. Roberge

beginning of the window, $R(t)$, whose spells are untruncated at the beginning of, or within, the window. Formally, $\lambda(t) = N(t)/R(t)$. Starting with the exit rate, we can derive two interesting distributions:

1. *The distribution of new spells.* This distribution yields the frequency of the duration of a new spell. Imagine that we were to draw 100 new spells at random. Let $D(t)$ be the proportion of households whose spells last exactly t windows. To obtain the proportion of new spells which will end up lasting t windows, it is sufficient to multiply the proportion of new spells still ongoing after t-1 windows by the conditional probability of leaving during window t. Recursively, we obtain:

$$D(1) = \lambda(1),$$

$$D(2) = \lambda(2)[1 - D(1)],$$

$$\qquad \qquad \vdots \qquad \qquad \qquad \qquad \qquad \qquad (1)$$

$$D(t) = \lambda(t)\left[1 - \sum_{j=1}^{t-1} D(j) \right].$$

The first term on the right-hand side of the last expression is simply the conditional probability of exit in window t. The second term is the probability of remaining ("surviving") after t-1 windows.

2. *The distribution of ongoing spells.* Imagine that we were to draw 100 spells at random out of all those ongoing at a particular point in time. How many of them would eventually have a total spell length of t windows? Note first that the probability of drawing at random, among all ongoing spells, a spell of long duration is higher than it is for one of shorter duration. For example, even if the same proportion of households began one- and ten-year spells at every point in time ($D(1)$ and $D(10)$ would then be equal), the longer spells would necessarily constitute a greater share of a sample of ongoing spells at a particular point in time (a share about ten times greater). Let $F(t)$ be the proportion of ongoing

spells at any instant that will end up having a duration of t windows. This proportion can be estimated in the following manner:

$$F(t) = \frac{tD(t)}{\sum_{j=1}^{\infty} jD(j)} . \qquad (2)$$

These two estimated distributions shall be useful for understanding the dynamics of welfare participation. Off-assistance spells are similarly used to estimate the re-entry rates and the distribution of off-welfare durations.[5]

Unobserved Heterogeneity

An important element of the welfare participation dynamics is the relation between spell duration and exit rates. A negative relation is referred to as "negative duration dependence" in the literature. Many factors may be responsible for negative duration dependence. For example, a lengthening spell on welfare may send a bad signal to potential employers concerning the beneficiary's level of motivation. Similarly, the erosion of human capital may have the effect of diminishing the number of job offers or simply the employment prospects of the welfare recipient. Furthermore, the individual's tastes may change over the course of the spell so as to reduce the rate of exit (e.g., discouragement). Finally, it is possible that a lengthy stay on welfare may modify demographic choices (e.g., marriage rates, fertility, separation) which in turn can decrease the probability of exit.

Decreasing exit rates may also be due to "unobserved heterogeneity" within the welfare population. A decreasing profile of exit rates is then a purely statistical artifact with no connection to negative temporal dependence. To see how, imagine that within a population comprising households

---

[5]Given information about the beginning and the length of repeated spells on welfare, it is possible to characterize the duration of off-assistance spells. After transformation of the data, calculating the re-entry rate after the end of a spell on welfare is analogous to finding the exit rate: it is the ratio of the number of spells off-aid which end (return to welfare) over the number of spells which could be ending. From these rates, we can derive distributions that are analogous to the two described above.

J.-Y. Duclos, B. Fortin, G. Lacroix and H. Roberge

with different exit probabilities but with no "negative temporal dependence", an exit rate for the first window is calculated from the behaviour of the entire sample. For subsequent windows, let the exit rate be derived from the behaviour of the households whose spells have not ended. These estimates will show progressively smaller exit probabilities, since the higher-rate groups will disproportionately have already left the sample. This observation could wrongly suggest negative temporal dependence. We must therefore be prudent when inferring causal explanations for the behaviour of the exit rates across time.

Descriptive Analysis of Welfare Dynamics

This section provides a detailed analysis of the exit rates from social assistance along with their two associated distributions. First, we examine the entire sample in order to characterize the behaviour of the "average" welfare recipient. Subsequently, the analysis is repeated for various socio-demographic groups. Unless otherwise stated, our data covers the interval from 1979 to 1993, so that the calculated exit rates and durations represent averages over several business cycles and in a changing environment.

Welfare Exit Rates

Table 4 and Figure 1 illustrate exit rates for the entire sample. As can be seen, these rates remain constant for the first two windows and then decrease significantly. The windows cover a six-month period, though the data is monthly. In calculating exit rates for these windows, we are in fact computing an average of the exit rates for the months it comprises. This table shows that many households exit welfare soon after entry. In fact, over 34% of new entrants leave within the first six months.[6] Of those remaining, 33.9% leave within the following six months. Conditional exit rates diminish regularly and then stabilize at around 8%.

---

[6]This is, however, low relative to the 75% found for British Columbia by Barrett and Cragg (1998).

Table 4: Welfare Exit Rates, Total Sample

Windows (months)	Exit rates
1 to 6	0.3404
7 to 12	0.3392
13 to 18	0.2486
19 to 24	0.2003
25 to 30	0.1723
31 to 36	0.1509
37 to 42	0.1416
43 to 48	0.1265
49 to 54	0.1250
55 to 60	0.1108
61 to 66	0.1053
67 to 72	0.1006
73 to 78	0.0966
79 to 84	0.0901
85 to 90	0.0893
91 to 96	0.0878
more than 96	0.0800

Figure 1: Welfare Exit Rates

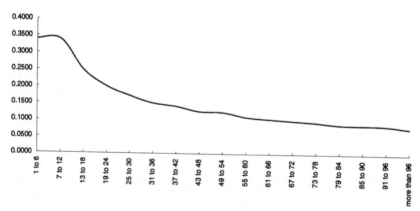

J.-Y. Duclos, B. Fortin, G. Lacroix and H. Roberge

Table 5 and Figure 2 decompose the exit rates among five household types: single men and women, couples with and without children and single-parent families. The exit rate for the first six-month window varies between 25.4% for single-parent families and 40.6% for couples without children. Thus, barely one single-parent household in four manages to get off welfare in the first six months, while four in ten couples with children do so. Exit rates remain fairly constant during the first two windows for all of the groups in the table, then drop substantially beginning with the third window. They converge to 8% for single men and women and for single-parent families, for childless couples they rapidly converge to 14%, while for couples with children they converge more slowly to 11%.

Figure 3 decomposes exit rates by age groups. It is of interest to note that increasing exit rates are found primarily among young people. In fact, these rates for 18-24 year olds climb from 39.6% to 43.9% from the first to the second window before falling back to 36.5% in the third. This group demonstrates relatively high exit rates — above 30% for many windows. However, very few individuals in this group have spells which last more than five years. The 25-30 and 31-45 age groups present a constant exit rate for the first two windows while the 46+ group is characterized by a declining rate as of the first window. As can be seen, the exit rates profile is highly correlated with age.

Figure 4 presents a breakdown of exit rates by level of education. As expected, more education implies higher exit rates. The picture may, however, be complicated by the existence of a negative correlation between age and level of education. Since members of the younger age groups generally have more schooling than their elders (see Table 1), and since young people tend to have higher exit rates, the variations in exit rates attributable to education may in fact be partly explained by age.

Figure 5 presents exit rates for spells beginning in each year from 1979 to 1993 and for windows of 1-6 months and 7-12 months. As can be seen, these two series of exit rates are positively correlated and serve to illustrate the impact of business cycles on the dynamics of welfare participation. We can distinguish two cycles, starting with the recession of the early 1980s and that of the late 1980s. It would nevertheless be inappropriate to attribute all the variations in exit rates to macroeconomic fluctuations. Several factors, perhaps in conjunction with these cycles, may play a role. The 1989 reform of the Quebec welfare system entailed a sizable jump in benefits to singles and childless couples under the age of 30. With the abolition of discrimination based on age, these claimants became eligible for the same benefits as

Table 5: Welfare Exit Rates by Type of Households

Windows (months)	Single men	Single women	Single heads	Couples (without children)	Couples (with children)
1 to 6	0.3627	0.3330	0.2543	0.4064	0.3605
7 to 12	0.3864	0.3407	0.2291	0.3889	0.3585
13 to 18	0.2957	0.2806	0.1709	0.2580	0.2486
19 to 24	0.2391	0.2150	0.1381	0.2074	0.2155
25 to 30	0.2047	0.1965	0.1248	0.1787	0.1799
31 to 36	0.1758	0.1646	0.1073	0.1621	0.1706
37 to 42	0.1554	0.1671	0.1045	0.1410	0.1625
43 to 48	0.1396	0.1399	0.0989	0.1532	0.1385
49 to 54	0.1230	0.1305	0.1084	0.1493	0.1415
55 to 60	0.1154	0.1150	0.0840	0.1453	0.1355
61 to 66	0.0984	0.1246	0.0863	0.1491	0.1188
67 to 72	0.1017	0.1234	0.0740	0.1436	0.1184
73 to 78	0.0836	0.1002	0.0844	0.1533	0.1134
79 to 84	0.0871	0.847	0.0788	0.1417	0.1040
85 to 90	0.0862	0.0934	0.0776	0.1548	0.0963
91 to 96	0.0697	0.0922	0.0740	0.1390	0.1157
more than 96	0.0700	0.0900	0.0700	0.1300	0.1050

Figure 2: Welfare Exit Rates by Type of Households

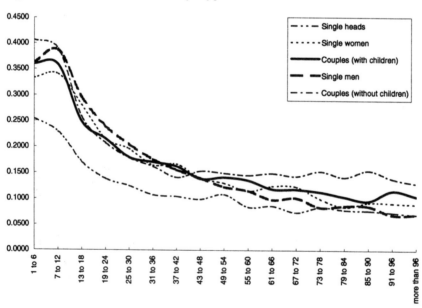

J.-Y. Duclos, B. Fortin, G. Lacroix and H. Roberge

Figure 3: Welfare Exit Rates by Age

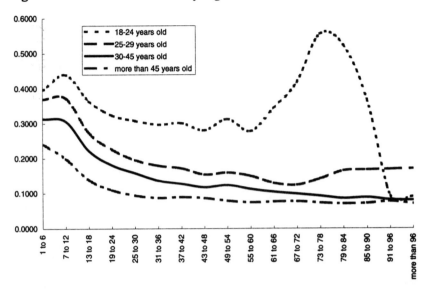

Figure 4: Welfare Exit Rates by Education

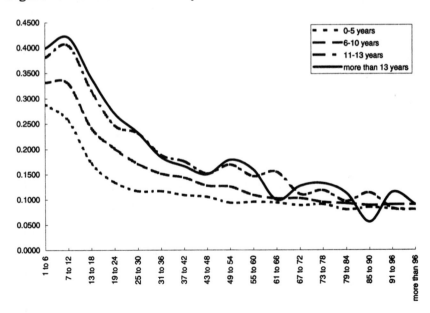

The Dynamics of Welfare Participation in Quebec 205

Figure 5: Welfare Exit Rates, Years 1979-1993

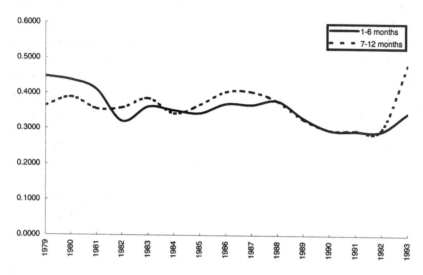

their elders, yielding them an increase in income support of nearly 100%. It is possible that this increase in the benefits scale is partly responsible for the fall in exit rates. Furthermore, we should note that the unemployment insurance (UI) program became significantly less generous after 1989, measured in terms of the ratio of the maximum number of weeks of benefits to the minimum number of weeks of work required to qualify. This type of change renders work less attractive to individuals with a weak attachment to the labour market, especially to the extent that they anticipate periods of unemployment in the future. Finally, the real minimum wage stagnated at an historic low in the period between 1986 and 1993.[7] *A priori*, the effect of the minimum wage on the exit rate is ambiguous. A low minimum wage undermines the attractiveness of work, reducing the supply of unskilled labour, but it simultaneously increases its demand. All these factors combine to explain, at least partly, the observed fall in the rate of exit from 1989.

---

[7]Between 1975 and 1993, the minimum wage averaged $4.84 in 1986 dollars. In 1976-77 it peaked at $6.00, and then fell to a low of $3.97 in August 1986. It has since hovered around $4.30 in 1986 dollars.

J.-Y. Duclos, B. Fortin, G. Lacroix and H. Roberge

One way of partially isolating the effect of the 1989 reform which does not rely on sophisticated statistical techniques is to examine the profile of exit rates beginning before 1989 and to compare it with the post-1989 data.[8] Assuming that the business cycle, the UI program and the minimum wage affect all age groups equally, observed changes in the exit rate across age groups may be attributable to the reform. Needless to say, to the extent that changes in the economic environment do not affect all age groups equally, the observed effects may not be entirely due to the reform. The analysis is presented in Figures 6 to 8 for each period. We see that before 1989 young people had exit rates significantly higher than those of their elders. These exit rates fell after 1989 to levels that are significantly closer to their elders'. It is of interest to note that exit rates for the 31-45 age group did not really change across the two periods.[9] We thus observe across the two periods an increase or stagnation of exit rates for the 30+ age group along with a significant decline for the under 30 age groups. Of course, the recession of 1989-93 may well have hurt young people moreso than others, but the variations in their exit rates are large enough to suspect that the reform probably had a significant impact on the duration of their spells.

Average Durations on Welfare

The preceding section provided a detailed analysis of the exit profiles of several socio-demographic groups. This information may be condensed into a measure of average duration. Recall that the exit rate, λ, representing the probability of exit from welfare during window t, given that the household received benefits until at least window t-1, can be written as:

$$\lambda(t) = \frac{N(t)}{R(t)} . \tag{3}$$

---

[8]Spells beginning before 1989 and continuing past December 1989 are censored.

[9]In fact, exit rates for the over 45 age group increased after 1989.

Figure 6: Welfare Exit Rates, 18-24 Years Old

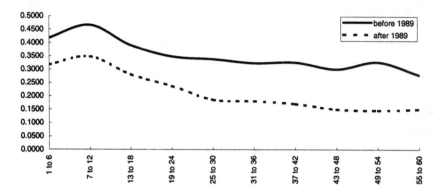

Figure 7: Welfare Exit Rates, 25-29 Years Old

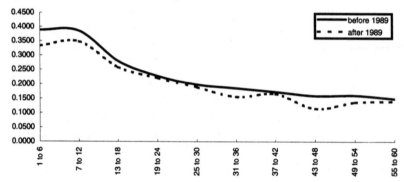

Figure 8: Welfare Exit Rates, 30-45 Years Old

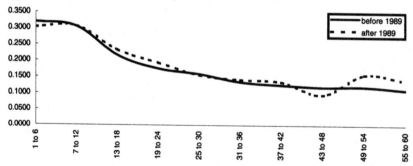

The expression $R(t)$ represents "survival" until t. We can easily show that $R(t)$ may be expressed as:

$$R(t) = \prod_{t_j < t} [1 - \lambda(t_j)], \quad t \geq 0. \tag{4}$$

Finally, we can also show that the expected duration on welfare may be expressed as a function of $R(t)$:

$$E(t) = \sum_{j=0}^{\infty} R(j) \tag{5}$$

This last expression simply says that the expected duration is the sum of the survival functions over all the periods. In the preceding section, exit rates were calculated for only 17 windows. Consequently, to calculate expected durations, we need to make some further assumptions concerning the survival rate beyond the windows used. Two approaches have been proposed in the literature:

1. One may assume that the exit rate of the last window considered remains constant for all subsequent windows (e.g., Bane and Ellwood, 1983).
2. One can use the exit rates from the windows we have been considering to estimate a second- or third-order autoregressive function. The estimated parameters may be used to predict the exit rate for subsequent windows (e.g., Katz and Meyer, 1990).

We use the second approach in this paper. In all cases, third-order autoregressive functions were used to calculate the exit rate for subsequent windows.[10] Using this, we find that the expected duration of a spell on welfare is slightly less than two years. Table 6 disaggregates this variable over various types of households. Except for single-parent families, it is around 22 months. Single women have slightly longer spells than single men (23.49 versus 21.28 months) and couples with children also have spells

---

[10]Expected durations were computed using more disaggregated monthly exit rates.

Table 6: Expected Durations

	On Welfare (months)	Out of Welfare (months)
By type of household		
Single men	21.28	73.44
Single women	23.49	92.47
Single heads	40.81	67.24
Couples (without children)	19.70	91.95
Couples (with children)	22.57	77.78
By age		
18-24 years old	12.82	76.48
25-29 years old	20.00	72.38
30-45 years old	29.29	74.81
More than 45 years old	48.92	98.91
By education		
0-5 years	37.30	85.71
6-10 years	26.10	72.88
11-13 years	18.33	87.16
More than 13 years	17.14	91.31

marginally longer than childless couples (22.57 versus 19.70 months). Furthermore, it is interesting to note that the average duration of spells for single-parent families is essentially the same as that obtained by Bane and Ellwood (1983) in their study of Aid to Families with Dependent Children (AFDC). In fact, our results show that the expected duration is 41 months, while the corresponding figure was 48 months in their study.

Table 6 also clearly indicates the positive correlation between the duration of spells and the age of claimants on one hand, and the negative correlation between this duration and the level of education on the other. Welfare spells for 18-24 year-olds have a mean duration of barely 12.8 months, while claimants over age 45 have spells of more than 49 months on

J.-Y. Duclos, B. Fortin, G. Lacroix and H. Roberge

average. Also, they are much longer for individuals with little schooling than for their more educated counterparts (37.30 versus 17.14 months).

Distributions of New and Ongoing Spells

Earlier we introduced two distributions that can be calculated directly from the exit rates. The first, $D(t)$, is the distribution of the length of a spell randomly selected among all starting spells, and the second, $F(t)$, is the distribution of the length of a spell randomly selected among all ongoing spells. Table 7 presents these estimated distributions for the entire sample, illustrating the flow and stock effects of participation in the welfare program. Thus, there is a 34% probability that a new spell will end within six months (column $D(t)$). Over half of the new spells (56%) will end within twelve months. Thus, few of the new spells will be of long duration.[11] Conversely, spells lasting more than five years account for 54% of the spells ongoing at any point in time (column $F(t)$), and spells longer than eight years account for 39%.

Table 7 also presents these estimates for different household types. The distribution of new and ongoing spells for single women is slightly tilted forward compared to that of men. This simply confirms that they have marginally longer durations than men do. Similarly, the distribution for couples with children is slightly offset from that of childless couples. The most striking information in this table, however, concerns single-parent families. Over half of ongoing spells at any time will eventually have a duration of over eight years. Only 25% of new spells will end in less than six months. Again, these results have a remarkable resemblance to those found by Bane and Ellwood (1983). In their study, 29% of single-parent families beginning a spell on welfare leave it within six months, and 19% within the following six months (17% in our study). Moreover, long spells (8+ years) account for 45.7% of the ongoing spells at any time.

Another way of illustrating the distribution of welfare spells is by plotting their Lorenz curve (Figure 9). On the horizontal axis, we first order spells by their lengths, starting with the shortest ones and ending with the longest. On the vertical axis, we express the proportion of the aggregate

---

[11]They are even fewer in British Columbia, where only 10% of new spells are still ongoing after one year (Barrett and Cragg, 1998).

Table 7: Distributions of New Spells (D(t)) and of Ongoing Spells (F(t)) by Types of Households

Windows (months)	Single men		Single women		Single heads		Couples (without children)		Couples (with children)		Total sample	
	D(t)	F(t)	D(t)	F(t)	D(t)	F(t)	D(t)	F(t)	D(t)	F(t)	D(t)	F(t)
1 to 6	36.2700	5.1139	33.3000	4.2536	25.4300	1.8657	40.6400	6.1900	36.0500	4.7911	34.0400	4.0106
7 to 12	24.6253	10.4162	22.7247	8.7084	17.0840	3.7602	23.0851	10.5484	22.9261	9.1407	22.3736	7.9082
13 to 18	11.5633	8.1519	12.3395	7.8810	9.8244	3.6039	9.3589	7.1274	10.1985	6.7770	10.8356	6.3832
19 to 24	6.5852	6.4994	6.8017	6.0818	6.5821	3.3803	5.5824	5.9518	6.6429	6.1799	6.5600	5.4103
25 to 30	4.2898	5.4435	4.8799	5.6101	5.1267	3.3852	3.8123	5.2260	4.3504	5.2036	4.5127	4.7851
31 to 36	2.9300	4.5443	3.2845	4.6150	3.8577	3.1133	2.8402	4.7586	3.3834	4.9461	3.2712	4.2396
37 to 42	2.1347	3.9127	2.7855	4.6256	3.3539	3.1989	2.0700	4.0988	2.6729	4.6180	2.6064	3.9921
43 to 48	1.6196	3.4254	1.9424	3.7218	2.8425	3.1281	1.9320	4.4140	1.9079	3.8035	1.9988	3.5324
49 to 54	1.2278	2.9430	1.5584	3.3841	2.8074	3.5015	1.5944	4.1283	1.6793	3.7941	1.7252	3.4555
55 to 60	1.0103	2.7064	1.1941	2.8981	1.9397	2.7038	1.3200	3.8200	1.3805	3.4860	1.3381	2.9954
61 to 66	0.7620	2.2563	1.1450	3.0714	1.8254	2.8123	1.1577	3.7030	1.0464	2.9204	1.1308	2.7977
67 to 72	0.7101	2.3027	0.9927	2.9164	1.4301	2.4132	0.9488	3.3237	0.9190	2.8090	0.9665	2.6192
73 to 78	0.5243	1.8483	0.7066	2.2564	1.5104	2.7704	0.8674	3.3029	0.7760	2.5781	0.8347	2.4587
79 to 84	0.5006	1.9058	0.5374	1.8535	1.2912	2.5577	0.6789	2.7917	0.6309	2.2640	0.7034	2.2375
85 to 90	0.4523	1.8494	0.5424	2.0094	1.1713	2.4921	0.6365	2.8116	0.5235	2.0175	0.6343	2.1673
91 to 96	0.3342	1.4607	0.4855	1.9223	1.0303	2.3433	0.4831	2.2810	0.5684	2.3416	0.5680	2.0744
more than 96	4.4606	35.2200	4.7798	34.1910	12.8928	52.9701	2.9923	25.5230	4.3439	32.3294	5.9000	38.9437

J.-Y. Duclos, B. Fortin, G. Lacroix and H. Roberge

Figure 9: Lorenz Curve of the Distribution of Welfare Spells

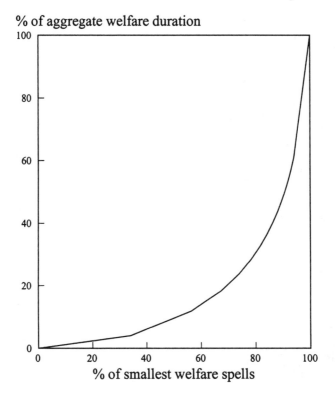

% of aggregate welfare duration

% of smallest welfare spells

welfare duration (or of ongoing spells, and thus approximately of aggregate welfare spending) accounted for by a certain percentage of the smallest spells. We find that the 50% shortest welfare spells account for only 10% of the total ongoing welfare spells and spending. Conversely, the 50% longest spells account for 90% of total welfare outlays. Figure 9 also indicates that the 20% shortest spells contribute to little more than 2% of aggregate welfare spending, whereas the longest 20% account for around 70% of aggregate welfare duration.

Rates of Welfare Re-entries

One of the key elements of the overall dynamics of welfare participation concerns the rate of re-entry to welfare after having exited. Table 8 and Figure 10 present such rates of re-entry for the entire sample. We find that

Table 8: Welfare Re-entry Rates

Windows (months)	Re-entry rates	D(t)	F(t)
1 to 6	0.2182	0.2182	0.0453
7 to 12	0.1057	0.0826	0.0515
13 to 18	0.1042	0.0729	0.0756
19 to 24	0.0733	0.0459	0.0667
25 to 30	0.0604	0.0351	0.0655
31 to 36	0.0508	0.0277	0.0633
37 to 42	0.0434	0.0225	0.0606
43 to 48	0.0394	0.0195	0.0607
49 to 54	0.0344	0.0164	0.0577
55 to 60	0.0302	0.0139	0.0547
61 to 66	0.0287	0.0128	0.0557
67 to 72	0.0268	0.0116	0.0554
73 to 78	0.0242	0.0102	0.0529
79 to 84	0.0212	0.0087	0.0488
85 to 90	0.0207	0.0083	0.0501
91 to 96	0.0198	0.0078	0.0502
more than 96	0.0190	0.3860	0.0853

Figure 10: Welfare Re-entry Rates

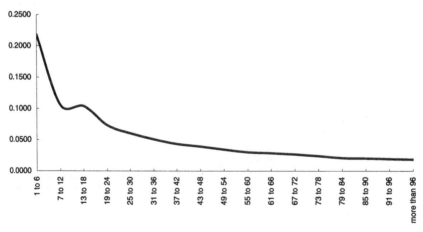

22% of households leaving welfare at any point in time will return within six months, and another 11% within the following six-month period. In British Columbia, a full 50% return within a year (Barrett and Cragg, 1998). Re-entry rates slowly decline to about 2%. Thus, the longer the person is off assistance, the less likely he or she is to return. Column 3 of Table 8 contains information on the distribution of new off-welfare spells. It reveals that over 42% of these exiting welfare participants will return to welfare within two years. Furthermore, 38.6% of households leaving welfare at any point in time will remain off welfare for at least eight years.

Figures 11, 12 and 13 provide information on re-entry rates and contain disaggregations analogous to those of Figures 2, 3 and 4. The main results are as follows:

1. While single women have a longer average duration on welfare than men, the latter have higher re-entry rates.
2. Childless couples have both higher exit rates and lower re-entry rates than couples with children.
3. Single-parent households have re-entry rates which are barely higher than the overall re-entry rates.
4. The re-entry rates of the age groups 18-24, 25-30 and 31-45 are practically identical. The 46+ age group presents a return profile lower than the other groups.
5. The rates of re-entry decomposed by level of education are virtually identical.

Figure 11: Welfare Re-entry Rates by Age

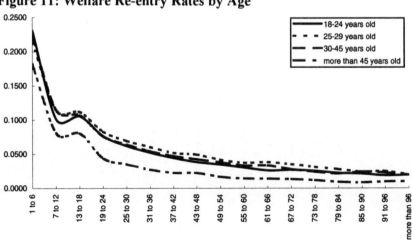

Figure 12: Welfare Re-entry Rates by Education

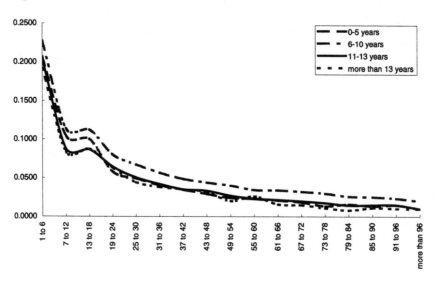

Figure 13: Welfare Re-entry Rates by Type of Households

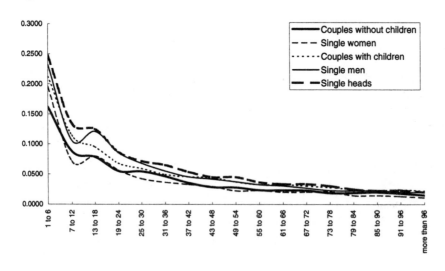

J.-Y. Duclos, B. Fortin, G. Lacroix and H. Roberge

Other results, not shown here, indicate that re-entry rates profiles are counter-cyclical, unlike exit rates. We also found two peaks of monthly re-entry rates at about 12-13 months and 7-18 months,[12] so there appear to be marked increases in returns to welfare after about one and one-and-a-half years off aid. Since we do not have the reasons for entry and exit, it is difficult to explain this phenomenon. Nonetheless, to the extent that individuals quit welfare to take a job, the increase in re-entry rates may be related to the parameters of the unemployment insurance program. In fact, depending on the year and the region, the minimum number of weeks of work required to qualify for the program varies between 10 and 12, with benefits being paid for 42 to 52 weeks. Consequently, individuals quitting welfare to take a job providing the required number of weeks, and then exhausting their insurance benefits, would indeed cause a peak in re-entry rates at about 12-13 months.

A possible explanation for the 18-month peak is the existence of the "Programme d'aide à l'intégration à l'emploi". Under this program, a firm hiring a welfare recipient may have a part of the wage reimbursed for a period of up to 26 weeks. During this probation period the individual contributes to the unemployment insurance program, and thus may become eligible for benefits. At the end of this period the trainee may not receive a permanent job offer, and may then receive unemployment insurance benefits for up to 42 weeks. In all, this individual will have been off-assistance for about 17-18 months, corresponding to the second peak.

Mean Durations of Off-Welfare Spells

Table 6 shows the mean durations of off-assistance spells for different socio-demographic groups. Taken together, the profile of off-aid durations differs somewhat from the on-aid profile. Thus, while the length of spells on welfare is slightly shorter for men than for women, the off-welfare spells of the latter are considerably longer. Also, couples with children have on-aid spells which are longer than those of childless couples, and off-aid spells which are shorter. Moreover, the 18-24, 25-30 and 31-45 age groups seem

---

[12]Barrett and Cragg (1998) also find a peak in re-entry rates at about 11 months in their sample from British Columbia. They attribute it partially to seasonality.

to have off-aid durations which are similar to, but lower than, those observed for the 46+ age group. Finally, there does not appear to be a strong correlation between the level of education and the expected length of off-assistance spells.

Overall Rates of Welfare Dependence

The descriptive analysis of the preceding sections has shed some light on the dynamics of participation in welfare for the period 1979-93. It has, among other things, allowed us to identify groups whose behaviour is characterized either by lengthy spells on welfare or by frequent returns to welfare. Now, the results presented thus far do not combine these two essential components of the dynamics of welfare participation into a synthetic measure of dependence. Such a measure is required if we wish to compare objectively different groups characterized by varying average durations on and off-welfare.

There are several ways to define welfare dependence. For our purposes, we shall propose a measure which combines the advantages of computational simplicity with an intuitive interpretation. We define the *rate of dependence* as follows. Let DW_i be the average duration of on-welfare spells for group i, DOW_i the corresponding off-welfare average, and $DT_i = DW_i + DOW_i$ the total mean duration of an on-aid / off-aid cycle. One measure of the rate of dependence, τ_i, is thus:

$$\tau_i = \frac{DW_i}{DT_i}, \qquad (6)$$

$$= DW_i \cdot \frac{1}{DT_i} \qquad (7)$$

The rate of dependence thus corresponds to the proportion of an entire cycle which is spent on welfare. The second term on the right-hand side of equation (7) is a measure of the frequency with which a given group begins a new cycle. For example, if $Dt_i = 100$, then $1/DT_i = 0.01$, and group i has one chance in 100 of starting a new cycle in any month. Multiplying this by DW_i

J.-Y. Duclos, B. Fortin, G. Lacroix and H. Roberge

gives us the expected proportion of a period of time we expect a member of group i to spend on welfare after he/she has entered welfare for the first time. It should be noted that a group having a high average duration of welfare spells and a long cycle (rare returns) may have the same value for its rate of dependence as a group with a shorter average length of welfare spells combined with a shorter cycle (frequent returns).

Table 9 presents dependence rates by household type. The table shows that single men exhibit a dependence rate higher than that of women, despite the fact that their welfare spells are shorter on average. Their greater dependence is explained by more frequent re-entries into welfare. Single-parent families clearly have a high rate of dependence because their longer spells combine with more frequent returns; once they have claimed welfare a first time, we expect single parents to spend on welfare 37.7% of the subsequent time periods. Finally, childless couples show a dependence rate that is significantly lower than couples with children because they return to welfare much less frequently.[13]

Tables 10 and 11 present overall welfare dependence rates by age group and education level, respectively, for men and women. We see that men and women are quite different in their behaviour vis-à-vis welfare. While the

Table 9: Dependence Rates by Household Types

	DW	DOW	τ
Single men	21.279	73.440	0.224
Single women	23.486	92.467	0.202
Single-parent families	40.807	67.240	0.377
Childless couples	19.699	91.952	0.176
Couples with children	22.571	77.782	0.224

[13]Lacroix (1997) also shows that, despite the fact that they stay off welfare longer, Quebec welfare recipients exhibit greater welfare dependence than in British Columbia, except for single parents (this is due to a significantly greater DW_i).

Table 10: Dependence Rates by Age Groups

	Men				Women			
	18-24	25-30	31-45	46+	18-24	25-30	31-45	46+
DW	11.215	15.064	23.300	44.625	14.683	25.280	35.930	53.688
DOW	72.951	68.782	71.022	93.002	80.566	76.526	79.414	105.680
τ	0.133	0.180	0.247	0.324	0.154	0.248	0.312	0.337

Table 11: Dependence Rates by Levels of Education

	Men				Women			
	≤6	7-11	12-14	15+	≤6	7-11	12-14	15+
DW	32.958	21.001	15.869	17.295	42.473	31.887	20.669	16.930
DOW	80.292	68.994	84.656	88.360	92.537	77.613	89.579	95.182
τ	0.291	0.233	0.158	0.164	0.315	0.291	0.187	0.151

length of welfare spells is shorter for men than for women in all groups, the former systematically return to social assistance more quickly. Nonetheless, this higher frequency does not entirely compensate for their shorter welfare spells, so that women's rate of welfare dependence is generally higher than men's. Rates of dependence are strongly correlated positively with age and negatively with education. Rising from less than 6 years of education to more than 15 decreases the proportion of time spent on welfare by as much as 15% for men or women.

Conclusion

The growth in expenditures on Canadian social assistance programs and the increase in the number of claimants up until recently has led to many calls for thorough reforms of the programs. To our knowledge very few studies

J.-Y. Duclos, B. Fortin, G. Lacroix and H. Roberge

have examined the dynamics of welfare participation in Canada. A detailed understanding of these dynamics is, nevertheless, essential for any enlightened discussion of possible reforms.

To contribute to a better understanding of the features and of the effects of the Quebec social assistance program, we use in this paper a representative sample of welfare recipients between the years 1979 and 1993, made available to us by the Ministère de la solidarité sociale. Descriptive tools then enable us to characterize the durations, exit and re-entry rates for several categories of households and thus to identify high-risk groups.

We find that the majority of starting spells (56%) will last for less than one year. Exit rates tend to decrease quite sharply with the length of the spell. While most new spells are of fairly short duration, it remains that a large proportion of ongoing spells are of long duration. We estimate, for instance, that 70% of aggregate welfare duration and spending is accounted for by the 20% longest spells.

Overall, young people leave welfare faster than their elders and more educated individuals sooner than their less educated counterparts. It appears that the business cycle has a significant influence on that dynamic. Thus, the exit rate in the first six months of 1986, a year of economic growth, was 37%, while the corresponding number for the first six months of 1991 was barely 29%. Results also show that the dynamics of welfare participation varies significantly with gender. Single men leave welfare more rapidly than do single women, and single-parent families (which are almost all headed by women) leave the least quickly of all family types. The expected welfare duration of single men is below that of single women (21 versus 23 months), and that length is twice as long for single-parent households as for any other household type; 53% of the ongoing spells for single parents will extend over 96 months, compared to only 34% for single women. This clearly suggests that, for policy, it is not so much the gender of the head that matters, but rather whether it is or is not in single parenthood.

The important welfare reform that occurred in Quebec in 1989 eliminated discrimination on the basis of age. As a consequence, the benefits scale for single individuals under age 30 more than doubled between 1988 and 1990, rising from $2,072 to $5,108 annually (1986 dollars). Conversely, it fell slightly for the 30 plus age group, from $5,495 to $5,108. The exit rate of participants over age 30 remained relatively stable before and after 1989. After 1989, we nevertheless witness a sharp drop in the exit rates for the under 30 age group. The reform thus appears to have had an important impact on the exit rates of the younger group.

Between 1979 and 1993, we estimate that the expected length of an ongoing welfare spell was 25.5 months, but that of a starting (or new) spell was around 17 months. Returns onto welfare generally occur shortly after exit and at a rate that diminishes with time. Single-parent households take an average of only 67 months to return to welfare once they have left; single women and childless couples return after 92 months on average. Re-entry is faster for young people and varies little with education.

Finally, our results indicate that overall welfare dependence (taking into account the combined incidence of exits and returns) is almost twice as large for single-parent households as for any other types of households. Single men return more quickly to welfare than do single women, and the rate of welfare dependence for single men also exceeds that for single women. Male-headed households, however, have lower welfare dependence rates than do female-headed ones (which are largely composed of single parents), whatever the age of the head. Finally, welfare dependence rates increase significantly with age and decrease with the claimant's level of education.

References

Allen, D.W. (1993), "Welfare and the Family: The Canadian Experience", *Journal of Labor Economics* 11, S201-S221.

Bane, M.J. and D.T. Ellwood (1983), "The Dynamics of Dependence: The Routes to Self Sufficiency", report prepared for the U.S. Department of Health and Human Services.

_____ (1994), *Welfare Realities: From Rhetoric to Reform* (Cambridge, MA: Harvard University Press).

Barrett, G.F. and M.I. Cragg (1998), "An Untold Story: The Characteristics of Welfare Use in British Columbia", *Canadian Journal of Economics* 31, 165-188.

Blank, R.M. and M.J. Hanratty (1993), "Responding to Need: A Comparison of Social Safety Nets in Canada and the United States", in D. Card and R.B. Freeman (eds.), *Small Differences that Matter* (Chicago: Chicago University Press), 190-231.

Canada. Human Resources Development Canada (1994), *Canada Assistance Plan: Annual Report 1992-93* (Ottawa: Human Resources Development Canada).

Charette, M.F. and R. Meng (1994), "The Determinants of Welfare Participation of Female Heads of Household in Canada", *Canadian Journal of Economics* 27, 290-306.

Dooley, M.D. (1994), "The Use of Social Assistance by Canadian Lone Mothers", mimeo, Department of Economics, McMaster University.

Lacroix, G. (1997), "Reforming the Welfare System: In Search of the Optimal Policy Mix", paper prepared for the IRPP conference "Adapting Public Policy to a Labour Market in Transition".

Katz, L.F. and B.D. Meyer (1990), "The Impact of the Potential Duration of Unemployment Benefits on the Duration of Unemployment", *Journal of Public Economics* 41, 45-72.

Moffitt, R. (1992), "Incentive Effects of the U.S. Welfare System: A Review", *Journal of Economic Literature* 30, 1-61.

Social Assistance and the Employment Rate of Lone Mothers: An Analysis of Ontario's Live Experiment

Constantine Kapsalis

Introduction

The percentage of lone mothers who are working (employment rate) is of particular policy interest for two important reasons: first, lone mothers are at high risk of relying on social assistance and changes in their employment rate can have a significant impact on welfare caseloads; second, a large percentage of poor children live in households with a female sole supporter. Consequently, the employment rate of lone mothers affects both welfare costs and child poverty.

The objective of this study is to provide further insight into the effect of changes in social assistance benefit rates on the employment rate of lone

The author wishes to thank for their constructive comments: Martin Dooley of McMaster University; Philip Merrigan of the University of Quebec in Montreal; Allen Zeesman and Michael Hatfield of the Applied Research Branch, Human Resources Development Canada; and Richard Chaykowski of Queen's University. The author is solely responsible for the conclusions expressed in this study, as well as for any errors or omissions.

mothers, by taking into account the impact of recent changes in social assistance benefit rates.

A previous study by this author (Kapsalis, 1996), based on regression analysis using the 1988-90 longitudinal Labour Market Activity Survey (LMAS) and data on social assistance benefit rates, estimated that an increase of $1,000 in annual benefit rates was associated with a reduction of 1.9 percentage points in the employment rate of lone mothers with young children (under age 16).

But if benefit increases produce *declines* in the employment rate, would benefit reductions produce equivalent *increases*? A live experiment of this scenario has just occurred in Ontario, with the annual social assistance benefit rate for a lone parent with one young child falling from $14,652 in 1994 to $11,484 in 1996, as a result of a 21.6% reduction in benefit rates by the Ontario government in October 1995.

Based on the results of the author's previous study, a reduction of this magnitude ($3,168) should have been associated with an increase in the employment rate of lone mothers in Ontario by six percentage points (3,168 * (1.9/1000)) — that is, from 46.6% in 1994 to 52.6% in 1996. The increase actually observed was 5.7 percentage points, which is very close to the predicted increase. This result is particularly noteworthy since the employment rate of mothers of young children in two-parent families rose by only 0.5 percentage point over the same period.

The success of the author's previous study in correctly predicting the change in the employment rate of lone mothers in Ontario, and the confirmation of the empirical coefficients by this study, provide compelling evidence of the effect of social assistance benefits on the employment rate of lone mothers.

This study updates the results of the previous study by incorporating Ontario's most recent experience. The study uses Labour Force Survey and benefit rate time-series data covering the period 1986-96.

While cross-sectional data (e.g., LMAS or Survey of Consumer Finances (SCF)) are more powerful, time-series data are more timely; time-series data were employed in this study so as to be able to provide an immediate assessment of the recent changes in social assistance benefits in Ontario. However, it should be noted that, despite the different type of data and the different period covered, the results of this study and the previous one based on LMAS are virtually identical.

In what follows, the second section provides a selective review of related literature, the third section examines trends in social assistance benefits and employment rates, the fourth section presents the empirical findings while the final section concludes the study.

Literature Review

The issue of work effort of social assistance recipients has attracted particular attention in the economic literature. To a large extent this has been in response to the significant increase in welfare caseloads during the last 15 years.

There is considerable dissatisfaction with social assistance and social programs in general. A recent study concluded that social assistance programs focus on the immediate problem of income need and do little to encourage self-reliance. There is a lack of emphasis on training and the benefit structure discourages work effort, acting as a "welfare trap". The situation is exacerbated by a focus on the non-working poor and the neglect of the working poor (Grady, 1995).

A number of hypotheses have been put forward to explain the increase in caseload rates including rapid skill deterioration and labour replacement due to technological change and globalization; shift of macroeconomic policy emphasis from economic stability to controlling inflation and reducing the deficit; and changing social values (Richards, 1995; Brown, 1995).

However, welfare caseloads are also sensitive to program changes. A recent study of the determinants of welfare participation of female heads of households (i.e., lone females and lone mothers) in Canada, using the LMAS data for 1990, found that the elasticities of welfare participation with respect to both welfare benefits and earned income exemption are relatively high (Charette and Meng, 1994).

The previous study by this author concluded that, while economic conditions are a significant determinant of welfare caseloads and the work effort of social assistance recipients:

> what can be said with considerable certainty is that higher social assistance benefits do have a negative effect on the employment rates of lone mothers. Therefore, efforts to improve the income situation of lone mothers should be combined with work incentives to avoid a self-defeating reinforcement of long-term dependency on social assistance. (Kapsalis, 1996, p. 23)

Several previous studies, although limited in number and with less than ideal data, have reached similar conclusions. Using data from the Survey of Consumer Finances for three different years, Dooley (1994b) found that a 10% increase in the benefit rate would lead to a two-to-four percentage point reduction in the proportion of lone mothers who work at least one week in the market. Similarly, Allen (1993) analyzed the likelihood of market work using a single cross-section from the 1986 census. Most of his estimates are similar to Dooley's.

It is important, however, to recognize that lone mothers are not a homogeneous group and there are significant differences between younger and older mothers. In particular, Dooley (1995) found that over the last 15 years lone mothers over age 34 exhibited growing wages, market work and earnings along with a falling incidence of both poverty and social assistance income. The picture for the younger age group, on the other hand, was one of stagnant wages, declining market work and earnings accompanied by unchanging poverty rates and rising reliance on social assistance.

Because of data limitations, this study did not explicitly take into account the age of the mother. However, this was done to some extent indirectly by controlling for the age of the youngest child, which is correlated with the age of the mother.

It is also important to point out that, while the results of this study confirm that cutting benefits would lead to greater market work and earnings by lone mothers, there may be better ways to achieve the same results. Dooley (1995), for example, suggests various "financial strategies" including lowering the tax-back rate on welfare payments, extending non-cash welfare benefits to other low-income families, and replacing child-based benefits with an enriched child tax credit. He also suggests "service strategies" in the form of providing clients with training, counselling and other employment services.

Model Description

This study develops a model that allows one to explore the relationship between social assistance benefit rates and the employment rate of lone mothers. In this section the model is explained against the backdrop of recent trends in employment rates and benefit rates. In the following section the model is estimated empirically using time-series data.

Over the period 1986-96, the social assistance benefit rates, in constant dollars, for single parents with one young child followed a much different pattern among the provinces. In particular:

1. rates in constant dollars remained virtually unchanged in Newfoundland, Nova Scotia and New Brunswick, while they declined by about 10% in PEI, Manitoba and Saskatchewan (see Appendix A);
2. rates increased by 15% in British Columbia and declined by 22% in Alberta (Figure 1); and
3. rates ended up just below where they started in Ontario and somewhat higher in Quebec, but both provinces experienced wide swings, especially Ontario (Figure 1).

Generally, assuming there is no change in labour market conditions, an increase in social assistance benefit rates is expected to lead to a decrease in the number of working lone mothers.

There are two types of lone mothers to consider. First, some lone mothers who were already on social assistance might choose to "spend" part

Figure 1: Index of Social Assistance Benefits in Constant Dollars for Lone Mothers with One Child Under 16 (Among Selected Provinces)

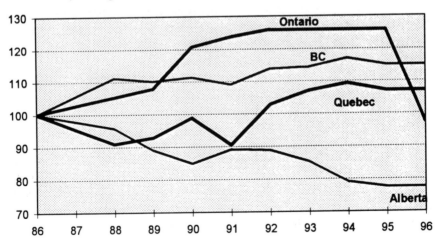

Source: Appendix A.

Social Assistance and the Employment Rate of Lone Mothers 229

of the increase in benefits by devoting more hours to child care, their own education, or other personal activities and, therefore, have fewer hours to devote to market work. Some of these mothers might even withdraw from the labour force altogether.

Second, an increase in social assistance benefits might also affect the behaviour of some lone mothers in low-wage jobs who were not initially on social assistance. Such lone mothers might now deem it in their best interest to reduce their hours of work so as to qualify for benefits. And once on social assistance, the high implicit tax rates on earned income may further influence them to reduce their hours of market work.

In reality, the connection between the level of social benefits and the employment rate of lone mothers is much more complex than the above simple exposition may suggest. For example, changes in work effort may take the form of an adjustment in the hours of work rather than a withdrawal from the labour force. In that regard, the employment rate is a cruder measure of work effort than the hours of work. The main attraction of the employment rate is the more ready availability of data. Also, changes in work effort may be affected by changes in labour market conditions. For example, higher benefits in an environment of improving labour markets would be less likely to create work disincentives. Finally, the negative effect of higher benefit rates on work effort would be muted by work incentives (such as the exemption of part of the earnings from the calculation of need or the provision of subsidized daycare).

In its simplest form, the basic model predicts that the difference between the employment rate of mothers with a spouse minus the employment rate of lone mothers will tend to move in the same direction as changes in the level of social assistance benefits. The underlying rationale is straightforward. The basic premise is that the labour market conditions facing both groups of mothers are similar and that, in the absence of changes in the level of social assistance benefit rates, the employment rates of the two groups would move in the same direction.

On the other hand, the potential effect of changes in social assistance benefits would be quite dissimilar between the two groups because of their different exposure to social assistance. For example, while 3% of mothers with younger children and a spouse present received social assistance in Ontario in 1990, the corresponding rate among lone mothers was 35%.[1]

The employment rates of lone mothers and mothers with spouses may move in different directions for other reasons. For example, the employment rate of married mothers will be affected by changes in the earnings of their spouses (a phenomenon known in the economic literature as "second earner effect"). However, when major changes in social assistance benefits take place, one would expect the effect of the benefit change to dominate other factors and provide a more clear picture of the effect of benefits on the employment rate of lone mothers.

Figure 2 shows that, even in its simplest form, the model conforms with Ontario's experience over the period 1986-96. All numbers in Figure 2 are expressed as an index with 1986 as the base year. As stipulated, an increase in the level of social assistance benefits is associated with an increase in the gap between the employment rate of mothers with a spouse over the employment rate of lone mothers.

**Figure 2: Employment Rate Index versus SA Benefit Index
Mothers with Children Under 16: Ontario**

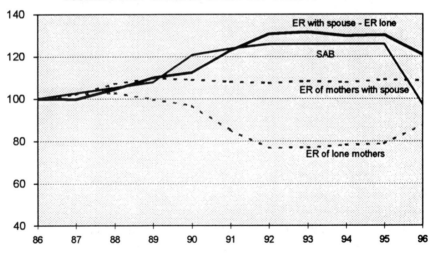

[1]Estimates based on the 1990 Labour Market Activity Survey. While the incidence of social assistance is underreported in the LMAS, the above estimates do provide an indication of the wide difference in incidence between the two groups of mothers.

The above depiction of the model also conforms with the experience of the rest of the provinces whose benefit rates experienced significant changes; that is, Quebec, Alberta and British Columbia. However, the simple model breaks down in the case of the remaining provinces whose benefit rates in constant dollars did not experience significant changes.[2]

Model Estimation

In this section, the basic model described above is used as the basis for developing a time-series model that estimates the relationship between the employment rate of lone mothers on the one hand, and social assistance and labour market conditions on the other. The basic specification of the various time-series models estimated here was the following:

$$ERATE = b_0 + b_1 * SAB + b_2 * MERATE + b_3 * CHILD{<}3 + b_4 * CHILD3\text{-}5$$

where: ERATE is the percentage of lone mothers who worked for some time during the year; SAB is the level of social assistance benefit rates for a single parent with one child, in constant dollars; MERATE is the employment rate of mothers *with* a spouse and similar age of youngest child; CHILD<3 is a dummy variable that equals 1 if the youngest child is under 3, and zero otherwise; and CHILD3-5 is a dummy variable that equals 1 if the youngest child is 3 to 5, and zero otherwise.

The source of the data, except for benefit rates, was the Labour Force Survey annual averages. The source of data for benefit rates was the National Council of Welfare (1986, 1989-96) and Sarlo (1992).[3] The regression results were weighted by the number of lone mothers in each province.

The data are pooled cross-sectional time series. For each province and each year, three types of lone mothers were selected depending on the age of the youngest child: under 3; age 3-5; and age 6 or over. The total number of observations was 330 (10 provinces; times 11 years covering the period 1986-96; times three types of lone mothers).

---

[2]See Appendix B for the same type of charts for the remaining nine provinces.

[3]For details see Table A1 in Appendix A.

The time-series model bears several similarities to the cross-sectional model developed by the author in the previous study (Kapsalis, 1996). Although fewer control variables are used in the time-series model than in the cross-sectional model, the time-series model has the advantage of exploiting data from a longer period and providing more up-to-date results.

Table 1 presents the results of two alternative estimates of the time-series regression models — one based on data from all provinces, and one based on data from provinces that experienced significant changes in their social assistance benefit rates over the period 1986-96:

1. According to the first regression, an increase in social assistance benefits by $1,000 (in $1995) will lead to a reduction in the employment rate of lone mothers with young children by 1.2 percentage points.
2. According to the second regression, the decrease in the employment rate will be 1.9 percentage points — identical to the result previously found using the 1988-1990 LMAS data (Kapsalis, 1996).

Several additional models were estimated and tested. However, they all led to similar results. For example:

1. The inclusion of the provincial unemployment rate in the regression reduced the effect of MERATE, but had virtually no effect on the SAB coefficient.

Table 1: Multiple Regression Results

Period covered: 1986-1996 Dependent Variable: ERATE (Employment Rate of Lone Mothers)				
		Provinces Included in Regression		
		All provinces		Quebec, Ontario, Alberta and B.C.
Independent Variables		B coeffic.	t-statistic	B coeffic.	t-statistic
SAB	Benefit rate in thousands 1995$	-1.21	-6.20	-1.90	-9.09
MERATE	ERate of mothers with spouse	0.78	12.45	0.93	12.35
CHILD<3	Presence of child under age 3	-22.48	-19.43	-19.90	-15.25
CHILD3-5	Presence of child age 3-5	-8.82	-9.05	-7.39	-7.09
CONSTANT		22.32	5.67	20.43	4.58
Adjusted R-square		0.84		0.86	
Standard Error		5.98		5.50	
F-statistic		427.67		421.00	
Observations		330		132	

2. The restriction of the sample to Ontario and Quebec only produced very similar results to those including Alberta and British Columbia as well.

The results were sensitive to the inclusion (or not) of provinces with no significant change in social assistance benefits (i.e., Atlantic provinces, Manitoba and Saskatchewan). This is not surprising. Effectively, the results suggest that the model does not perform well when there are no significant changes in social assistance benefits. However, the model appears to work well when benefits increase (British Columbia), decrease (Alberta), or swing up and down (Quebec and Ontario).

Also, not surprisingly, the presence of young children was found to have a very substantial impact on the employment rate of lone mothers. On the other hand, the inclusion of the provincial unemployment rate (not shown here) had virtually no effect on the coefficient of social assistance benefits, but considerably reduced the coefficient of the employment rate of mothers with a spouse (MERATE).[4]

Conclusion

The results of this analysis largely confirm the results of the author's previous study (Kapsalis, 1996). In fact, one of the two regression models estimated here produced an identical coefficient for the effect of social assistance benefits on the employment rate of lone mothers — that is, each $1,000 of an increase in social assistance benefit rates (expressed in 1995 dollars) was found to lead to a 1.9 percentage point decline in the employment rate of lone mothers with young children.

The fact that this study, using a different source of data over a different period of time, produced similar results provides further confidence about the relationship between social assistance benefit rates and the employment rate of lone mothers.

---

[4]The inclusion of the provincial URATE in the first regression (all provinces) reduced the coefficient of social assistance benefits from -1.21 to -1.05. In the case of the second regression model, the coefficient was reduced from -1.90 to -1.72. By contrast, the reduction of the MERATE coefficient was significant: from 0.778 to 0.398 in the first regression, and from 0.935 to 0.629 in the second regression.

Constantine Kapsalis

At the same time, the study also shows that labour market conditions have a strong effect. Each percentage point increase in the employment rate of mothers with a spouse (which can be viewed as an indicator of the labour market conditions faced by lone mothers) is associated with a virtually equivalent (0.93 percentage point) increase in the employment rate of lone mothers.

Looking ahead, while the connection between social assistance benefit rates and employment rates appears to be well established, a better understanding of the employability of lone mothers will be constructive. Two areas of investigation are particularly promising:

- The recently completed International Adult Literacy Survey (IALS) provides a unique opportunity for linking poverty and reliance on social assistance to the level of literacy.
- Similarly, analysis of Survey of Consumer Finance data at the 78 economic region level provide an opportunity for disentangling provincial benefit rates from local labour market conditions.

The results of the study have important policy implications. Lone mothers are at high risk of relying on social assistance, and changes in their employment rate can have a significant impact on welfare caseloads. Moreover, because a large percentage of poor children live in households with a female sole supporter, the employment rate of lone mothers affects both welfare costs and child poverty.

While the study confirms that cutting benefits would lead to greater market work and earnings by lone mothers, there may be better ways to achieve the same results. This may include Dooley's (1995) suggestions of lowering the tax-back rate on welfare payments, extending non-cash welfare benefits to other low-income families, replacing child-based benefits with an enriched child tax credit, or providing lone mothers with training, counselling and other employment services.

Appendix A: Social Assistance Benefit Rates

Table A1: Constant Dollar Social Assistance Benefit Rates for Single Parents with One Child Under 16 (1995$)

YEAR	NFLD	PEI	NS	NB	QUE	ONT	MAN	SASK	ALTA	BC
86	11,342	11,582	10,695	9,142	10,781	12,263	10,496	11,669	11,849	10,410
87	11,186	11,291	10,802	9,371	10,288	12,583	10,156	11,459	11,595	10,990
88	11,030	11,000	10,909	9,600	9,795	12,902	9,816	11,249	11,341	11,570
89	11,108	11,206	11,017	8,928	10,000	13,210	10,286	11,625	10,546	11,457
90	11,090	11,296	10,938	8,789	10,656	14,804	10,161	11,293	10,060	11,577
91	11,211	11,204	10,804	8,591	9,749	15,164	9,990	10,869	10,556	11,343
92	11,168	11,379	10,803	8,653	11,069	15,439	11,064	10,744	10,528	11,851
93	11,532	11,317	10,617	8,684	11,534	15,422	9,930	10,630	10,113	11,898
94	11,499	11,088	10,754	9,030	11,770	15,415	9,838	10,599	9,385	12,176
95	11,262	10,564	10,560	9,476	11,528	15,415	9,636	10,381	9,192	11,964
96	11,262	10,564	10,560	9,476	11,528	11,930	9,636	10,381	9,192	11,964

Note: When changes in benefit rates occur in the middle of the year, the annual rate is estimated by taking a weighted average.

Sources: 1986, 1989-95: National Council of Welfare "Welfare Incomes 1995". Winter 1996-97.

1988: Based on Sarlo (1992).

1986, 1987: Estimates obtained through interpolation between 1986 and 1988.

1996: It was assumed benefit rates remained the same in all provinces except Ontario. In Ontario the benefit rate was set equal to the level introduced in October 1995.

Table A2: Constant Dollar Social Assistance Benefit Rates Index for Single Parents with One Child Under 16 (1986=100)

YEAR	NFLD	PEI	NS	NB	QUE	ONT	MAN	SASK	ALTA	BC
86	100	100	100	100	100	100	100	100	100	100
87	99	97	101	103	95	103	97	98	98	106
88	97	95	102	105	91	105	94	96	96	111
89	98	97	103	98	93	108	98	100	89	110
90	98	98	102	96	99	121	97	97	85	111
91	99	97	101	94	90	124	95	93	89	109
92	98	98	101	95	103	126	105	92	89	114
93	102	98	99	95	107	126	95	91	85	114
94	101	96	101	99	109	126	94	91	79	117
95	99	91	99	104	107	126	92	89	78	115
96	99	91	99	104	107	97	92	89	78	115

Constantine Kapsalis

Appendix B: Employment Rates versus Benefit Rates

**Figure B1: Employment Rate Index versus SA Benefit Index
Mothers with Children Under 16: Newfoundland**

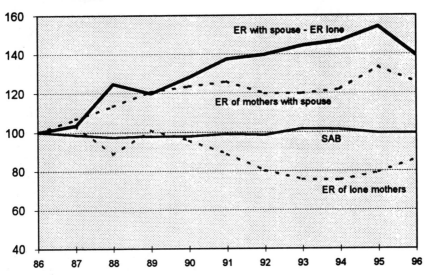

**Figure B2: Employment Rate Index versus SA Benefit Index
Mothers with Children Under 16: PEI**

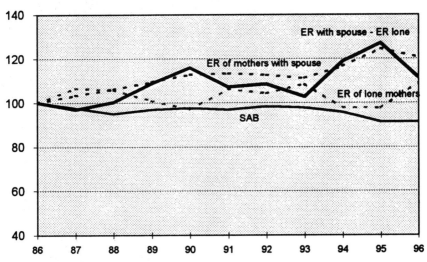

Social Assistance and the Employment Rate of Lone Mothers   237

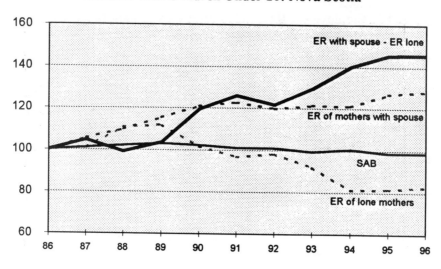

**Figure B3: Employment Rate Index versus SA Benefit Index
Mothers with Children Under 16: Nova Scotia**

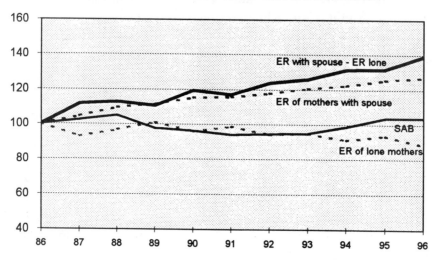

**Figure B4: Employment Rate Index versus SA Benefit Index
Mothers with Children Under 16: New Brunswick**

Constantine Kapsalis

Figure B5: Employment Rate Index versus SA Benefit Index Mothers with Children Under 16: Quebec

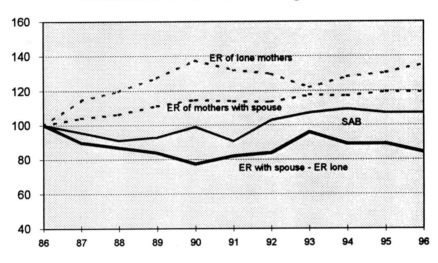

Figure B6: Employment Rate Index versus SA Benefit Index Mothers with Children Under 16: Ontario

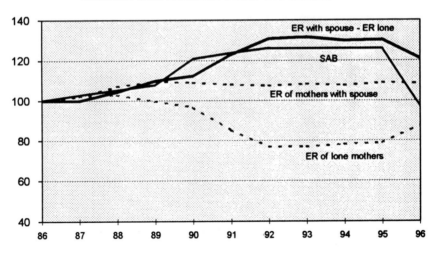

Same as Figure 2 in the main body of the study.

Social Assistance and the Employment Rate of Lone Mothers   *239*

Figure B7: Employment Rate Index versus SA Benefit Index Mothers with Children Under 16: Manitoba

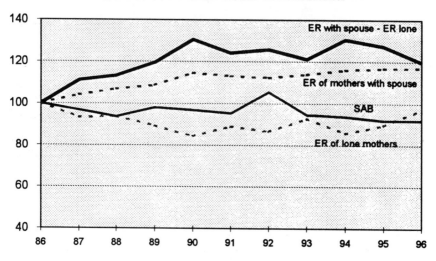

Figure B8: Employment Rate Index versus SA Benefit Index Mothers with Children Under 16: Saskatchewan

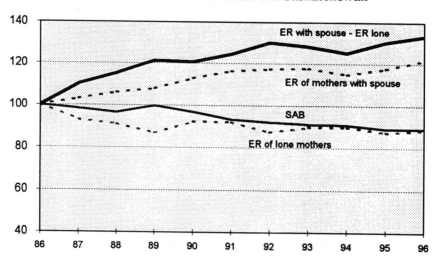

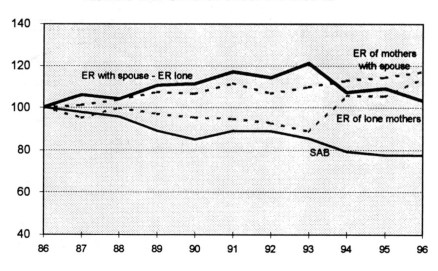

**Figure B9: Employment Rate Index versus SA Benefit Index
Mothers with Children Under 16: Alberta**

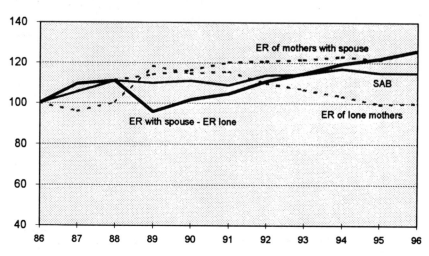

**Figure B10: Employment Rate Index versus SA Benefit Index
Mothers with Children Under 16: BC**

: Employment Rates

loyment Rate of Lone Mothers with Children Under 16,
-96

	NFLD	PEI	NS	NB	QUE	ONT	MAN	SASK	ALTA	BC
1986	38.9	53.2	46.1	46.5	39.2	59.7	57.6	59.2	61.6	50.7
1987	40.2	56.7	46.5	43.2	44.8	61.0	53.7	55.1	58.6	48.7
1988	34.5	56.3	51.0	45.0	46.9	61.3	54.0	53.9	61.5	50.9
1989	39.3	53.7	51.5	47.0	49.9	59.5	51.4	51.4	59.7	60.0
1990	37.2	51.6	46.8	44.6	53.9	57.7	48.5	54.6	58.7	58.1
1991	34.5	56.5	44.6	45.9	51.7	50.8	51.3	54.5	58.3	58.6
1992	31.2	55.4	45.3	43.8	50.8	45.8	49.9	51.7	57.1	55.7
1993	29.4	57.7	42.4	44.1	47.7	45.9	53.5	53.1	54.6	54.2
1994	29.3	52.0	37.4	42.4	50.2	46.6	49.4	53.2	65.1	52.5
1995	30.8	51.9	37.6	43.6	51.1	47.0	51.6	51.7	64.9	50.4
1996	33.5	58.1	38.1	41.0	53.0	52.3	56.0	52.4	70.1	50.7

Source: Statistics Canada, Labour Force Survey, Annual Averages
(CD 71F0004xCB).

Constantine Kapsalis

References

Allen, D. (1993), "Welfare and the Family: The Canadian Experience", *Journal of Labour Economics* 11(1), S201-223.

Ashenfelter, O. (1983), "Determining Participation in Income Tested Social Programs", *Journal of the American Statistical Association* 78, 517-525.

Brown, D. (1995), "Welfare Caseload Trends in Canada", in J. Richards and W.G. Watson (eds.), *Helping the Poor — A Qualified Case for 'Workfare'*, The Social Policy Challenge No. 5 (Toronto: C.D. Howe Institute), 37-81.

Human Resource Development Canada (1994), *Improving Social Security in Canada: A Discussion Paper* (Ottawa).

Charette, M. and R. Meng (1994), "The Determinants of Welfare Participation of Female Heads of Household in Canada", *Canadian Journal of Economics* 27(2), 290-306.

Dooley, M. (1994a). "Women, Children and Poverty in Canada", *Canadian Public Policy/Analyse de Politiques* 20(4), 430-443.

_____ (1994b), "The Converging Market Work Patterns of Married Mothers and Lone Mothers in Canada", *Journal of Human Resources* 29(2), 600-620.

_____ (1995), "Lone Mother Families and Social Assistance Policy in Canada", *Family Matters — New Policies for Divorce, Lone Mothers, and Child Poverty*, The Social Policy Challenge No. 8 (Toronto: C.D. Howe Institute).

Grady, P. (1995), "Income Security Reform and the Concept of a Guaranteed Annual Income", *Redefining Social Security*, Queen's University, Research Series.

Kapsalis, C. (1996), "Social Assistance Benefit Rates and the Employment Rate of Lone Mothers", Working Paper W-96-5E (Ottawa: Applied Research, Human Resources Development Canada).

National Council of Welfare (1986, 1989-96), *Welfare Incomes* (Ottawa: National Council of Welfare).

Richards, J. (1995), "The Study in Brief", in J. Richards and W.G. Watson (eds.), *Helping the Poor — A Qualified Case for 'Workfare'*, The Social Policy Challenge No. 5 (Toronto: C.D. Howe Institute), ix-xxvii.

Sarlo, C.A. (1992), *Poverty in Canada* (Vancouver: Fraser Institute).

_____ (1996), *Poverty in Canada*, 2d ed. (Vancouver: Fraser Institute).

Unions, Collective Bargaining and Labour Market Outcomes for Canadian Working Women: Past Gains and Future Challenges

Andrew Jackson and Grant Schellenberg

Introduction: Unions, Low Pay and Earnings Inequality

The major purposes of this paper are: first, to examine the impacts of collective bargaining on labour market outcomes for women workers in Canada, specifically with respect to pay, benefits coverage, the incidence of low pay and the extent of earnings inequality and second, to suggest ways in which positive impacts could be extended via the expansion of collective bargaining coverage.[1] This part of the paper briefly reviews the literature on the impacts

---

[1]This is an extensively revised draft of a paper presented at the "Women and Work" Conference sponsored by the John Deutsch Institute and the Canadian Workplace Research Network. While this paper has been a collaborative effort, Schellenberg is solely responsible for the regression analysis in the section on the Impacts of Collective Bargaining and the Appendix, and Jackson is solely responsible for the arguments advanced in the paper relating to trade union strategy and public policy. The Canadian Labour Congress financially supported the work on the microdata file of the 1995 Statistics Canada Survey of Work Arrangements held by the Centre for International Statistics at the Canadian Council on Social

of collective bargaining on earnings, low pay, and earnings inequality, and the next part provides some background description of the labour market position of Canadian working women. Particular attention is paid to the situation of the majority of women who continue to work in lower paid, often insecure and part-time, clerical, sales and service jobs. The central conclusion of the empirical analysis in the third section, mainly based on data from Statistics Canada's 1995 Survey of Working Arrangements, is that collective bargaining coverage, controlling for other factors, has significant positive impacts in terms of raising pay and access to benefits and in terms of reducing the incidence of low pay among women workers. However, the level of collective bargaining coverage for women is very low in precisely those sectors of the economy where women in low paid and insecure jobs are most concentrated; namely, in private services and in smaller enterprises. Promoting better labour market outcomes for women workers accordingly requires a major extension of collective bargaining. The fourth section of the paper briefly considers ways in which this could be achieved through trade union action and through changes to public policy.

The 1996 *OECD Employment Outlook* comprehensively documented profound differences in the degree of earnings inequality and the incidence of low pay in the advanced industrial countries, noting that these two labour market characteristics are closely related in that "the incidence of low pay tends to be highest in those countries where earnings inequality is the most pronounced" (OECD, 1996, p. 60). While there is significant variation between countries, a generalized pattern is that continental European countries, particularly in Northern Europe, have a strikingly more equal distribution of earnings and a much lower incidence of low pay among both working women and men than do the United States, the United Kingdom and Canada. To indicate the extremes, the earnings gap between the top and bottom deciles of women earners in Canada is double that in Sweden (i.e., the ratio between the upper limit of decile 9 and the bottom limit of decile 2 is 3.7 compared to 1.8), and the incidence of low pay among full-time women workers (defined as earning below two-thirds of the economy wide median wage) is 34.3% in Canada compared to just 8.4% in Sweden. OECD

Development which is the major statistical basis for the analysis. The paper has benefited from the comments of Penni Richmond, Director of the Women's and Human Rights Department of the Canadian Labour Congress, Richard Chaykowski and Lisa Powell of Queen's University, and Brenda Lautsch of Simon Fraser University.

countries such as Canada and Sweden are exposed to broadly comparable forces of "structural" change, such as exposure to international trade and investment flows and to rapid technological change, but differ significantly in terms of labour market institutions. This suggests that institutions such as collective bargaining can have significant impacts on the quality of jobs as well as on the level of inequality between wage earners.

As the OECD notes, a major explanation for large differences between countries is labour market institutions: "different institutional settings with regard to wage bargaining, legal minimum wages and the generosity of unemployment and other related benefits appear to account for some of the wide variation across countries in the overall incidence of low pay" (OECD, 1996, p. 76). More specifically, it was established in the OECD analysis that there is a high and negative correlation between collective bargaining coverage and the incidence of low pay. Similarly, a major set of Canada-U.S. comparative studies has shown that labour market institutions, broadly defined, have significantly attenuated income inequality in Canada compared to the United States (Card and Freeman, 1993). Among those studies, Lemieux (1993) demonstrated that the higher level of unionization in Canada compared to the United States was one important factor explaining the lower level of wage inequality and somewhat lower incidence of low pay among Canadian compared to American workers in the mid-1980s. He calculates that the pattern and extent of unionization in Canada compared to the United States explained 40% of the difference in the wage inequality among men in Canada compared to the United States.

The impact of unionization and collective bargaining on the quality of employment in terms of pay, benefits, security and other outcomes is a complex and controversial subject. However, there is a substantial consensus that collective bargaining raises pay and benefits for unionized workers compared to otherwise comparable non-union workers, particularly lower skilled workers (the wage premium effect) and promotes greater equality of wages and working conditions within the unionized sector by compressing wage and benefit differentials (the compression effect). Chaykowski (1995) provides evidence on the impact of Canadian unions on pay and access to benefits, and on pay differentials within and between firms. Collective bargaining generally reduces the incidence of low pay and promotes equality between workers by simultaneously lifting the wage floor and by compressing wage differentials in the unionized sector; but collective bargaining can also increase inequality in the labour market as a whole by creating a pay gap between union and non-union workers. The impact of collective bargaining on the incidence of low pay and on inequality in the labour market as a whole is thus crucially determined by three major variables: the wage premium effect (the impact of unionization on wages and differentials of union compared to non-union workers); the compression effect (the impact on earnings distributions in the unionized sector); and by the extent of collective bargaining coverage among the labour force as a whole.

A crucial institutional difference between many continental European countries and North America is that collective bargaining coverage is much higher in the former because of generally higher unionization rates, and because many non-union workers are covered by informal or legal extensions of collective agreements. Union wage premiums, by contrast, have generally been found to be higher in the United States. It can be observed that, because of the impacts on the labour costs of union compared to non-union employers operating in competitive markets, relatively low collective bargaining coverage combined with a high union wage premium is likely to considerably increase employer hostility to unions and decrease the prospects for long-term union survival and growth compared to wide coverage and a lower wage premium (Chaykowski and Slotsve, 1996).

Recent empirical work in the United States has found that the inequality reducing wage compression effects of collective bargaining within the unionized sector outweigh the inequality increasing wage premium effect among male workers. Declining unionization has thus implied increasing wage inequality, and it has been estimated by Card (1992) and Freeman (1993) that about one-fifth of the increase in earnings inequality among U.S. men in the 1980s can be attributed to the sharp fall in unionization over the decade.

The impacts of collective bargaining on wage inequality among women have been found to differ because of the historically lower rate of union-ization among women (though this is no longer true of Canada), and because unionization among women, unlike men, tends to be more heavily con-centrated among highly educated workers. This is, in turn, a function of the relatively high unionization rates in public or quasi-public services such as health and education which employ a large proportion of women with high levels of education, and very low unionization rates in private services which employ a high proportion of women, such as retail trade, personal services and accommodation and food services. Fortin and Lemieux (1996) have found that changes in labour market institutions, broadly defined, account for about one-third of the increase in wage inequality among American men and

Andrew Jackson and Grant Schellenberg

women in the 1980s, but that the fall in collective bargaining coverage specifically had little impact on inequality among women.

Lemieux (1993) found, on the basis of Canadian data for 1986, that unionization significantly raised the wages of unionized compared to non-unionized women, that the unionization rate of women increased with skill level, and that unionization compressed wages among unionized women. The "wage raising" effect of unionization among women was not entirely offset by the wage compression effect in the unionized sector, so unionization very slightly increased wage inequality among women. Unionization did, however, very modestly improve the position of women relative to men in the overall wage distribution. In both the United States and Canada, research has shown that unionization has little impact on the overall gap between the wages of women and men, in significant part because the unionization rate has been much higher for men, thus concentrating the income gains of collective bargaining among male workers (particularly blue collar workers). However, the impact of unionization on inequality of earnings between men and women was found to be small in Canada in 1984 (30 cents per hour), and was concentrated in the private sector where the unionization rate of women is low. Unionization has considerably reduced earnings differences between men and women in public services where the unionization rate of women is high (Maki and Ng, 1990). The impact of collective bargaining on earnings inequality between women and men will increase if the unionization rate of women in private services increases, and/or if more women work in relatively highly unionized blue collar occupations.

There is, then, evidence that the pattern and extent of unionization are major influences on the distribution of earnings and the incidence of low pay, and that these patterns are different for women and men. Higher rates of unionization and collective bargaining coverage among women could potentially have a significant impact on the very high incidence of low pay among Canadian women workers, on high levels of inequality of earnings among Canadian women, and on the still significant earnings gap between women and men. These issues are clearly of public concern, but the impact of unionization on women workers in the 1990s has not been extensively studied. A central purpose of this paper is to document the independent impact of collective bargaining coverage on the level of wages, the incidence of low pay, and the distribution of wages, with a specific focus on the impacts upon women. The data are presented so as to facilitate comparisons with the impacts on men.

It would be argued by some that the gains of unionization come at the expense of employment, particularly for the lower skilled. However, the OECD analysis of low-paid work and earnings inequality found that "there is little evidence to suggest that countries where low-paid work is less prevalent have achieved this at the cost of higher unemployment rates and lower employment rates for the more vulnerable groups in the labour market such as youth and women" (OECD, 1996, p. 76). Freeman has similarly concluded on the basis of numerous recent studies that union wage effects (higher wages, particularly for the low paid, and greater compression in the distribution of wages) do not come at the expense of productivity and are not responsible for the aggregate level of unemployment, largely because collectively bargained wages flexibly respond to shifting market realities (Freeman, 1992, 1994). According to the 1995 *World Employment Report* of the International Labour Organization (ILO), it is wrong to view labour market regulation as the fundamental cause of unemployment, and it is important to recognize that such regulation has important positive impacts for society in terms of greater equality and less poverty. The ILO report takes particularly strong issue with the widespread view that labour market "rigidities" have been an important source of the unemployment problem in Europe, and emphasizes the many negative features of "flexible" U.S.-style labour markets from the point of view of workers. Collective bargaining procedures which secure steady employment at decent wages in a relatively non-polarized labour market are seen as an important source of social well-being, rather than as a barrier to job creation. In recent years, the ILO has also drawn attention to the positive role of labour market regulation and collective bargaining in addressing the specific labour market problems faced by women.

In Canada, the labour movement has made the extension of collective bargaining among women, particularly lower paid women, a major priority. The widely distributed 1997 Canadian Labour Congress (CLC) document *Women's Work*, which was based on extensive discussions with women workers and union leaders and activists across the country, was intended to closely examine the impact of recent economic restructuring on women's work and women's lives as a basis for critical reflection on current trade union practices and on public policies. The report documented the increased precariousness of women's jobs which has come with the shift to temporary, contract and involuntary part-time work, particularly among women clerical, sales and service workers in the private sector, and the loss of reasonably secure and well-paid jobs for women, particularly in public and social services and in manufacturing that has been another result of economic restructuring. While noting the continued progress of women in the labour market in some key respects, such as declining earnings differentials between full-time, full-year working men and women and increased entry of women into managerial and professional occupations, central themes of the report included: the increase in insecurity and the continued high prevalence of both insecurity and low pay for many women; and the continued large inequalities which exist between working women and men.

The report noted (with some reference to broad aggregate data) that unionization had raised wages for women workers, particularly women working in part-time and other "non-standard" jobs, and also documented important equality gains for women which have been made through the collective bargaining process. However, as the report also highlighted, rates of unionization are very low for women (and men) in the private service sector of the economy, and collective bargaining coverage is particularly low for workers in small firms and in "precarious" jobs, such as contract and casual employment. These are precisely the areas of employment for women which are expanding most rapidly. In short, the labour movement has tempered its recognition of some success in terms of bargaining positive outcomes for working women with recognition of relative failure in terms of extending collective bargaining to the most insecure and vulnerable women workers, including most visible minority and aboriginal women. The fact that unions are most absent where they are most needed has led the CLC to argue that organizing women, particularly women in private services, must be made a central priority and the report made a number of recommendations for trade union and government action which are noted later in the paper. Similar recommendations were also made by Alexandra Dagg in her capacity as the labour representative on the Advisory Group on the Changing Workplace appointed by the federal minister of labour in 1996 (HRDC, 1997).

Women in the Canadian Labour Market: An Overview

The labour market experience of Canadian women is very different from that of men, and profound (though declining) inequalities between men and women continue to exist with respect to pay and benefits, and with respect to hours worked on both a weekly and annual basis. Inequality of earnings between men and women is driven in large part by differences in hourly pay.

Average hourly earnings of women are, on average, 82% those of men ($13.63 versus $16.58)[2] and the incidence of low wages is much higher among women than men. If low wage is defined as earning less than two-thirds of the economy-wide median hourly wage, the incidence of low pay among all women in 1995 was 33.6%, or more than half again as high as the 21.5% rate among men. This wage threshold is also approximately the same as that required to place a full-time earner above the Statistics Canada Low Income Cut-Off for a single person.

The effect of differences in hourly pay on wage and salary income are compounded by the effects of hours worked. Just 52% of women workers work on a full-time, full-year basis, compared to 66% of men (Statistics Canada, 1996). As a result, the difference between the annual earnings of men and women is greater than the difference of hourly earnings. Women's median annual earnings in 1996 were 61% those of men — $17,408 versus $28,510, while women working full-time, full-year earned 73.4% as much as men ($30,717 versus $41,848) (ibid.). The major difference between annual hours worked by women and men flows from the far higher incidence of part-time work among women: one in four (24%) adult women work part-time, compared to just one in twenty (6%) of adult men. While the higher incidence of part-time work is partly driven by choice and by the gendered distribution of responsibilities for child care and domestic labour, it also represents a lack of access to desired hours of work. In recent years, at least one in three women part-time workers have been underemployed in the sense that they wanted, but could not find, full-time jobs. Hours of work in part-time jobs also tend to be more variable than those of full-time workers — one in three part-timers have no regular work schedule but work the weekly hours requested by the employer. Also, the incidence of paid overtime on a weekly basis is significantly higher among men than women (18.4% versus 9.4%) and weekly overtime hours average significantly higher for men (5.5% versus 3.2%). However, the jobs of women tend to be more stable than those of men in the sense that the incidence of layoffs is much lower.

Many of these differences in pay and hours worked result from the very different occupational distribution of women and men, as well as differences in the jobs held by women and men within occupational categories. As indicated in Table 1, a majority of working women (53%) work in generally

---

[2]Data from the 1995 Survey of Work Arrangements. This is the source of other labour market data unless otherwise indicated.

Andrew Jackson and Grant Schellenberg

Table 1: Composition of Female and Male Employment and Incidence of Unionization, by Selected Characteristics, Canada 1995

	Women		Men	
	Composition of Employment	*% Unionized*	*Composition of Employment*	*% Unionized*
All	100%	36	100%	40
Aged 15 to 24	20	13	21	16
Aged 25 to 44	55	38	53	42
Aged 45 to 69	25	44	26	51
Less than high school	18	26	24	40
High school/some post-sec.	34	28	31	36
Certificate/diploma	31	40	29	44
University degree	17	49	16	40
Full-time	70	39	87	43
Part-time	30	27	13	18
Management/administration	13	24	13	24
Professional	25	62	14	48
Clerical	28	32	6	45
Sales	10	11	7	15
Services	15	24	13	37
Blue collar	9	34	46	47
Firm size less than 20	24	6	21	10
Firm size 20 to 99	15	27	18	28
Firm size 100 to 500	20	50	18	47
Firm size more than 500	41	50	43	59
Public sector	19	79	16	80
Private sector	81	24	84	32
Agriculture/primary	2	na	5	33
Manufacturing	11	29	24	47
Construction	1	na	8	37
Distributive services*	7	37	16	41
Retail Trade	14	13	11	19
FIRE*/business services	14	12	9	16
Community services*	29	64	9	69
Personal and other services*	16	9	11	12
Public administration	6	76	7	76

Notes: Distributive services includes transportation, communications (including postal services), utilities and wholesale trade. FIRE includes financial services, insurance and real estate. Community services includes health, education and religious organizations. Personal services and other services includes recreation, food, and accommodation; private households and miscellaneous services. na - Sample size too small to provide reliable estimate.

low-paid, often part-time, clerical, sales and service occupations — double the proportion of men (26%). While clerical work has been in decline, it is notable that more than one-quarter of women (28%) still work in clerical jobs, which are overwhelmingly held by women. Sales and services jobs are much more evenly divided between women and men and their share of total employment has been rising. Fully one-half (48.6%) of women in clerical, sales, and services occupations were low-paid workers in 1995 (again defined as earning less than two-thirds of the economy-wide median hourly wage) and annual earnings for women clerical, sales and service workers averaged just $17,184; 31.6% of these women were underemployed in the sense that they reported a desire to work more hours than currently worked, and 20.4% worked an irregular or on-call schedule.

Thirty-eight percent of women work in generally better paid managerial/ administrative and professional occupations (13% and 25% respectively), and this proportion has been steadily rising, driving much of the decreased earnings inequality between women and men. The increased entry of women into these occupations was, historically, closely associated with the growth of public and social services, notably health care and education. About two in three women in these higher paid occupations work in non-market services (very broadly defined to include health, education and social services), in part because the incidence of professional occupations non-market services is much higher than in private services and, in part, because two out of three workers in non-market services are women. Clearly, the lack of job growth in public and social services in recent years — indeed actual reductions in employment in public administration and in institutional health care — has negatively impacted upon a major source of good jobs for working women. By the same token, future prospects for women in the labour market will very much depend upon the quality of jobs in growing private services.

The pay gap between full-time, full-year working women and men has been declining in the 1980s and 1990s, in part due to the falling real earnings of men. There remain, however, very significant differences between the distribution of annual earnings among men and women. In 1996, just 6.3% of women earned more than $50,000 compared to 20.4% of men, and 45.3% of women earned less than $15,000 per year compared to 28.9% of men. Table 2 shows that the proportion of women falls at each step in the decile distribution of annual earnings — with women making up 62% of the lowest income decile and just 17% of the top decile. However, as indicated in the table, the proportion of women in the upper part of the earnings distribution has increased significantly since 1984.

Table 2: Gender Composition of Earnings Deciles in 1984 and 1994, All Earners

1984 Earnings Deciles	Annual Earnings (in 1994 $)	Gender Composition of Earnings Deciles (% women)		Percentage Point Change
		1984	1994	1994 minus 1984
1 lowest	$3,393 or less	60.5	61.6	1.1
2	$3,394-$7,234	56.4	59.4	3.0
3	$7,235-$11,988	60.6	58.3	-2.3
4	$11,989-$16,974	56.3	59.2	2.9
5	$16,975-$22,177	55.7	55.7	0.0
6	$22,178-$27,714	53.7	52.3	-1.4
7	$27,715-$33,948	40.0	47.9	7.9
8	$33,949-$41,020	30.0	34.0	4.0
9	$41,021-$51,072	19.2	28.8	9.6
10 highest	$51,073 or more	11.5	17.2	5.6
Total	All levels	44.4	46.6	2.2

Source: Scott and Lochead (1996).

Picot (1996) has recently documented trends in the earnings distribution of men and women in the 1980s and 1990s. He finds that, unlike for men, there has been little or no increase in earnings inequality among women since 1981, and that there has been a modest increase in the real median annual earnings of women. The real annual earnings of lower paid women have also increased, but it is emphasized that this has been largely driven by increases in the number of weeks worked over a year rather than by increases in hourly pay. There has also been some shifting of women into higher hourly paid jobs.

In summary, there has been a decline in the earnings inequality of women compared to men, but women remain concentrated in relatively low hourly wage occupations and in jobs which offer fewer hours of work than those occupied by men. These differences are also reflected in access to non-wage benefits: 47.8% of women belong to employer-sponsored pension plans, compared to 54.3% of men; women average 11.6 days of paid vacation per year compared to 13.4 for men; 49.8% of women belong to a dental plan compared to 59.4% of men; 53.5% of women have a health plan compared to 63.9% of men; and 55.8% of women have access to paid sick leave compared to 58.1% of men.

It should be noted that visible minority, disabled and aboriginal women — who comprise respectively 8%, 6% and 3% of all women workers — have still lower earnings than other women. On average, visible minority women workers earned 9% less per hour in 1993 than did all women workers, workers with disabilities earned 8% less, and aboriginal workers earned 12% less.[3] The incidence of unemployment is also significantly higher for these equity seeking groups. Unfortunately, little detailed analysis has been undertaken of the specific barriers encountered by minority women in the labour market and the Survey of Work Arrangements does not allow for such analysis.

The collective bargaining coverage rate for women workers is now quite comparable to that of men — 36% compared to 40% (see Table 1).[4] However, this is in large part a reflection of the fact that there is a very high unionization rate among women working in public administration (76%) and in community services (64%). More than one in three women work in these predominantly non-market sectors — double the proportion of men. The incidence of collective bargaining coverage for women in professional occupations is both high and is higher than for men — 62% versus 48% — reflecting the disproportionate concentration of women professionals in the non-market sector. By contrast, the collective bargaining coverage of women in sales and service occupations is very low at 11% and 24%, respectively. Coverage is both low and somewhat lower than for men in retail trade (13% versus 19%), financial and business services (12% versus 16%), and personal services (9% versus 12%). Coverage is 34% in blue-collar jobs, but just 9% of women work in such jobs.

As will be documented below, collective bargaining has particularly significant positive impacts upon labour market outcomes for women, holding other factors constant. However, these gains are relatively narrowly

---

[3]Unpublished data from the 1993 Statistics Canada, Survey of Labour and Income Dynamics.

[4]Collective bargaining coverage is somewhat higher than the unionization rate since it includes workers who are not union members, but who are covered by the terms of a collective agreement.

Andrew Jackson and Grant Schellenberg

concentrated on a minority of women because of low bargaining coverage. In the private services sector, the gains of collective bargaining apply to only a small minority of workers, and to an even smaller minority of women.

Impacts of Collective Bargaining Coverage on Canadian Women Workers

Union Wage Premium

There is a consensus within the literature that unionization is associated with a substantial and consistent wage premium in Canada. As Chaykowski and Slotsve (1996) show, such a premium has been consistently reported in studies over the last two decades. Evidence from the 1995 Survey of Work Arrangements (SWA) confirms the presence of the union wage premium. The average wage of women in unionized jobs was more than $5.00 (or 31%) higher than the average wage of women in non-unionized jobs, while for men, the wage difference was about $4.50 — or 24%. The wage premium associated with unionization is shown for selected subgroups of women and men in Table 3. It is notable that the apparent union wage premium tends to be higher for less-educated workers, though this is more clearly the case for men than for women. This is consistent with the fact that managerial and professional occupations in the private sector have very low rates of unionization.

The positive impact of unionization on hourly wages is confirmed using ordinary least squared (OLS) regression. Table 4 shows OLS estimates of hourly wage equations run separately for women and men.[5] The equations

---

[5]The OLS analysis was undertaken using the 1995 Survey of Work Arrangements. SWA respondents who were paid employees in their main job were asked about their hourly wages; 16,358 (or 82%) provided valid information. From this group, 625 individuals were excluded because of missing values on one or more of the independent variables included in the equation, resulting in a sample of 15,733. A number of regression equations were run using both hourly wages and the log of hourly wages as the dependent variable. An analysis of residuals indicated that the hourly wage variable was acceptable for use in the OLS equation; the log of hourly wages resulted in only minor improvement in the distribution of error terms.

Table 3: Average Hourly Wages of Women and Men, by Unionization and Selected Characteristics, Canada 1995

	WOMEN			MEN		
	Union	Non-Union	"Union Premium"	Union	Non-Union	"Union Premium"
All	16.68	11.58	30.6%	18.98	14.45	23.9%
Age 15 to 24	11.23	8.11	27.8	11.83	8.64	27.0
Age 25 to 44	16.92	12.71	24.9	18.79	15.80	15.9
Age 45 to 69	17.37	12.71	26.8	20.93	18.15	13.3
Less than high school	12.16	8.30	31.7	16.23	10.80	33.5
High school grad.	14.60	10.73	26.5	17.34	12.40	28.5
Certificate/diploma	16.56	12.05	27.2	19.87	15.45	22.2
University degree	21.38	17.18	19.6	23.12	21.73	6.0
Full-time	16.90	12.61	25.4	19.29	15.60	19.1
Part-time	15.95	9.62	39.7	12.71	8.52	33.0
Managerial/admin.	18.59	16.51	11.2	23.00	21.41	6.9
Professional	19.49	15.45	20.7	22.47	18.49	17.7
Clerical	14.47	11.21	22.5	16.55	12.26	25.9
Sales	12.04	9.09	24.5	13.51	10.90	19.3
Services	12.18	7.40	39.2	16.20	8.93	44.9
Blue collar	12.87	9.37	27.2	18.32	13.17	28.1
Firm size less than 20	12.42	10.41	16.2	16.48	11.62	29.5
Firm size 20 to 99	15.03	11.13	25.9	17.00	13.12	22.8
Firm size 100 to 500	16.36	11.99	26.7	18.39	15.92	13.4
Firm size + 500	17.53	13.10	25.3	19.82	18.06	8.9

Note: The "union premium" is simply the difference between the average union and non-union wage divided by average union wage, expressed as a percentage.

Andrew Jackson and Grant Schellenberg

Table 4: Ordinary Least Squared Estimates of Wage Equation: Unstandardized Regression Coefficients (standard errors in parentheses)

	Women	Men
Unionized	1.241	1.145
	(.136)	(.147)
Age	.239	.397
	(.031)	(.038)
Age-squared	- .003	- .004
	(.000)	(.000)
Married	.489	1.513
	(.116)	(.142)
Less than high school	- .939	- 1.192
	(.164)	(.172)
Certificate or diploma	.556	1.475
	(.131)	(.154)
University degree	4.136	4.313
	(.169)	(.208)
Part-time	.271	- .801
	(.123)	(.225)
Firm size less than 20	- 1.512	- 2.833
	(.145)	(.179)
Firm size 20 to 99	- 1.213	- 2.276
	(.156)	(.176)
Firm size 100 to 499	-.804	- 1.067
	(.141)	(.167)
Job tenure less than one year	-.296	- .429
	(.143)	(.168)
Job tenure 6 to 10 years	1.531	1.496
	(.148)	(.183)
Job tenure 11 to 20 years	2.740	2.797
	(.168)	(.192)
Job tenure more than 20 years	3.912	3.619
	(.227)	(.237)
Constant	9.758	8.563
	(.611)	(.740)
Adjusted R^2	.539	.535
Observations	7,861	7,872

Notes: The specification also includes four region dummies, four industry dummies and six occupation dummies.
Reference categories for dummy variables: education (excluded high-school or some postsecondary); firm size (500 or more); job tenure (1-5 years).
Source: 1995 Survey of Work Arrangements micro data file.

include variables for unionization, age, education, marital status, part-time /full-time hours, firm size, job tenure, occupation, industry and region. As would be expected, higher hourly wages are positively associated with increasing age, higher levels of education, longer job tenure and employment in larger firms. Likewise, unionization is associated with a positive effect, as evidenced by the wage premium of $1.24 for women and $1.15 for men. The difference reported between the wage premium for women and men is not statistically significant. One unexpected finding is that, among women, part-time employment is positively associated with hourly wages. This is not the case among men. To examine this in closer detail, an interaction term combining part-time hours and unionization was subsequently included in the equations. For women, the coefficient of the interaction term was positive (0.680) and significant, and its inclusion in the model made the part-time variable insignificant. For men, the inclusion of the interaction term had little effect on other coefficients. This suggests that unionization is a particularly important factor associated with wage gains for women in part-time jobs.

A second set of regression equations was run to assess the impact of unionization on the hourly wages of women and men within occupational categories. The unstandardized regression coefficients are shown in Table 5.[6] (The results of the analysis are presented in Appendix Table A1.) Unionization has a positive impact on hourly wages for women within all five occupational categories, with this generally in the range of $1.00 to $2.00. Similarly, unionization has a positive effect on the hourly wages of men in all categories, with the exception of those in professional occupations.

Incidence of Low Pay

As noted above, the OECD reports striking national differences in the incidence of low-wage employment among full-time workers. The incidence of low-wage employment is 25% in the United States and 23.7% in Canada, compared to 13.3% in Germany, and just 5.2% in Sweden. The incidence of low pay among women workers, higher than for men in all countries, is

---

[6]Separate equations were run for men and women in each of professional, clerical, sales, service and blue-collar occupations using the same specifications as noted above. The regression equations were also run using the log of hourly wages as the dependent variable. This led to the same end results.

Andrew Jackson and Grant Schellenberg

Table 5: Change in Hourly Wage Associated with Unionization, Canada, 1995 by Sex and Occupation

	WOMEN	MEN
Professional	1.11	na
Clerical	1.62	0.83
Sales	0.85	1.53
Services	2.37	1.47
Blue collar	1.67	2.25

Note: Unadjusted regression coefficients. See Appendix. Union variable not significant for men in professional occupations; significant at 0.1 for men in clerical occupations.

32.5% in the United States, 34.3% in Canada, 25.4% in Germany and just 8.4% in Sweden.

The incidence of low-wage employment among women and men in union and non-union sectors is shown in Table 6. While almost one-half of all non-unionized women work in low-wage jobs, this is the case for less than 10% of women who are unionized. Striking differences are evident when comparisons are made between unionized and non-unionized women in specific age groups, in specific occupations and so on (e.g., 85% of women in non-union services job are low pay compared to 26% of those who are unionized). The same pattern is evident among men, although non-unionized men stand a better chance than non-unionized women of finding jobs above the low-wage cut-off and the incidence of low pay among non-unionized men tends to be somewhat lower than among women, particularly in sales and service occupations. The importance of unionization as a protective factor against low-wage employment is confirmed using logistic regression.[7] After

---

[7] A logistic regression model was run in which SWA respondents were categorized into two groups on the basis of the hourly wage in their main job — those in jobs paying less than $9.93 per hour (two-thirds the economy-wide median wage) and those in jobs paying more. Those in "low-wage" jobs were

Table 6: Share of Women and Men in "Low-Wage" Jobs, by Unionization and Selected Characteristics, Canada 1995

	Women		Men	
	Union	Non-Union	Union	Non-Union
All	9	47	6	32
Aged 15 to 24	47	76	40q	72
Aged 25 to 44	6	36	5	19
Aged 45 and over	5	41	na	18
Less than high school	22	78	11q	50
High school/some post-sec.	13	50	7q	39
Certificate/diploma	5	39	na	22
University degree	na	16	na	11
Full-time	7	37	4	23
Part-time	15	67	na	77
Managerial/admin.	na	14	na	7q
Professional	na	20	na	18
Clerical	8q	40	na	36
Sales	na	70	na	51
Services	26q	85	na	72
Blue collar	21q	68	5	29
Firm size less than 20	na	56	na	42
Firm size 20 to 99	12q	50	12q	35
Firm size 100 to 500	9	44	6q	26
Firm size more than 500	6	37	5q	22

Notes: Low wages jobs are those that pay less than two-thirds of the economy-wide median wage. This includes jobs paying less than $9.33 per hour.
q - sample less reliable due to small sample size.
na - unable to provide reliable estimate because of small sample size.

coded as one and those in non-low wage jobs as zero. The personal and job characteristics used in the ordinary least square regression equations discussed above were included in the logistic model, and separate equations were run for women and men. The model correctly classified 88% of men and 87% of women as low-wage or non-low-wage workers.

Andrew Jackson and Grant Schellenberg

factors such as age, education and firm size are taken into account, unionization still significantly reduces the *relative odds* of working in a low-wage job, with this being the case for both women and men (regression results are shown in Appendix Tables A3 and A4).

Wage Inequality

As noted above, there is evidence that unionization and collective bargaining have an impact on the overall distribution of earnings. One summary measure of inequality is the ratio between the top and bottom deciles of the earnings distribution. (The top of Decile 9 compared to the bottom of Decile 2.) In the United States, the top decile of male earners earn at least 4.5 times more than the bottom decile, compared to a ratio of 3.7 in Canada, 2.8 in Germany and 1.8 in Sweden. The top decile of women earners in the United States earn at least 4 times more than the bottom decile, compared to a ratio of 3.7 in Canada, 2.8 in Germany and 1.8 in Sweden.

Table 7 provides an overview of wage dispersion among unionized and non-unionized women and men in Canada. The Decile 9/Decile 1 ratio for unionized women is 2.50 compared to 3.30 for non-unionized women —

Table 7: Dispersion of Hourly Wages, by Sex and Unionization, Canada 1995

	WOMEN		MEN	
	Union	Non-Union	Union	Non-Union
Decile Limits ($s):				
Decile 9	25.00	19.78	27.00	25.48
Decile 5	16.00	10.00	18.75	12.50
(median)				
Decile 1	10.00	6.00	11.00	7.00
Decile 9/decile 5	1.56	1.98	1.44	2.04
Decile 1/decile 5	0.63	0.60	0.59	0.56
Decile 9/decile 1	2.50	3.30	2.45	3.64

ratios that are approximately comparable to those for men. The wage compression impact of unionization is a major reason for the observed relationship between unionization and the reduced incidence of low pay.

Non-Wage Benefits

Occupational pensions, medical and dental plans and paid holidays are important aspects of the compensation package and noticeable differences between workers in union and non-union jobs are evident (see Table 8). For example, women in unionized jobs are more than twice as likely to be included in pension plans than women in non-unionized positions, and the situation is similar when medical and dental plan coverage is considered. Differences between unionized and non-unionized workers remain when other factors, such as age, hours of work and occupation are taken into account. Likewise, when logistic regression is used to identify the factors associated with benefit coverage, the positive impact of unionization remains. As Lipsett and Reesor report, *"Union status and firm size are major factors in determining the probability of [employer-sponsored pension plan] coverage (significant at the 0.001 level). Their effects are as expected, with unionized workers and those working in large firms having better odds of ESPP coverage than their counterparts"* (Lipsett and Reesor, 1997). Currie and Chaykowski (1995) have documented the significant gender gap in benefits coverage in the unionized private sector in Canada, but show that the gap narrowed, 1986-90.

Equality Issues and Collective Bargaining

Gains for working women flow from the fact that pay and other forms of discrimination have been directly addressed in bargaining as unionized women have pushed forward an equality agenda. Table 9 provides data on the incidence of collective agreement provisions of particular importance to women, such as provisions regarding maternity leave, sexual harassment, and family responsibilities. Half of workers covered by major collective agreements now have the protection of a formal sexual harassment clause, more than double the level of 1985; 60.5% of major collective agreements contain a non-discrimination clause; and 27.6% of workers covered by major

Andrew Jackson and Grant Schellenberg

Table 8: Receipt of Non-wage Benefits, by Sex, Union Status and Selected Characteristics, Canada 1995

	Women		Men	
	Union	*Non-Union*	*Union*	*Non-Union*
% WITH PENSION PLAN -All	79	31	83	35
Age 25 to 44	80	38	83	41
Age 45 to 69	83	34	89	46
Full-time	85	41	85	41
Part-time	60	9	31q	na
Management/administration	89	54	91	58
Professional	84	36	90	46
Clerical	81	32	88	39
Sales	na	21	57q	33
Service	62	9	82	15
Blue collar	61	22	80	27
% WITH MEDICAL PLAN - All	78	40	87	49
Age 25 to 44	80	48	88	56
Age 45 to 69	80	43	91	60
Full-time	86	54	89	56
Part-time	50	11	31q	na
Management/administration	88	69	94	77
Professional	79	45	88	60
Clerical	80	43	85	49
Sales	na	27	69q	48
Service	61	13	84	21
Blue collar	79	34	87	40
% WITH DENTAL PLAN - All	72	38	79	46
Age 25 to 44	75	46	81	55
Age 45 to 69	72	37	82	55
Full-time	80	51	82	53
Part-time	46	10	29q	na
Management/administration	87	65	81	73
Professional	71	44	77	58
Clerical	76	41	84	47
Sales	na	26	63q	44
Service	54	12	79	19
Blue collar	69	28	80	39

Notes: q - Estimate less reliable due to small sample size.
na - Sample size too small to provide reliable estimate.

Table 9: Employees Covered by Collective Agreements with 500 or More Employees: Percent of Employees Covered by Clauses Pertaining to Selected Issues, Canada 1985 and 1998

Clauses Regarding	1985	1998	% Point Change
Anti-discrimination provision	56.1	60.5	+ 4.4
Affirmative action	5.9	11.8	+ 9.9
Sexual harassment	20.6	51.7	+ 31.1
Equal pay	5.4	27.6	+ 22.2
Job sharing	2.6	9.5	+ 6.9
Flexitime	17.5	34.9	+ 17.4
Day care facilities	3.4	6.0	+ 2.6
Seniority during maternity leave	47.0	52.0	+ 5.0
Paid maternity leave UI/EI supplement	37.0	52.8	+ 15.8
Max. maternity leave - with and without pay			
1 to 16 weeks	0.3	0.4	+ 0.1
17 weeks	16.6	22.8	+ 6.2
18 to 25 weeks	27.5	24.0	+ 3.5
26 weeks or more	17.6	21.5	+ 3.9
Length not specified	7.0	4.2	+ 2.8
No provision	30.9	27.1	+ 3.8
Seniority during adoption leave	34.8	48.1	+ 13.3
Paid adoption leave UI/EI supplement	20.3	30.2	+ 9.9
Max. adoption leave - with and without pay			
1 to 16 weeks	26.2	19.2	- 7.0
17 weeks	7.1	8.7	+ 1.6
18 to 25 weeks	3.4	13.9	+ 10.5
26 weeks or more	15.9	21.9	+ 6.0
Length not specified	0.9	1.8	+ 0.9
No provision	46.3	34.5	-11.8
Paid leave - illness in family	22.5	24.2	+ 1.7
Unpaid leave - illness in family	8.7	17.8	+ 9.1
Unpaid extended parental leave	9.7	28.2	+ 18.5
Unpaid extended paternity leave	21.7	47.2	+ 25.5
Unpaid personal reasons leave	34.1	52.9	+ 18.8

Source: Special tabulations prepared by Human Resources Development Canada, Workplace Information Directorate.

Andrew Jackson and Grant Schellenberg

collective agreements have access to a provision calling for equal pay for work of equal value, compared to just 5.4% in 1985. Many unions have negotiated formal job evaluation plans and elimination or compression of pay grades occupied by lower paid women. Bargaining has resulted in progress on equity issues in the absence of legislative provisions, and has often made the resolution of such issues subject to grievance and arbitration procedures.

Another area of readily documentable progress has been with respect to paid maternity leaves. Today, the majority of workers covered by major collective agreements have access to such leaves, often at up to 76% to 100% of normal pay. Provision for paid leaves in excess of 17 weeks have become much more common.

Gains have been made in terms of provisions allowing workers to take time off work to attend to parental responsibilities and family care, although in most cases such leave has been provided on an unpaid basis. Several unions have also been able to bargain significant funds for child care. The Canadian Auto Workers, for example, have bargained 4.5 cents per hour for child care, which has been used to establish programs that accommodate the needs of shift workers. The Canadian Union of Postal Workers has also bargained significant funds which have been used to develop innovative, community-based child-care services. In some cases, the gains made by unions through collective bargaining have been trend setting and have exerted pressure on governments to improve labour standards. For example, provisions for parental and adoption leave were negotiated within many large collective agreements well before legislation on these issues was passed in any jurisdiction (White, 1993, pp. 87-89).

Given that one in four adult women work part-time, contract provisions pertaining to part-time workers are particularly relevant to women: 70% of collective agreements have specific part-time provisions, up from 56% in 1985; and gains for part-time workers have been made on several issues, including sick leave, holiday time, severance pay, hours of work, health and welfare, and the prorating of benefits (Schellenberg, 1996).

The unionization rate for women working part-time in 1997 was 26%, though unionization rates are very low in small workplaces (7.2% in workplaces with less than 20 employees) and in private services. In 1997, as indicated by Labour Force Survey data, unionized women part-time workers earned 94.3% of the hourly wage of full-time unionized workers, while non-unionized women part-timers earned just 75.5% of the hourly wage of non-unionized women full-time workers. The wage gap is lower for women than for men working part-time. Unionization has also brought major gains with respect to benefits; 56.7% of unionized part-timers belong to a pension plan, below the 86.6% coverage for full-time unionized workers, but well above the pension coverage rate of just 7.4% for non-union part-time workers. The comparable data for health plan coverage are 88.9%, 47.8% and 9%.

As suggested by the data, negotiation of equal pay and at least pro-rated benefits for part-timers has been a major priority for many unions over the past decade. Some unions have also been in the forefront of bargaining "flexible" part-time working time arrangements which particularly suit the needs of women (given the gendered division of household labour, child care and elder care). "Flexitime" and compressed workweek provisions are now common, though not generally more prevalent in unionized than in non-union workplaces. In addition, some unions (e.g., the Communications, Energy and Paperworkers Union at the *Toronto Star*, and CUPE in the City of Winnipeg) have bargained for a worker's right to reduce hours to part-time status, with no loss of pay and benefits, with a right to return to a full-time job. While exceptional, such rights to reduce hours are clearly an important part of genuine worker "flexibility".

Of course, unionization also gives to working women the normal protections of a collective agreement, notably access to a grievance and arbitration process regarding discipline, dismissal and promotions; protection against layoff; and other rights and protections. In practice, even legislated minimum employment standards are much easier to access in a unionized environment. Most importantly, unions are an instrument of democratization, giving workers a collective, independent voice in workplace governance.

Women activists in the labour movement have increasingly moved into leadership positions, though the CLC Report on Women's Work stresses that much more has to be done to open up the labour movement to participation by women and other equality seeking groups, and to push issues of concern to women higher up the collective bargaining and political agenda.

Future Challenges: Collective Bargaining and the Future of Women's Work

Job growth for women in the 1990s has been heavily concentrated in the private services sector, primarily in very small firms and in self-employment. Between 1992 and 1996, the number of self-employed women (in unincorporated enterprises) rose by 32.7%, representing 141,000 jobs; the

Andrew Jackson and Grant Schellenberg

number of women private sector employees rose by 6.5%, representing 275,000 jobs, and the number of women public sector employees fell by 2.2% or 25,000 jobs lost.[8] Recent job growth for women has also been disproportionately in part-time jobs and the incidence of temporary work has been rising rapidly. While recent trends have been overlaid by a very slow recovery from the recession of the early 1990s and by the restructuring of public services, it seems highly likely that these broad trends will continue. Some women will find well-paid professional and managerial jobs in private services, but it also seems likely that a very large proportion of working women will continue to be employed in relatively low-pay clerical, sales and service occupations. Indeed, the professional and managerial share of women's jobs may well decline if growth in public and social services does not resume.

Through the past three decades, the overall unionization rate in Canada has remained remarkably steady at about one in three paid workers. In 1997, it stood at 31%, though the overall picture of stability is modified somewhat if it is taken into account that the proportion of self-employed workers in the workforce has been growing very rapidly (Statistics Canada, 1997). Today, almost one-half (45%) of union members are women, up from just 25% in 1972. Since 1972, 86% of the growth of union membership was among women, a function of the rising participation rate of women, the decline of the employment share of traditionally male-dominated industries, and the entry of women into fast growing public and social services. However, with a public services recession, very slow overall job growth, and the dispro- portionate concentration of job growth in self-employment and small firms, the total number of women union members has grown by just 0.6% over the 1992 to 1997 period (Lipsig-Mummé and Laxer, 1998).

As noted above, unionization rates are very low in most parts of the private services sector — retail trade, accommodation and food services, finance and business and personal services — and are particularly low in small workplaces. These are precisely the sectors in which most women in the private sector work and where the potential gains from collective bargaining, as documented above, are greatest. Clearly, a key challenge facing the labour movement is to find ways to maintain and improve access to collective bargaining and the benefits, rights and protections it affords in the context of a structural shift of employment to relatively low-paid sectors

---

[8]Labour Force Survey data.

where levels of precarious and contingent work are high. Given the large potential gains from the spread of collective bargaining, this should also be viewed as a challenge for public policy. A lot of analytical attention has been paid to the dismal employment trends of the 1990s, but there has been too little debate over positive policy prescription.

The unionization rate is determined by the pace of structural change which adds and subtracts employment in unionized workplaces, and by the pace of new organization. The obstacles to union organizing in private services are not insuperable. Coverage is significant in some parts of the retail trade, such as grocery stores and larger retail chains, and in the hotel industry. There have been successful and widely publicized recent organizing drives in fast food restaurants, small retail operations, and other small workplaces. Several unions have made new organizing a major priority, and it is often not appreciated that the relatively steady membership of some unions masks constant new organizing to offset membership losses in other workplaces. The membership of large industrial unions such as the USWA, UFCW, CAW and the CEP has shifted from larger industrial workplaces towards the service sector as a result of mergers and organizing, and public sector unions such as CUPE, NUPGE and the PSAC have been organizing workers in privatized public services and in social services delivered by the private sector. Much of this new organizing has involved women. The commitment of Canadian unions to new organizing has generally been significantly higher than in the United States, though major changes in the United States may be underway.

While Canadian unions have tended to have a stronger "organizing culture" than U.S. unions, much more could and should be done to increase the resources and efforts devoted to new organizing, particularly among women workers. The CLC Women and Work Report drew particular attention to the need for unions to hire women organizers and to focus more on issues of particular concern to women — such as pay and employment equity and dealing with harassment in both organizing campaigns and in collective bargaining. The report also called up on unions to adopt forms of organizing which have proven to be successful in building unions among lower paid service sector workers in both the United States and Canada. One key lesson from recent experience is the importance of a high level of rank and file mobilization and leadership, including both current and prospective members of the union, as opposed to top-down organizing by professional, full-time union staff. The "movement" dimension of union building has also been in the forefront in community-based campaigns which attempt to build support for workplace organizing efforts at the level of the local geographical community, as well as within ethnic and other communities of identity. These new organizing methods are in many ways a conscious return to the social movement building efforts which marked earlier periods of rapid unionization (Bronfenbrenner and Friedman, 1998). The CLC report also called for higher levels of co-operation among affiliated unions in organizing efforts and consideration of associate membership and other forms of "pre union" organization. Women and social movement activists have questioned the unionization of jobs, as opposed to building labour organizations that link workers who can, and do, move frequently between jobs.

The overall picture suggests that new organizing is running below the rate needed to maintain, let alone increase, the overall unionization rate. Available data shows that organizing of new members in the 1990s has been running significantly below the growth in the labour force (Lipsig-Mummé and Laxer, 1998). One important caveat does have to be added: where labour legislation has been reasonably facilitative of organizing, as in British Columbia today and in Ontario under the New Democratic Party (NDP) government, the number of new certifications has significantly increased, sometimes at or near the level that would increase the unionization rate.

The fundamental reality is that union representation in the small firm, private services sector, is low and is likely to remain low in the absence of public policy support. The key barriers are not worker rejection of unions or lack of union interest in organizing, but are structural.[9] As a practical matter, it is extremely difficult to establish collective bargaining in sectors that are dominated by small firms and that are both labour intensive and highly competitive. A "community of interest" is hard to establish among workers where turnover is high, the hours of work are highly variable, and there is close supervision of workers by owners and managers. Further, small enterprise employers strongly resist unionization because of the loss of "flexibility" in hiring and firing and, most importantly, because unionization threatens to raise wages and benefits in highly competitive, labour-intensive sectors, posing the issue of survival of the enterprise in the short term. While many larger employers have established stable bargaining relationships and accept the legitimacy of the process — and even cite some benefits — the structural situation is different in the very competitive and predominantly non-union parts of the private services sector.

---

[9]This section draws heavily on Dagg (1997). See also Wial (1993).

Employers have significant resources at their disposal to resist union-ization: short-term and contract workers can be easily dismissed, the hours of part-timers can be changed, and work can be restructured through the use of franchisees, contractors, and subcontractors in order to disguise the real nature of the employment relationship. Precisely because their jobs are so precarious, precarious workers fear employer reprisal or workplace closure if they join a union. Unions themselves find it difficult to organize and to represent small bargaining units, given stretched staff and resources and the high costs of bargaining and representation in small units. The highly competitive reality of the small business, the private service sector, also means that it is difficult for unions to make significant gains for members. Wages and benefits and hours are an important part of the competitive equa-tion unless they can be generalized across employers. This is particularly true of contract services awarded by competitive tendering. A single fast food outlet or retail store will also be reluctant to raise wages above the prevailing industry level. Further, chains will not want to make precedent-setting agree-ments in a single workplace. The structural reality is that isolated bargaining units are difficult to maintain because of the underlying economics of the situation.

A fundamental solution to this set of structural problems in the small firm, private services sector, is to facilitate union organization and collective bargaining at a broader level than that of the individual firm and workplace, defined both sectorally and geographically. This has been done on the initiative of the union in the "Justice for Janitors" campaigns of the Service Employees International Union in some U.S. cities which "took wages out of competition" through broad, city-wide, organizing of cleaning staff. How-ever, this is very difficult if there is no compulsion on employers to bargain as a group. In Canada, multi-employer or sectoral bargaining almost always requires the consent of both the employers and the unions involved (though there are important exceptions such as the institutional construction industry where multi-employer bargaining has sometimes been legislatively man-dated). A different solution to the same underlying problem has been the juridical extension model of many European countries and Quebec. Here, once a certain threshold of unionization and collective bargaining coverage has been passed in a sector and/or geographical area, some of the key provisions of the agreement such as on wages and hours are extended by law to non-union employers. This again effectively takes wages out of competi-tion and facilitates the spread of unionization by lowering the incentive for non-union employers to resist union representation.

Andrew Jackson and Grant Schellenberg

Recently, proposals have been made to encourage, through facilitative labour legislation, the growth of the broader-based bargaining model in the small employer, private services sector, where unions have been historically underrepresented. One proposal made by task force members Baigent and Ready to the BC government in 1992 was to require (rather than simply allow) employers to bargain as a group once a certain level of union representation had been reached in a sectoral/geographically defined unit. Such a unit would consist of all employers in a certain industry within a local labour market as defined by the Labour Board. Under this model, once two or three bargaining units had been certified and contracts negotiated, any new certification would be followed by the application of the collective agreement already negotiated. Employers bound by the same agreement would be required to ultimately bargain as a group. Such a mechanism would make it easier to extend collective bargaining in traditionally unorganized sectors and to take the gains of unionization out of the competitive equation. It makes organization of small workplaces a more viable proposition for unions. It is also a proposal that raises major questions regarding how unions would cooperate and relate to each other, if more than one union represented workers in a particular sector.

Short of a major change, legislation could facilitate broader-based bargaining to cover closely related units which could readily be covered by the same contract. For example, it should not be necessary for an individual union to bargain a separate contract for every unit of a single large employer or every franchised unit of a large operation. Broader-based bargaining could be mandated for large companies operating directly or through franchises in traditionally underrepresented sectors. Labour Codes could also allow for collective agreements in the same sector to be consolidated if a single union made an application.

The broader-based sectoral/geographical model of union representation and bargaining is also relevant to the changing labour market for women in that it would allow for the development of multi-employer pension and benefits plans, creating the larger units which make such plans possible while reflecting the fact that many workers move frequently between jobs, but in the same sector and area. The model might also facilitate joint union/multi-employer training programs, and labour exchanges which would help employers recruit trained workers. All of these institutions have been developed in the construction sector where multi-employer bargaining has provided stability of wages and benefits and promoted training in a context where workers move frequently between jobs and between different employers.

Advocacy of broader-based bargaining is moving slowly onto the labour movement and public policy agenda, primarily because it responds to the needs of working women. The Canadian Labour Congress Report on Women's Work noted that *"in developing strategies to counter the phenomenon of contracting-out and precarious forms of employment, women questioned the effectiveness of workplace by workplace bargaining. The increasing polarization between unionized jobs protected by collective agreements and low-paid, non-unionized jobs has turned workers against each other .... Broader-based bargaining will move towards larger and more centralized bargaining units which potentially cover sectors of the economy. Such bargaining structures can be legislated or can happen through union co-operation."*

Collective bargaining results in enhanced wages and other benefits for working women, particularly women in relatively low-paid and precarious jobs. Yet collective bargaining is very weakly established in the fast growing private services sector where most women's jobs are likely to be found in the future. It has been suggested that a shift to broader-based bargaining could help resolve this problem. Broader-based bargaining should be actively considered by unions, employers and governments as a means of extending the benefits of collective bargaining to historically unrepresented workers, particularly women, who are increasingly excluded for structural reasons.

Appendix

Table A1: Estimated Non-Standardized Regression Coefficients, Hourly Wages of Women within Occupational Categories (standard errors of coefficients in parentheses)

WOMEN	Professional Occupations	Clerical Occupations	Sales Occupations	Service Occupations	Blue Collar Occupations
Constant	4.276	6.447	9.945	7.349	7.750
Age	.449	.268	.151	.122	.161
	(.091)	(.048)	(.067)	(.041)	(.085)
Age-squared	-.005	-.003	-.002	-.002	-.002
	(.001)	(.000)	(.000)	(.000)	(.001)
Married	.907	.557	.782	.110*	.928
	(.269)	(.195)	(.291)	(.184)	(.352)
Less than high school	-3.834	-1.003	-.359	-.289*	-.254*
	(.772)	(.261)	(.340)	(.193)	(.354)
Post-sec. certificate/diploma	2.196	-.015*	.163	.684	.707*
	(.416)	(.188)	(.305)	(.210)	(.421)
University degree	6.072	1.239	2.919	.977	4.570
	(.423)	(.340)	(.427)	(.443)	(.905)
Atlantic	-3.116	-2.269	-2.522	-2.040	-1.938
	(.495)	(.333)	(.481)	(.272)	(.664)
Quebec	-.253*	-.994	-.291*	-.665	-.064*
	(.316)	(.215)	(.326)	(.229)	(.380)
Prairies	-2.008	-.994	-1.320	-1.100	-1.307
	(.354)	(.234)	(.345)	(.221)	(.461)
British Columbia	.553*	.649	.797	1.402	1.641
	(.414)	(.265)	(.361)	(.243)	(.611)
Firm size less than 20	-3.153	-.043*	-1.434	-.826*	-2.347
	(.417)	(.229)	(.298)	(.210)	(.462)

	(1)	(2)	(3)	(4)	(5)
Firm size 20 to 99	-1.409	-.311*	-.450*	-.993	-2.904
	(.379)	(.256)	(.381)	(.235)	(.443)
Firm size 100 to 499	-.864	-.436*	-.932	-.752	-2.091
	(.300)	(.244)	(.371)	(.244)	(.399)
Job tenure less than 1 year	.286*	-.909	-.501*	.073	-.082*
	(.379)	(.232)	(.280)	(.192)	(.417)
Job tenure 6 to 10 years	2.391	1.128	.914	.787	1.461
	(.351)	(.242)	(.407)	(.238)	(.431)
Job tenure 11 to 20 years	3.217	1.988	3.637	1.460	2.775
	(.392)	(.259)	(.461)	(.322)	(.525)
Job tenure more than 21 years	4.272	2.965	3.749	3.130	5.118
	(.498)	(.372)	(1.071)	(.598)	(.711)
Part-time job	1.184	.400	-.976	-.110*	.227*
	(.288)	(.194)	(.269)	(.173)	(.423)
Unionized	1.105	1.618	.850	2.371	1.668
	(.327)	(.215)	(.429)	(.231)	(.370)
Traditional service industries	-1.526	-2.891	-3.697	-1.839	-1.471
	(.817)	(.285)	(.525)	(.771)	(.487)
Dynamic service industries	-.848*	-.172*	1.260	2.136	1.226
	(.726)	(.262)	(.564)	(.873)	(.541)
Non-market service industries	-.884*	.039*	3.498*	1.023*	.432*
	(.607)	(.287)	(2.150)	(.782)	(.810)
Adjusted R Square	.360	.373	.547	.534	.355
N	2025	2189	742	1105	698

Note: All estimates significant at 0.05 level of confidence or better except "*" which are not significant.

Andrew Jackson and Grant Schellenberg

Table A2: Estimated Non-Standardized Regression Coefficients, Hourly Wages of Men within Occupational Categories (standard errors of coefficients in parentheses)

MEN	Professional Occupations	Clerical Occupations	Sales Occupations	Service Occupations	Blue Collar Occupations
Constant	-1.648	5.404	7.692	8.860	6.987
Age	.813 (.132)	.479 (.115)	.448 (.126)	.226 (.071)	.372 (.047)
Age-squared	-.008 (.002)	-.006 (.001)	-.005 (.002)	-.003 (.000)	-.004 (.000)
Married	1.190 (.415)	2.079 (.431)	1.313 (.485)	1.542 (.331)	1.349 (.181)
Less than high school	-.230* (1.112)	-1.110 (.520)	-.568* (.533)	-1.399 (.309)	-.803 (.197)
Post-sec. certificate/diploma	2.611 (.610)	.484* (.466)	.222* (.497)	.837 (.325)	1.962 (.187)
University degree	5.520 (.594)	4.027 (.614)	1.248 (.638)	.365* (.496)	2.376 (.482)
Atlantic	-4.483 (.762)	-4.081 (.764)	-2.004 (.745)	-2.710 (.492)	-2.345 (.299)
Quebec	-1.228 (.461)	-2.369 (.466)	-2.169 (.511)	-1.192 (.329)	-1.403 (.195)
Prairies	-3.385 (.540)	-2.330 (.571)	-.835* (.518)	-1.339 (.344)	-.566 (.224)
British Columbia	-.308* (.595)	.256* (.587)	.488* (.624)	.834 (.406)	2.250 (.251)
Firm size less than 20	-4.053 (.624)	-1.894 (.731)	-1.299 (.503)	-.995 (.361)	-2.643 (.225)

Firm size 20 to 99	-2.343	-1.446	-1.554	-.493*	-2.273
	(.603)	(.582)	(.576)	(.358)	(.224)
Firm size 100 to 499	-.620*	-1.642	-.133*	.223*	-1.430
	(.454)	(.524)	(.552)	(.362)	(.225)
Job tenure less than 1 year	-.241*	-1.144	-.649*	-.274*	-.685
	(.552)	(.523)	(.453)	(.327)	(.215)
Job tenure 6 to 10 years	1.636	1.461	2.308	1.987	1.189
	(.566)	(.587)	(.601)	(.410)	(.236)
Job tenure 11 to 20 years	3.433	3.252	2.487	3.362	2.017
	(.616)	(.605)	(.719)	(.455)	(.244)
Job tenure more than 21 years	3.502	5.614	3.404	7.011	2.824
	(.731)	(.717)	(.954)	(.549)	(.307)
Part-time job	1.077*	-1.071*	-.670*	-.884	-1.757
	(.704)	(.632)	(.522)	(.346)	(.336)
Unionized	.469*	.832**	1.534	1.470	2.248
	(.475)	(.446)	(.499)	(.362)	(.183)
Traditional service industries	-1.399*	-1.874	-5.922	-3.245	-2.069
	(.854)	(.588)	(.670)	(.604)	(.257)
Dynamic service industries	1.540	.428*	-3.444	-2.416*	-.682
	(.585)	(.535)	(.674)	(.642)	(.188)
Non-market service industries	-1.581	.586*	-2.846*	.606*	-2.009
	(.602)	(.667)	(3.942)	(.610)	(.362)
Adjusted R Square	.432	.564	.544	.641	.460
N	1172	534	436	965	3687

Note: All estimates significant at 0.05 level of confidence or better except "*" which are not significant, and "**", significant at 0.1.

Andrew Jackson and Grant Schellenberg

Table A3: Results of Females' Logistic Regression Model on Low-Wage Employment

	Coefficient	Standard Error	Significance	Odds Ratio
Age 15 to 24	.996	.126	.000	2.708
Age 25 to 34	.233	.102	.022	1.263
Age 35 to 44*				
Age 45 to 54	.294	.118	.013	1.342
Age 55 to 69	.591	.168	.000	1.805
Less than high school	.707	.108	.000	2.028
High school /Some post-sec.*				
Certificate/Diploma	-.325	.091	.000	.723
University Degree	-1.068	.142	.000	.344
Married*				
Never Married	.425	.099	.000	1.529
Separated/Widowed/Divorced	.027	.138	.846	1.027
Management/Administrative*				
Professional	.438	.165	.008	1.55
Clerical	.950	.134	.000	2.587
Sales	1.368	.159	.000	3.926
Services	2.091	.157	.000	8.010
Blue Collar	2.400	.176	.000	10.998
Firm size less than 20	.820	.098	.000	2.270
Firm size 20 to 99	.548	.109	.000	1.731
Firm size 100 to 500	.412	.110	.001	1.510
Firm size more than 500*				
Non-Unionized*				
Unionized	-1.340	.103	.000	.247
Full-time*				
Part-time	.384	.084	.000	1.467
Job tenure less than one year	.520	.093	.000	1.681
Job tenure 1 to 5 years*				
Job tenure 6 to 10 years	-.755	.104	.000	.470
Job tenure 11 to 20 years	-1.448	.141	.000	.235
Job tenure more than 20 years	-1.650	.229	.000	.192
Atlantic	1.434	.147	.000	4.194
Quebec	.529	.098	.000	1.698
Ontario*				
Prairies	.852	.106	.000	2.344
British Columbia	-.416	.124	.000	.660
Goods-producing industries*				
Dynamic service industries	-.150	.133	.257	.861
Traditional service industries	-1.871	.130	000	6.497
Non-market service industries	-.336	.145	.021	.715

Notes: * Excluded category. An odds ratio below one indicates the specific category of the independent variable has a negative impact on the likelihood of being in a low-wage job, relative to the reference (excluded) category. An odds ratio above one indicates the specific category of the independent variable has a positive impact on the likelihood of being in a low-wage job, relative to the reference (excluded) category.

Table A4: Results of Males' Logistic Regression Model on Low-Wage Employment

	Coefficient	Standard Error	Significance	Odds Ratio
Age 15 to 24	1.227	.133	.000	3.410
Age 25 to 34	.214	.115	.063	1.239
Age 35 to 44*				
Age 45 to 54	.008	.154	.959	1.008
Age 55 to 69	.488	.186	.009	1.629
Less than high school	.586	.105	.000	1.797
High school /Some post-sec.*				
Certificate/Diploma	-.350	.101	.001	.705
University Degree	-.517	.152	.001	.596
Married*				
Never Married	.816	.095	.095	2.262
Separated/Widowed/Divorced	.112	.199	.000	1.119
Management/Administrative*				
Professional	.654	.198	.001	1.923
Clerical	1.047	.208	.000	2.850
Sales	1.389	.200	.000	4.014
Services	1.932	.183	.000	6.901
Blue Collar	.856	.170	.000	2.354
Firm size less than 20	.732	.111	.072	2.080
Firm size 20 to 99	.760	.115	.000	2.140
Firm size 100 to 500	.245	.125	.050	1.278
Firm size more than 500*				
Non-Unionized*				
Unionized	-1.078	.106	.000	.340
Full-time*				
Part-time	1.055	.114	.000	2.873
Job tenure less than one year	.626	.091	.000	1.870
Job tenure 1 to 5 years*				
Job tenure 6 to 10 years	-.451	.121	.001	.636
Job tenure 11 to 20 years	-.919	.164	.000	.398
Job tenure more than 20 years	-1.676	.286	.000	.187
Atlantic	1.055	.147	.000	2.872
Quebec	.607	.102	.000	1.835
Ontario*				
Prairies	.444	.110	.000	1.559
British Columbia	-.585	.142	.000	.557
Goods-producing industries*				
Dynamic service industries	.207	.110	.060	1.230
Traditional service industries	1.127	.111	.000	3.089
Non-market service industries	.176	.169	.298	1.192

Notes: * Excluded category. An odds ratio below one indicates the specific category of the independent variable has a negative impact on the likelihood of being in a low-wage job, relative to the reference (excluded) category. An odds ratio above one indicates the specific category of the independent variable has a positive impact on the likelihood of being in a low-wage job, relative to the reference (excluded) category.

Andrew Jackson and Grant Schellenberg

References

Bronfenbrenner, K. and S. Friedman, eds. (1998), *Organizing to Win* (Ithaca, NY: Cornell University Press).

Card, D. (1992), "The Effect of Unions on the Distribution of Wages: Redistribution or Relabelling?" NBER Working Paper No. 4195 (Cambridge, MA: National Bureau of Economic Research).

Card, D. and R. Freeman, eds. (1993), *Small Differences that Matter: Labour Markets and Income Maintenance in Canada and the U.S.* (Chicago: The University of Chicago Press).

Chaykowski, R. (1995), "Union Influences on Labour Market Outcomes and Earnings Inequality", in K. Banting and C. Beach (eds.), *Labour Market Polarization and Social Policy Reform* (Kingston: School of Policy Studies, Queen's University).

Chaykowski, R. and G. Slotsve (1996), "Union Wage Premiums and Union Density in Canada and the U.S.", *Canadian Business Economics* 4(3), 46-59.

Currie, J. and R. Chaykowski (1995), "Male Jobs, Female Jobs, and Gender Gaps in Benefits Coverage in Canada", in S.W. Polachek (ed.), *Research in Labor Economics,* Vol. 14 (Greenwich, CT: JAI Press), 171-192.

Dagg, A. (1997), "Worker Representation and Protection in the 'New Economy'", in *Report of the Advisory Committee on the Changing Workplace* (Ottawa: Department of Human Resources Development).

Fortin, N. and T. Lemieux (1996), "Institutional Changes and Rising Wage Inequality: Is There a Linkage?" unpublished paper.

Freeman, R. (1992), "Is Declining Unionization in the United States Good, Bad or Irrelevant?" in L. Mishel and P.B. Voos (eds.), *Unions and Economic Competitiveness* (New York: M.E. Sharpe for the Economic Policy Institute).

_____ (1993), "How Much Has Deunionisation Contributed to the Rise in Male Earnings Inequality?" in S. Danziger and P. Gottschalk (eds.), *Uneven Tides: Rising Inequality in America* (New York: Russell Sage Foundation).

_____, ed. (1994), *Working Under Different Rules* (New York: Russell Sage Foundation).

HRDC (1997), *Report of Advisory Committee on the Changing Workplace* (Ottawa: Department of Human Resources Development).

Lemieux, T. (1993), "Unions and Wage Inequality in Canada and the United States", in D. Card and R. Freeman (eds.), *Small Differences that Matter: Labour Markets and Income Maintenance in Canada and the U.S.* (Chicago: The University of Chicago Press).

Lipsett, B. and M. Reesor (1997), "Employer Sponsored Pension Plans — Who Benefits?", Working Paper W-97-2E (Ottawa: Applied Research Branch, Human Resources Development Canada).

Lipsig-Mummé, C. and K. Laxer (1998), *Organizing and Union Membership: A Canadian Profile* (Ottawa: Canadian Labour Congress).

Maki, D. and I. Ng (1990), "Effects of Trade Unions on the Earnings Differential Between Males and Females: Canadian Evidence", *Canadian Journal of Economics* 23(2), 305-311.

OECD (1996), "Earnings Inequality, Low Paid Employment and Earnings Mobility", in *OECD Employment Outlook, 1996* (Paris: OECD).

Picot, G. (1996), "Working Time, Wages and Earnings Inequality Among Men and Women in Canada, 1981-93", paper presented to Labour Market Institutions and Labour Market Outcomes Conference.

Schellenberg, G. (1996), *The Changing Profile of Part-time Employment* (Ottawa: CCSD).

Scott, K. and C. Lochead (1996), *Are Women Catching Up in the Earnings Race?* (Ottawa: Canadian Council on Social Development).

Statistics Canada (1996), *Earnings of Men and Women, 1996*, Cat. No. 13-217 (Ottawa: Statistics Canada).

_____ (1997), *A Statistical Portrait of the Trade Union Movement*, Cat. No. 75-001XPE (Ottawa: Statistics Canada).

White, J. (1993), *Sisters and Solidarity: Women and Unions in Canada* (Toronto: Thompson Educational Publishing).

Wial, H. (1993), "The Emerging Organizational Structure of Unionism in Low Wage Services", *Rutgers Law Review* 45(3), 671-738.

The Impact of Labour Market Transformations on the Effectiveness of Laws Promoting Workplace Gender Equality

Marie-Thérèse Chicha

In the late 1980s, and especially in the first half of the 1990s, several authors (Standing, 1989; OECD, 1994) called attention to the increasing risk posed by structural changes in the labour market for the application of laws promoting workplace gender equality. The expression *implicit deregulation* has been used as a way of pointing to the relative ineffectiveness of these laws stemming from growing difficulties in their application. The underlying idea is that the significant changes in the labour market resulting from globalization and technological change imply greater precariousness, especially for women. Several studies have documented the deterioration of working conditions for women, notably, intensified work pace, de-skilling and increased risks to occupational health and safety (CLC, 1997; Appay, 1997; Spalter-Roth and Hartmann, 1998). However, no study has systematically examined the potential or observed effects of these changes on the goals and

I would like to thank Rick Chaykowski and Lisa Powell from Queen's University for their insightful comments which helped improve the paper. The research on which this paper is based benefits from a Social Science and Humanities Research Council grant.

methodological criteria of laws promoting workplace equality. These laws fall into two main categories: pay equity and employment equity.

The aim of this paper, therefore, is to suggest how some of the potential effects of labour market changes can be analyzed by examining their impact on the methodological criteria of laws promoting workplace equality. The main question to be addressed is whether these laws, which were conceived on the basis of a traditional model of the labour market, are still appropriate in a context of labour market restructuring. A central feature of this restructuring is the search by organizations for greater flexibility at all levels. The relatively stable and precise boundaries that delimited the employer's identity, the status of workers, work schedules, job content, job skills and compensation methods are giving way to a workplace characterized by imprecise, continuously changing contours.[1] Thus, the paper identifies certain lines of inquiry that, of course, will eventually need to be tested empirically in a variety of workplaces. The present analysis contributes to a broader re-examination of labour law in the context of economic change. And although the questions raised may appear to be hypothetical, if the trends identified here become more pronounced, they may become a major impediment to the application of laws promoting workplace gender equality.

The paper begins by explaining why it is necessary to reinforce laws promoting workplace gender equality in today's labour market. This is followed by a brief historical sketch of the relevant laws and a general outline of their goals and methodology. The paper then examines how certain essential criteria can become ineffective in the new organizational context. The conclusion offers some suggestions for future avenues of research.

The Need for Pay and Employment Equity Laws

Although equality laws have been in effect for over 20 years in some jurisdictions, their goals are far from being fulfilled. Occupational segregation still predominates in a majority of workplaces. According to the most recent Canadian census, female workers are still concentrated in just a few

---

[1] Many authors have recently stressed various limitations of labour law protection of workers' rights in the context of changing employment relationships and have suggested new lines of inquiry. See, e.g., Brault, 1997; Carnevale, Jennings and Eisenmann, 1998; duRivage, Carré and Tilly, 1998; Vallée, 1998.

occupations. About one-third of the female labour force can be found in ten predominately female occupations such as receptionist, cashier, secretary, nurse, etc. (Statistics Canada, 1998). The most recent annual report of the Canadian Human Rights Commission (1997) indicates that, due to workplace discrimination, many competent women are excluded from high level jobs in private as well as in public organizations. Other studies substantiate the enduring presence of workplace practices in hiring or promotion that deprive women, as well as other target groups, of equal access to jobs (Henry, 1994; Samuel, 1997). Moreover, the wage gap between men and women, which is another major indicator of inequality, is decreasing very slowly. A recent study by Scott and Lochhead (1997) shows that the wage gap decreased from 46% in 1981 to 35% in 1995 for all workers, and from 36% to 27% for those who work full-time all year round. In other words, on average in 1995, a woman working full-time for the entire year earned $0.73 for every dollar earned by a man in the same situation. Moreover, the narrowing of the gap that has been observed is partly the result of slower growth in male salaries due to the poor performance of the manufacturing sector.

Two important facts — the difficult and slow application of laws, as well as the vulnerability of women in the face of labour market trans-formations — help explain the persistence of labour market inequalities. Studies indicate that laws aimed at achieving employment or pay equity have had a limited impact. Among the explanatory factors cited by researchers in relation to the federal Employment Equity Act are the lack of strict control over the implementation of programs by the government and the low level of commitment to equity on the part of the heads of many firms (Jain and Hackett, 1989; Leck, 1991; Poole and Rebick, 1993). Other studies of the federal government have arrived at similar conclusions (Samuel, 1997; Chicha and Saba, 1999). At the provincial level (as in Quebec where affirm-ative action programs have existed for 14 years), recent studies indicate that results are uneven and that, on the whole, the progress made does not meet initial expectations. Only a minority of firms have been able to reach 50% or more of their own numerical goals for target group representation (Chicha, 1998).

According to Gunderson's (1995) study of the pay equity situation in Ontario, wage adjustments resulting from the Pay Equity Act reached 2.2% of payroll in the public sector while in private firms it did not exceed the 1.1% threshold. Gunderson notes that:

this occurs in spite of the evidence that wage discrimination is greater in the private sector than the public sector. This suggests that the absence of adjustments in the private sector because of the finding of no pay equity wage gap likely reflects the stronger resistance of the profit-maximizing private sector to such legislative initiatives. (Gunderson, 1995, p. 28)

Similarly, Leck, St. Onge and Lalancette (1995) found that, in firms under federal jurisdiction, the wage gap between the sexes is decreasing very slowly in the lower and middle wage categories and that it is not changing in the higher categories.

This trend has been confirmed in other studies. Research carried out to date reveals that although laws aimed at establishing labour market equality have had an impact, the objectives sought have not yet been attained. Analysts are generally agreed that equity legislation can still play an important role and that they must therefore be strengthened.

Today, the need for this type of legislation has become all the more evident because the situation of working women has deteriorated in a number of ways as a result of changes in the labour market. As Scott and Lochhead point out:

Preliminary analysis shows that the women who made gains over the last decade were the beneficiaries of a pool of good jobs in the health, education and social services sectors. However, as the structure of the economy continues to change, with the continuing polarization of job opportunities, there is a real danger that women's economic advances will be halted. (1997, p. 2)

The polarization between good and bad jobs takes several forms. According to the Canadian Labour Congress (1997), in large segments of the female workforce, part-time jobs have been substituted for full-time jobs. In the clerical sector, there was a 13% decrease in the number of full-time positions between 1990 and 1995 while the number of part-time jobs increased by 2.2%. In the services sector, the number of women workers increased by 6.8% at the same time that the number of full-time jobs decreased. More specifically, the banking industry, which is a large employer of women, was one of the sectors to lose the most full-time jobs.

Not only are women workers increasingly working part-time, but they are also more likely to be in non-permanent jobs. In 1995, 57% of women workers had a non-permanent job, compared to 43% for men (Grenon and

Chun, 1997). In addition to this inequality in terms of temporary employment, there were also wage inequities. The average hourly wage gap between men and women in temporary jobs was 25%. While men earned an average of $17.28 per hour, women earned $12.85.

Lower wages, uncertain — and in some cases, insufficient — working hours, all point to a precarious situation for many women affected by labour market changes. This finding, combined with the real but still limited impact of equity laws, underlines the need for pursuing research studies aimed at making these laws more effective.

Goals and Methodology of Equity Laws

Pay Equity Legislation

The principle of pay equity was recognized as early as 1951 by International Labour Organization Convention 100, which was ratified by most western countries. Initially, interpretation of the principle was based on the objective of equal pay for equal work. However, the principle was subsequently broadened to include the objective of equal pay for work of equal value (Eyraud, 1993). The overall trend observed in Canada has been towards broadening the scope of the pay equity principle and abandoning the requirement that discrimination be proved as a prerequisite for imposing a pay equity program. This development originated from the finding that traditional approaches were relatively ineffective. In fact, the principle of pay equity was first implemented at the federal level and in Quebec through a model based on complaint mechanisms.

This type of application came to be viewed as both slow and costly, thus leading to the search for a new approach that eventually resulted in the adoption of what are called "proactive" laws (Chicha, 1997; Gunderson, 1994; McDermott, 1993). These laws impose a time frame and provide detailed methodological guidelines to organizations that are subject to them. Such an approach was chosen by Manitoba, Ontario, Nova Scotia, Prince Edward Island, New Brunswick and, more recently, Quebec. The laws adopted in Ontario and Quebec differ from the others in that they apply to both the public and private sectors,[2] thus making the challenge posed by labour market restructuring all the more important.

Applications of the laws, in the United States mainly as part of union-management agreements and in Canada by various human rights or pay equity commissions, are based on common practices in many work environments; in particular, evaluation methods centred on precise and stable job definitions. The need to adapt these methods to pay equity goals gave rise to a whole new body of research that sought to define non-discriminatory tools (Chicha, 1997; Remick, 1984; Sorensen, 1994: Steinberg and Haignere, 1985; Weiner, 1991).

Irrespective of whether the approach adopted was based on a complaint mechanism, negotiation or proactive programs, the basic methodological criteria of pay equity implementation is the same (see Table 1).

Table 1 illustrates the dimensions that need to be clearly defined to achieve equity goals: the employer, the employee, the job, job value and the wage. To date, the development of methodologies to apply all pay equity policies — whether through legislation or union-management negotiations — has been mainly based on the characteristics of a traditional labour market: an employment relationship with a single employer; stable, full-time employment; well-defined duties; and a basic salary determined by requirements of the duties to be performed.

Table 1: Essential Components of Pay Equity Implementation

- Identification of female- and male-dominated **jobs** for one employer.
- Evaluation methods that take four **job requirements** into account: responsibility, skill, effort and work conditions.
- **Comparisons** of **wages** for equivalent female- and male-dominated **jobs** for the **same employer**.
- Payment of wage adjustments to the employer's **workers**.

---

[2]Unlike the laws in the other provinces, which are limited to the public sector, broadly defined.

Employment Equity Legislation

The other significant type of law promoting workplace equality is employment equity legislation, which was largely inspired by affirmative action programs in the United States; specifically, by the regulations issued by the Office of Federal Contract Compliance Programs in the late 1960s and early 1970s (Leonard, 1994). The aim of these programs is to ensure that members of designated groups — women, visible minorities, Aboriginal peoples and persons with disabilities — are equitably represented in occupations from which they have historically been excluded because of discrimination.[3] A proactive form of these policies is contract compliance. By virtue of this obligation, any employer who wants to bid on a government contract or who is the recipient of a government grant is required to implement an employment equity program. Under the Quebec and federal employment equity programs, firms with 100 or more employees may be subject to this obligation. The methodological criteria used to implement these policies are summarized in Table 2.

Table 2: Essential Components of Employment Equity Implementation

---

- Determination of **required skills** for jobs in which women are underrepresented.
- Establishment of **numerical goals** for qualified women workers for the jobs in which they are underrepresented.
- Introduction of remedial measures, for example, **accelerated hiring** of qualified women.
- Review and elimination of discriminatory practices, particularly those related to **recruitment, selection and promotion**.
- Introduction of measures to facilitate the integration of women workers into the firm: for example, qualitative measures to help workers **reconcile work and family responsibilities**.

---

[3]Although employment equity programs are aimed at a number of designated groups, this article deals solely with those aimed at achieving employment equity for women. The analysis may be extended to programs promoting equality for other designated groups as well.

The key elements of the methodology are also centred on the notions of the job, the firm, and the skills required by the job. The assumption underlying these laws is that the firm will increase the representation of designated groups among its employees mainly through hiring and that a degree of flexibility will be introduced to meet certain needs of women workers, such as reconciling work and family responsibilities.

Three implicit requirements may be deduced from Tables 1 and 2. First, the methodological criteria refer to job requirements and not to the characteristics of individuals who hold the jobs. These laws therefore attempt to replace an individualist approach, which tends to give rise to prejudices and stereotypes with regard to women workers, with an objective approach centred on the essential characteristics of jobs and the skills that are really needed.

The second requirement is that a group approach be used. Measuring indirect discrimination resulting from an employment practice essentially involves a comparison of its impact on the members of two groups that can be distinguished by race, sex, age and so on. In order for the discriminatory impact of an employment practice to be measured, it must be collective in scope (Bosset, 1989). The standardization of employment practices that was prevalent in the 1960s and 1970s is necessary in order for employment equity and pay equity programs to be implemented.

The third requirement that emerges from Tables 1 and 2 is the need to carry out comparisons within each firm.[4] Estimating the effects of discrimination is essentially based on comparisons; that is, between the value and wages of predominantly female and predominantly male jobs in the firm. The larger the firm and the more diverse its jobs, the wider the choice of bases of comparison. Conversely, in a firm with a very limited number of occupations, it may be difficult to identify any reference point and thus impossible to measure the discriminatory effect of employment practices.

For a long time, these conditions were taken for granted and research therefore concentrated largely on improving the process of implementing laws. However, while there has been progress in this area, there have also been transformations in the labour market that are likely to make these laws partially inoperative. As several authors (Chaykowski and Verma, 1994;

---

[4]Under Ontario legislation, external comparisons (i.e., proxies) can be made in the public sector. The Quebec law extends this possibility to the private sector but, because no regulations have been adopted, this principle does not yet have any practical effect.

Marie-Thérèse Chicha

Long, 1989; Maschino, 1992) have pointed out, these transformations are affecting a range of issues, including work organization, compensation, qualifications, hours of work, work relations and worker participation. The aim of this paper is not to carry out a comprehensive review of the potential impact of these changes, but rather to highlight, through a number of examples, the divergence between the orientations of equity policies on the one hand, and labour market transformation on the other. We will consider some of the methodological criteria of equity policies and the potential or observed impacts on them of labour market transformation.

Drawing on comprehensive surveys, a number of researchers have developed typologies of these transformations (Betcherman *et al.*, 1994; Cappelli, 1995; Osterman, 1994; Piore, 1986). From an analytical point of view, the typology developed by Betcherman *et al.* allows a broader range of transformations to be considered. It includes the following elements, which are particularly relevant to the issue raised in this paper:

* non-traditional job designs, such as job enlargement, job enrichment and self-directed work teams;
* variable pay practices, such as skill-based compensation;
* alternative scheduling arrangements, including not only the flexible work schedules aimed at reconciling work and family responsibilities that Betcherman *et al.* identify, but also the full range of work schedules that are possible today; and
* non-standard employment, which modifies the classic employment relationship between employers and workers.

To these practices we will add an important contextual element that impacts on the effectiveness of equity laws: substantial job reductions in firms leading to a marked downturn in hiring.

Defining Jobs

The basic unit on which pay equity and employment equity programs are built is the concept of a job. Pay equity involves evaluating job requirements on the basis of four factors: responsibility, skill, effort and working conditions. Employment equity involves setting numerical goals for the representation of the designated groups based on the skills required for targeted jobs. To ensure that the objectives are reached, the basic unit must therefore be precisely defined and stable. Employers who are under the legal obligation to apply these programs are subject to audit, and non-compliance may result in sanctions. Stability is necessary both for planning these programs (which, in certain cases, can run as long as eight years) and for maintaining equality once it is achieved.

The growth of non-traditional job designs as a result of work re-organization is likely, at least partly, to thwart these two requirements. The definition of job duties in terms of the performance of tasks that are clearly defined, relatively fixed and, indeed, often routinized, is gradually becoming blurred in the face of new practices, particularly job enlargement and enrichment. Job enlargement can be defined as "the performance by each worker of several operations that were previously allocated to various specialized work stations"[5] (Maschino, 1992, p. 75). Job enlargement was used in 21.1% of the establishments surveyed by Betcherman *et al.* (1994).[6] Other studies show rates as high as 42.6% (Maschino, 1992).[7]

A recent case study of a food processing plant (Flecker, Meil and Pollert, 1998) provides a good illustration of the consequences of work reorganization. Operations such as colour and viscosity control and acidity testing, which had previously been part of quality control, were added to the packing area, thus enlarging the duties of the workers in that area. Similarly, the tasks of machine operators were enlarged by adding minor maintenance and repair tasks.

As to job enrichment, it can be defined as "the modification of employees' tasks to increase their responsibilities and control over the task"[8] (Maschino, 1992, p. 75). Surveys of firms have reported the use of job enrichment at rates varying from 21.4% (Betcherman *et al.*, 1994) to 49.5%

---

[5]Our translation.

[6]Based on data from a survey of 714 establishments across Canada drawn from the secondary sector (wood products, electrical and electronic products, fabricated metal products) and the tertiary sector (selected business services).

[7]Survey carried out in 1991 by the Quebec Ministry of Labour with 404 establishments drawn from different economic sectors and employing over 75 workers. The manufacturing sector was considerably overrepresented among the 202 respondents.

[8]Our translation.

Marie-Thérèse Chicha

(Maschino, 1992). The elimination of middle management jobs often results in this type of transfer of responsibilities.

Job rotation, which often accompanies teamwork, consists in gradually diversifying the skills of each team member, thereby allowing each worker to alternately carry out the tasks of another team member. In the plant referred to above, job rotation had the following result: "In the process area ... workers were given financial incentives to learn additional jobs, so that they could be assigned to the separator, the mixer, various process lines, and the control room as needed" (Flecker, Meil and Pollert, 1998, p. 18). Transformations such as the ones presented above from the manufacturing sector can also be found in the services sector (Walsh, 1997; Scott, O'Shaughnessy and Cappelli, 1996).

A common characteristic of these new forms of work is that they use "broad and flexible job definitions and often deploy workers anywhere within a family of jobs" (Betcherman et al., 1994, p. 33). They tend to make the rigid job descriptions traditionally used in firms obsolete (Cappelli, 1995; Piore, 1986). Thus, alongside these changes, firms have also been establishing new job classifications based on broadly defined responsibilities. Indeed, the number of job classes in a firm often falls drastically subsequent to this form of work reorganization, with decreases from 100 job classes to as few as five in one case (Cappelli, 1995) and from 3,600 to 2,000 in another (Batt, 1996).

These changes are affecting the conditions under which pay equity laws are being applied. Traditionally, evaluation has been based on a precise, comprehensive and relatively static description of all job dimensions. Responsibilities, qualifications, effort and working conditions must be clearly defined. The new forms of work organization, however, threaten to undermine these requirements. Job enlargement and enrichment, and especially job rotation, result in much broader definitions of the responsibilities and qualifications required for a job. The boundaries between job categories thus become less clear. As one manager put it, "Everything is so interdependent now that it's hard to determine when one job ends and when the other one begins" (Taplin, 1995, p. 426).

Evaluating job content in a context where tasks are being enhanced and elements are constantly changing raises the question of whether the evaluation methods that have been used so far are still suitable. Can existing methods take this new flexibility into account or should other approaches and tools, not currently provided for under existing legislation, be devised?

Defining the Employer and the Bases of Comparison

Both pay equity and employment equity rely on the ability to make adequate comparisons. More fundamentally, in order to measure discrimination, comparisons must be made according to gender, race, presence of a disability, age, etc. As in the case of pay equity, comparisons generally must be made for individual employers or within an establishment.

The growth of subcontracting can result in the transfer of entire segments of the production process to other employers, thus considerably reducing the possible bases of comparison. This can undermine the objectives of equity policies in two ways. First, the transfer of certain production segments may result in the transfer of entire families of jobs; for example, technical or sales jobs. If a firm had only a limited range of occupations to begin with, it may then become impossible to find male-dominated occupations to be used as comparators for measuring gender wage discrimination. A second consequence of contracting out activities is that the firm's size may be reduced to the point where it no longer falls within the scope of equity laws that apply to firms with a minimum number of employees. This would be the case for employment equity programs that operate through contract compliance and apply only to firms with 100 employees or more.[9]

Similar effects may result from the growth of non-standard forms of employment such as term employment, part-time employment, self-employment, placement through temporary job agencies or sharing of workers by a pool of employers. In some cases, it may become very difficult to determine exactly which party is responsible for applying the programs. Results may differ greatly depending on whether the job-placement agency or the firm using the employee's services is considered to be responsible. In fact, the male reference jobs, as well as their wages, will not be the same from firm to firm. They may not even exist if the employer deemed responsible is a temporary secretarial job-placement agency, which is not uncommon.

---

[9]The importance of net employment growth in small firms compared to large ones (Baldwin and Picot, 1994; Picot, Baldwin and Dupuy, 1994) may, of course, reinforce this result.

Marie-Thérèse Chicha

Determination of Compensation

Some firms have adopted new forms of compensation that tend towards greater individualization. These new compensation practices are gradually replacing the traditional methods of wage determination, which are mainly based on job requirements, with practices centred on the individual's performance. These are not entirely new (Chaykowski and Lewis, 1995). What is significant today, however, is that their use is becoming widespread and, instead of being applied selectively, they have become part of a global strategy of compensation management in firms (Tremblay, 1993).

Among the main compensation practices[10] identified by Betcherman *et al.* (1994), are profit-sharing (21.6% of establishments), employee stock option plans (14.1%), pay-for-skill/knowledge (14.5%) and productivity gain-sharing (6.5%). Pay-for-skill/knowledge best illustrates how pay equity goals may be negatively affected by the new forms of compensation. This practice compensates workers "for the skills or knowledge that they can demonstrate, regardless of whether the job they perform requires a particular skill/competency" (Milkovich and Newman, 1996, p. 99). Workers are paid higher wages for each new skill acquired. Thus, the wider the range of skills workers acquire at work, the higher their wages will be. The logic of the pay-for-skill/knowledge thus contradicts the logic of pay equity, which requires that wages be aligned with job requirements, including skills.

This problem of applying the principle of pay equity is not entirely new, since several laws require that overall compensation costs, including variable compensation, be compared. However, there are good grounds for thinking that, in practice, flexible compensation, which lacks precise benchmarks, will thwart the goals of pay equity. Two risks are of particular concern. First, in general, these compensation practices are applied selectively to certain jobs. It follows that the comparisons of compensation required by pay equity will then become more difficult because they are based on different principles within the same firm. Moreover, the effect of implementing these systems is to reduce the transparency of compensation practices. As Rubery (1994, p. 94) has pointed out, "Performance pay can be used to disguise other pay objectives and practices." It then becomes very difficult to determine the real compensation of the firm's various workers. As a consequence, workers'

---

[10]Compensation methods for non-managerial workers.

ability to exercise control over the content of the pay equity program and its compliance with the law is likely to be much more limited.

Hiring and Integrating Women Workers into Jobs Where They are Underrepresented

The main goal of employment equity programs is to increase the representation of women in jobs where they are few in number or absent. Up until now, the way to achieve this has been to focus on hiring, outreach recruiting and the review of selection practices to make them non-discriminatory. In order to recruit women, targeted interventions are carried out, for example, through associations and groups that promote workplace gender equality or through educational institutions. One of the aims of reviewing selection practices is to eliminate direct or indirect discriminatory interview questions. Personality tests are also reviewed or abolished to avoid any disproportionate impact on the designated groups.

The current massive reductions in the number of workers in many firms is limiting the impact of such measures geared towards recruitment. Job shortages are resulting in increased competition between job seekers, leading firms to raise the skills required of applicants. Thus, faced with a surplus of candidates, a number of American firms are reinstating hiring tests that they had previously abandoned to avoid charges of discrimination (Badgett, 1995).

Firms are now looking for new types of skills — called "soft skills" — among job applicants, thus adding a new element to selection criteria. Soft skills can be defined as: "...skills, abilities and traits that pertain to personality, attitude, and behaviour rather than to formal or technical knowledge" (Moss and Tilly, 1996, p. 253). However, because the evaluation of these skills is uncertain and subjective, there is a risk that it will be influenced by codes of cultural behaviour. In some cases, it has been observed that this type of evaluation can penalize those whose behaviour is different due to either socialization or culture (ibid.).

Increased competition has led to an upsurge in other potentially discriminatory practices; for example, recruiting through word-of-mouth to avoid wasting time over an enormous influx of applicants. The use of acting appointments to fill permanent positions as a way to short-circuit the normal recruitment process is also widespread (Samuel, 1997).

These few pieces of evidence suggest that we are currently witnessing a weakening or replacement of the non-discriminatory hiring practices that were developed as part of employment equity programs. The traditional recruitment tools of employment equity programs, which were suited to a conventional labour market, are encountering serious problems today. Integrating women into jobs where they are currently underrepresented should be supported by diversified interventions focusing, for instance, on company training programs (Chicha and Lambert, 1998) as well as on promotion practices (Henry, 1994).

Integrating Women Workers through Measures Aimed at Reconciling Work and Family Responsibilities

As shown in Table 2, one of the ways to increase the success of employment equity programs is to introduce support measures to meet women's specific needs, such as flexible work schedules or workplace daycare centres. This question, particularly the costs and benefits of these measures as well as the various ways of implementing them, has been the subject of in-depth and innovative study (Ferber, O'Farell and Allen, 1991; Guérin et al., 1994).

However, the model of employment to which most of these studies apply is often not specified explicitly. When the types of measures proposed are examined more closely, it can be seen that they are typically designed for the standard workweek of the labour market prevalent in the 1960s and 1970s. However, today the search by firms for flexibility is resulting in a diversification of work schedules. The most recent data show an increase in the percentage of employees who work shorter hours or overtime. In 1995, 24% of employees worked less than 35 hours per week, an increase of eight percentage points from 1976. During the same period, the percentage of employees working long hours (over 40 hours) increased from 19% to 22% (Statistics Canada, 1997).

More specific data show that the management occupational group is especially penalized in terms of flexibility and support for reconciling work and family responsibilities. According to 1992 data on how Canadians use their time, managers devote an average of 9.2 hours per day to paid work (Stone, 1995). Case studies (Lachance, 1997) show that to avoid being excluded, women in managerial positions must conform to the predominant model, which means long working hours over which they have very little control. The resulting stress level can be high for those who have family responsibilities (Stone and Marshall, 1997) and may discourage some women from applying for managerial positions (Weissman, 1997). In addition, the availability to work overtime may also be an implicit hiring criterion. As some researchers suggest: "... In many professional settings, long work hours (or other performance measures that entail long hours) are used to screen for valuable yet hard to observe characteristics of employees, such as commitment or ambition" (Landers, Rebitzer and Taylor, 1996, p. 216). This may account, at least in part, for the slow progress of women at the senior management level which, paradoxically, is given priority in employment equity programs.

At the other extreme, the increasing fragmentation of work schedules in personal services and retail sales services, as well as in some business services, leaves little scope for reconciling professional and family responsibilities. Case studies of employment in the retail sales sector reveal that more and more women workers are obliged to come in for short work shifts, or have had their workday cut by several hours (Cattanéo, 1997). There appears to be a growing managerial practice of structuring employees' hours of work on a basic minimum, then adding hours to meet variable business volume. Women are called in to work earlier than expected or are asked to stay later than planned. Thus, the greater flexibility for managers afforded by this type of fragmentation of working time affects employees severely (Soares, 1997). According to Horrell and Rubery (1991, p. 388), "There is little evidence that working time for women is arranged to fit with domestic constraints and women's preferences, except with respect to the total length of hours worked. Requirements for flexibility and for unsocial working hours suggest greater influence on the demand side."

In this context of flexibility, it is not surprising that the task of reconciling work and family has been described as a nightmare by some women workers (Cattanéo, 1997). Moreover, the situation has serious implications for occupational equality since it can effectively reduce access to continuing education, thus reducing opportunities for these workers to improve their skills. The new flexible work schedules can make it impossible for women workers to be both available at regular times for training courses and available for fragmented hours of work. This is, therefore, a considerable obstacle to implementing employment equity, but one that is generally ignored.

Marie-Thérèse Chicha

Conclusion

The preceding analysis shows that the use of laws promoting workplace gender equality may be limited in the future in many ways as a result of current labour market restructuring. The analysis has highlighted the increasingly obvious contradictions between the traditional model underlying equity laws and the changing reality of the workplace. These changes affect the basic criteria and tools of these laws, which were designed in the 1960s and 1970s, thereby creating the risk that they will become less and less effective. The boundaries between jobs are becoming blurred and less stable. Employment relationships are becoming increasingly complex and diversified. The use of new flexible compensation methods are gradually becoming more widespread in firms. Employment practices are putting increasing emphasis on subjective recruitment criteria. Finally, although practices favouring the reconciliation of work and family are making progress, the use of flexible work schedules to meet short-term fluctuations in production levels is also increasing.

Taken together, these changes reflect a fundamental trend towards a growing individualization of employment rules and practices. This individualization throws into doubt the suitability of the methodological foundations of equity laws, in which the concept of group and collective comparisons are so crucial.

To overcome the problems created by the new labour market trends, various complementary routes should be explored. Labour laws in general, not just equity laws, need to be amended. The definitions of employer and employee need to be revised so that they become more inclusive. Other changes, such as the definition of compensation, are more specific to equity. It is true that a number of pay equity laws use a broader definition of compensation that covers the new forms that are developing. However, as long as truly operational guidelines have not been decreed, there is a risk that the scope of these provisions will remain theoretical (for example, in organizations where several forms of compensation co-exist).

Another route, known as "mainstreaming", is currently creating a certain amount of interest. This approach, which was initially aimed at developing public policies and programs, can be transposed to the organizational level. Mainstreaming is based on the assumption that, given the speed of changes taking place in the human resources management practices of firms, equity laws always risk being significantly out of step with reality. Given this risk, the aim of a mainstreaming approach is that human resources managers should explicitly consider potential effects in terms of gender in all decisions related to new employment practices.

Thinking about these subjects is obviously still at a preliminary stage. For progress to be made, it is essential that the situation be thoroughly evaluated through empirical studies of work environments. What is needed are empirical studies of organizations that have applied pay equity or employment equity provisions. With regards to pay equity, the major elements of the changing nature of jobs must be studied. Can they still be evaluated through the evaluation plans used to implement pay equity? If not, which evaluation tools would be more appropriate? A large number of cases will certainly need to be studied in order to identify the new criteria and methods. As regards compensation, can comparison between, for example, the maximum of a conventional wage scale and the maximum of a skills-based wage scale really correct discriminatory wage gaps? Can these types of compensation truly be compared given that their structures are so different? Are firms, which are subject to employment equity laws, evaluating the new skills, like soft skills, in a non-discriminatory way? If so, what tools are they using? Thus, considerable field research is necessary in order to determine the nature and scale of the methodological obstacles contained in the current laws and to develop truly operational solutions.

In recent years, the scope of the federal Employment Equity Act has been widened and proactive pay equity laws with a theoretically universal impact have been adopted. Although these advances are essential, it is important to evaluate their real impact, which may prove to be limited if the tools on which these laws depend are not adapted to new workplace configurations. This is becoming a matter of great urgency given the persistence and, in some cases, the deterioration of women's labour market position.

References

Appay, B. (1997), "Précarisation sociale et restructurations productives", in B. Appay and A. Thébaud-Mony (ed.), *Précarisation sociale, travail et santé* (Paris: Institut de recherche sur les sociétés contemporaines), 509-553.

Badgett, M.V.L. (1995), "Affirmative Action in a Changing Legal and Economic Environment", *Industrial Relations* 34(4).

Baldwin, J. and G. Picot (1994), *Employment Generation by Small Producers in the Canadian Manufacturing Sector*, Research Paper Series No. 70 (Ottawa: Analytical Studies Branch, Statistics Canada).

Marie-Thérèse Chicha

Batt, R. (1996), "From Bureaucracy to Enterprise? The Changing Job and Careers of Managers in Telecommunication Service", in P. Osterman (ed.), *Broken Ladders: Managerial Careers in the New Economy* (Oxford: Oxford University Press), 55-80.

Betcherman G., K. McMullen, N. Leckie and C. Caron (1994), *The Canadian Workplace in Transition* (Kingston: IRC Press, Queen's University).

Bosset, P. (1989), *La discrimination indirecte dans le domaine de l'emploi - Aspects juridiques* (Montreal: Les Éditions Yvon Blais).

Brault, S. (1997), *Collective Reflection on the Changing Workplace: Report of the Advisory Committee on the Changing Workplace* (Ottawa: Public Works and Government Services Canada), ch. 4.

Canadian Labour Congress, CLC (1997), *Women's Work, A Report* (Ottawa: CLC).

Canadian Human Rights Commission (1997), *Annual Report 1997* (http://www.chrc.ca).

Cappelli, P. (1995), "Rethinking Employment", *British Journal of Industrial Relations* 33(4), 563-602.

Carnevale, A.P., L.A. Jennings and J.M. Eisenmann (1998), "Contingent Workers and Employment Law", in K. Barker and K. Christensen (eds.), *Contingent Work: American Employment Relations in Transition* (Ithaca: ILR Press), 281-305.

Cattanéo, N. (1997), "Le travail à temps partiel: entre rêve et cauchemar", in M. Maruani (ed.), *Salaires, compétences et qualifications. Réduction, diversification et éclatement des temps de travail. Les Cahiers du Mage* (Paris: CNRS), 71-80.

Chaykowski, R.P. and B. Lewis (1995), *Compensation Practices and Outcomes in Canada and the United States* (Kingston: IRC Press, Queen's University).

Chaykowski, R.P. and A. Verma (1994), "Innovation in Industrial Relations: Challenges to Organizations and Public Policy", in T.J. Courchene (ed.), *Stabilization, Growth and Distribution: Linkages in the Knowledge Era*, The Bell Canada Papers on Economic and Public Policy, Vol. 2 (Kingston: John Deutsch Institute, Queen's University), 367-401.

Chicha, M.-T. (1997), *L'équité salariale: mise en oeuvre et enjeux* (Montreal: Éditions Yvon Blais).

_____ (1998), *Portrait et analyse des programmes d'accès à l'égalité soumis à l'obligation contractuelle du Québec*, Rapport de recherche, Montreal.

Chicha, M-.T. and N. Lambert (1998), "On the Job Training for Non-Traditional Occupations: A Key to Gender Equality in the Work Place?" in V. Ferreira *et al.* (eds.), *Shifting Bonds, Shifting Bounds: Women, Mobility and Citizenship in Europe* (Certa Press), 291-304.

Chicha, M.-T. and T. Saba (1999), *Les gestionnaires et l'équité en emploi: résistance ou incompréhension?* Document de recherche (Montreal: École de relations industrielles, Université de Montréal), (à paraître).

Desjardins, A. (1996), "Le temps de travail", *Le marché du travail* (Novembre), 6-8 et 75-89.

duRivage, V.L., F.J. Carré and C. Tilly (1998), "Making Labor Law Work for Part-Time and Contingent Workers", in K. Barker and K. Christensen (eds.), *Contingent Work: American Employment Relations in Transition* (Ithaca: ILR Press), 281-305.

Eyraud, F. (1993), "Equal Pay: An International Overview", in F. Eyraud *et al.* (eds.), *Equal Pay Protection in Industrialised Market Economies: In Search of Greater Effectiveness* (Geneva: International Labour Organization), 1-21.

Ferber, M.A., B. O'Farell and L.R. Allen (1991), *Work and Families: Policies for a Changing Work Force* (Washington, DC: National Academy Press).

Flecker, J., P. Meil and A. Pollert (1998), "The Sexual Division of Labour in Process Manufacturing: Economic Restructuring, Training and «Women's Work»", *European Journal of Industrial Relations* 4(1), 7-34.

Grenon, L. and B. Chun (1997), "Non-permanent Paid Work", *Perspectives on Labour and Income* 9(3), 21-31.

Guérin, G., S. St-Onge, R. Trottier, M. Simard and V. Haines (1994), "Les pratiques organisationnelles d'aide à la gestion de l'équilibre travail-famille: la situation au Québec", *Gestion* (May), 74-82.

Gunderson, M. (1994), *Comparable Worth and Wage Discrimination: An International Perspective* (Geneva: International Labour Organization).

_____ (1995), "Gender Discrimination and Pay Equity Legislation", in L.N. Christofides, E.K. Grant and R. Swidinsky (eds.), *Aspects of Labour Market Behaviour: Essays in Honour of John Vanderkamp* (Toronto: University of Toronto Press), 22-39.

Henry, F. (1994), "The Marginalization of Racial Minorities in the Canadian Workforce", in D. Saunders (ed.), *New Approaches to Employee Management* (New York: JAI Press), 101-113.

Horrell, S. and J. Rubery (1991), "Gender and Working Time: An Analysis of Employers' Working Time Policies", *Cambridge Journal of Economics* 15, 373-391.

Jain, H. and R. Hackett (1989), "Measuring Effectiveness of Employment Equity Programs in Canada", *Canadian Public Policy/Analyse de Politiques* 15(2), 189-204.

Lachance, S. (1997), "Formation en entreprise et accès à l'égalité: la situation des conseillères en crédit commercial: Mémoire de maîtrise" (Montreal: École de relations industrielles, Université de Montréal).

Landers, R.M., J. B. Rebitzer and L.J. Taylor (1996), "Human Resources Practices and the Demographic Transformation of Professional Labor Markets", in P.

Osterman (ed.), *Broken Ladders: Managerial Careers in the New Economy* (Oxford: Oxford University Press), 215-245.

Leck, J. (1991), "Employment Equity Programs in Canada's Federal Jurisdiction", Ph.D. Dissertation, McGill University, Montreal.

Leck, J.D., S. St. Onge and I. Lalancette (1995), "Wage Gap Changes among Organizations Subject to the Employment Equity Act", *Canadian Public Policy/Analyse de Politiques* 21(4), 387-400.

Leonard, J.S. (1994), "Affirmative Action: Symbolic Accommodation and Conflict", in D. Saunders (ed.), *New Approaches to Employee Management* (New York: JAI Press), 13-33.

Long, R.L. (1989), "Patterns of Workplace Innovation in Canada", *Relations industrielles* 44(4), 805-826.

Maschino, D. (1992), "Les changements de l'organisation du travail dans le contexte de la mondialisation économique", *Le marché du travail*, 6-8, 73-80.

McDermott, P.C. (1993), "Equal Pay in Canada", in F. Eyraud *et al.* (eds.), *Equal Pay Protection in Industrialised Market Economies: In Search of Greater Effectiveness* (Geneva: International Labour Organization), 43-61.

Milkovich, G.T. and J.M. Newman (1996), *Compensation* (New York: Irwin McGraw-Hill).

Moss, P. and C. Tilly (1996), "«Soft» Skills and Race: An Investigation of Black Men's Employment Problems", *Work and Occupations* 23(3), 252-278.

OECD (1994), *Women and Structural Change: New Perspectives* (Paris: Organisation for Economic Cooperation and Development).

Osterman, P. (1994), "How Common is Workplace Transformation and Who Adopts it?" *Industrial and Labor Relations Review* 47(2), 173-188.

Picot, G., J. Baldwin and R. Dupuy (1994), *Have Small Firms Created a Disproportionate Share of New Jobs in Canada? A Reassessment of the Facts*, Research Paper Series No. 71 (Ottawa: Analytical Studies Branch, Statistics Canada).

Piore, M.J. (1986), "Perspectives on Labor Market Flexibility", *Industrial Relations* 25(2), 147-166.

Poole, P.J. and J. Rebick (1993), "Not Another Hundred Years: The Failure of the Federal Employment Equity Act", *Canadian Labour Law Journal* 1(4), 341-367.

Remick, H. (1984), "Major Issues in a priori Applications", in H. Remick (ed.), *Comparable Worth and Wage Discrimination: Technical Possibilities and Political Realities* (Philadelphia: Temple University Press).

Rubery, J. (1994), "Decentralisation and Individualisation: The Implications for Equal Pay", *Économies et Sociétés* 8(18), 79-97.

Samuel, J. (1997), *Visible Minorities and the Public Service of Canada* (Ottawa: Canadian Human Rights Commission).

Scott, E.D., K.C. O'Shaughnessy and P. Cappelli (1996), "Management Jobs in the Insurance Industry: Organizational Deskilling and Rising Pay Inequity", in P. Osterman (ed.), *Broken Ladders: Managerial Careers in the New Economy* (Oxford: Oxford University Press), 126-154.

Scott, K. and C. Lochhead (1997), *Are Women Catching up in the Earnings Race?*, Social Research Series No. 3 (Ottawa: Canadian Council on Social Development).

Soares, A. (1997), "Le (non) choix d'être caissière", in L. Mercier and R. Bourbonnais (eds.), *Le travail et l'emploi en mutation*, Les cahiers scientifiques no. 87 (Montreal: ACFAS), 125-146.

Sorensen, E. (1994), *Comparable Worth: Is it a Worthy Policy?* (Princeton: Princeton University Press).

Spalter-Ross, R. and H. Hartmann (1998), "Gauging the Consequences for Gender Relations, Pay Equity, and the Public Purse", in K. Barker and K. Christensen (eds.), *Contingent Work: American Employment Relations in Transition* (Ithaca: ILR Press), 69-100.

Standing, G. (1989), "Global Feminisation Through Flexible Labor", *World Development* 17(7).

Statistics Canada (1997), *Labour Force Update: Work Hours,* Cat. No. 71-005-XPB (Ottawa: Statistics Canada).

_____ (1998), *The Daily*, Cat. No. 11-001E (Ottawa: Statistics Canada).

Steinberg, R. and L. Haignere (1985), *Equitable Compensation: Methodological Criteria for Comparable Worth* (Albany: Centre for Women in Government, Institute for Government and Policy Studies, State University of New York).

Stone, L. (1995), "Utility of Integration of Data for Paid Work and Unpaid Work of Economic Value: The Case of Female Managers", *Statistical Journal of the United Nations* ECE 12, 133-145.

Stone, L. and K. Marshall (1997), *Canadian Women's Employment Patterns and Job-Family Tension*, paper presented at the Tri-National Conference on Women and Work in the 21st Century, Querétaro, Mexico.

Taplin, I.M. (1995), "Flexible Production, Rigid Jobs: Lessons from the Clothing Industry", *Work and Occupations* 22(4), 412-438.

Tremblay, M. (1993), "Rémunération des compétences. Une nouvelle option stratégique", *Info-ressources humaines* (Octobre), 21-23.

Vallée, G. (1998), "Pluralité des statuts de travail et protection des droits de la personne: quel rôle pour le droit du travail?" Document de recherche 98-03 (Montreal: École de relations industrielles, Université de Montréal).

Walsh, J. (1997), "Employment Systems in Transition? A Comparative Analysis of Britain and Australia", *Work, Employment and Society* 11(1), 116-133.

Weiner, N. (1991), "Job Evaluation Systems: A Critique", *Human Resource Management Review* 1(2), 119-132.

Weissman, E. (1997), "Cadres sup: le temps des femmes", *Alternatives Économiques* 152, 44-47.

Contributors

Gordon Betcherman	World Bank
Marie-Thérèse Chicha	Université de Montréal
Jean-Yves Duclos	Université Laval
Ross Finnie	Queen's University and Statistics Canada
Bernard Fortin	Université Laval
John Greenwood	Social Research and Demonstration Corporation
Andrew Jackson	Canadian Labour Congress
Constantine Kapsalis	Data Probe Economic Consulting Inc.
Guy Lacroix	Université Laval
Darren Lauzon	University of British Columbia
Norm Leckie	Ekos Research Associates Inc.
Brenda Lipsett	Human Resources Development Canada
Mark Reesor	Human Resources Development Canada and University of Waterloo
Hélène Roberge	Université Laval
Grant Schellenberg	Canadian Council on Social Development
Ted Wannell	Statistics Canada
Caroline L. Weber	Queen's University
Işik Urla Zeytinoğlu	McMaster University